BENCHMARK SERIES

Microsoft®

POWERPOINT

COMPREHENSIVE CERTIFICATION

2002

MICROSOFT OFFICE USER SPECIALIST

Microsoft® OFFICE

APPROVED COURSEWARE

Pierce College at Puyallup
Puyallup, Washington

NITA RUTKOSKY

EMCParadigm

Senior Developmental Editor	Sonja M. Brown
Associate Editor	Courtney Kost
Special Projects Coordinator	Joan D'Onofrio
Senior Designer	Jennifer Wreisner
Editorial Assistant	Susan Capecchi
Copy Editor	Sharon O'Donnell
Proofreader	Kathyrn Savoie
Indexer	Nancy Fulton

Publishing Team—George Provol, Publisher; Janice Johnson, Director of Product Development; Tony Galvin, Acquisitions Editor; Lori Landwer, Marketing Manager; Shelley Clubb, Electronic Design and Production Manager

Acknowledgments—The author and publisher wish to thank the following reviewers for their technical and academic assistance in testing exercises and assessing instruction:

• Kay M. Newton, Commonwealth Business College, LaPorte, Indiana
• David Parker, St. Charles Community College, St. Charles, Missouri
• Christie Jahn, Lincoln Land Community College, Springfield, Illinois

Special thanks to Christie Jahn for preparing Internet Projects and Job Study scenarios as part of the Unit Performance Assessment sections.

Library of Congress Cataloging-in-Publication Data
    Rutkosky, Nita Hewitt.
        Microsoft PowerPoint 2002: core and expert certification / Nita Rutkosky.
           p.cm. – (Benchmark series)
        ISBN 0-7638-1453-9
             1. Microsoft PowerPoint. 2. Business presentations. I. Title.
      II. Benchmark series (Saint Paul, Minn.)

Z52.5.M52 R945 2002
652.5'5369—dc21
                                      2081035792

Care has been taken to verify the accuracy of information presented in this book. However, the author, editor, and publisher cannot accept any responsibility for Web, e-mail, newsgroup, or chat room subject matter or content, or for consequences from application of the information in this book, and make no warranty, expressed or implied, with respect to its content.

Trademarks: Some of the product names and company names included in this book have been used for identification purposes only and may be trademarks or registered trademarks of their respective manufacturers and sellers. The author, editor, and publisher disclaim any affiliation, association, or connection with, or sponsorship or endorsement by, such owners.

Text: ISBN 0-7638-1453-9
Order Number: 05549

© 2002 by Paradigm Publishing Inc.
    Published by **EMC**Paradigm
    875 Montreal Way
    St. Paul, MN 55102

    (800) 535-6865
    E-mail: educate@emcp.com
    Web site: www.emcp.com

Printed in the United States of America
10 9 8 7 6 5 4 3 2 1

CONTENTS

WELCOME

You are about to begin working with a textbook that is part of the Benchmark Office XP Series. The word *Benchmark* in the title holds a special significance in terms of *what* you will learn and *how* you will learn. *Benchmark*, according to *Webster's Dictionary*, means "something that serves as a standard by which others may be measured or judged." In this text, you will learn the Microsoft Office User Specialist (MOUS) skills required for certification on the Core and/or Expert level of one or more major applications within the Office XP suite. These skills are benchmarks by which you will be evaluated, should you choose to take one or more certification exams.

The design and teaching approach of this textbook also serve as a benchmark for instructional materials on software programs. Features and commands are presented in a clear, straightforward way, and each short section of instruction is followed by an exercise that lets you practice using the new feature. Gradually, as you move through each chapter, you will build your skills to the point of mastery. At the end of a chapter, you are offered the opportunity to demonstrate your newly acquired competencies—to prove you have met the benchmarks for using the Office suite or an individual program. At the completion of the text, you are well on your way to becoming a successful computer user.

EMCParadigm's Office XP Benchmark Series includes textbooks on Office XP, Word 2002, Excel 2002, Access 2002, PowerPoint 2002, Publisher 2002, Outlook 2002, and FrontPage 2002. Note that the programs include the year 2002 in their name, while the suite itself is called Office XP (for "experience"). Each book includes a Student CD, which contains prekeyed documents and files required for completing the exercises. A CD icon and folder name displayed on the opening page of each chapter indicates that you need to copy a folder of files from the CD before beginning the chapter exercises. *(See the inside back cover for instructions on copying a folder.)*

Introducing Microsoft Office XP

Microsoft Office XP, released in May 2001, is a suite of programs designed to improve productivity and efficiency in workplace, school, and home settings. A suite is a group of programs that are sold as a package and are designed to be used together, making it possible to exchange files among the programs. The major applications included in Office are Word, a word processing program; Excel, a spreadsheet program; Access, a database management program; PowerPoint, a slide presentation program; and Outlook, a desktop information management program.

Using the Office suite offers significant advantages over working with individual programs developed by different software vendors. The programs in the Office suite use similar toolbars, buttons, icons, and menus, which means that once you learn the basic features of one program, you can use those same features in the other programs. This easy transfer of knowledge decreases the learning time and allows you to concentrate on the unique commands and options within each program. The compatibility of the programs creates seamless integration of data within and between programs and lets the operator use the program most appropriate for the required tasks.

The number of programs in the Office XP suite varies by the package, or edition. Four editions are available:

- **Standard:** Word, Excel, Outlook, PowerPoint
- **Professional:** Word, Excel, Outlook, PowerPoint, and Access
- **Professional Special Edition:** All Professional package programs plus FrontPage, Publisher, and SharePoint. This edition is available only for a limited time and only to current Office users.
- **Developer:** All Professional package programs (except SharePoint) plus Developer tools

New Features in Office XP

Users of previous editions of Office will find that the essential features that have made Office popular still form the heart of the suite. New enhancements focus on collaboration, or the ability for multiple users to work together on the same document from different locations over the Internet. Another highlight is the Smart Tag feature, which is an icon that when clicked offers a list of commands that are especially useful for the particular job being done. In Word, for example, a Smart Tag might offer the ability to turn off automatic capitalization or other types of automatic formatting. A more comprehensive kind of targeted assistance is offered in a new Task Pane, which is a narrow window that appears at the right of the screen to display commands relevant to the current task. Speech recognition technology is available with this edition, offering users the ability to dictate text into any Office program. This feature must be installed separately.

Structure of the Benchmark Textbooks

Users of the Core Certification texts and the complete application textbooks may begin their course with an overview of computer hardware and software, offered in the *Getting Started* section at the beginning of the book. Your instructor may also ask you to complete the *Windows 2000* and the *Internet Explorer* sections so you become familiar with the computer's operating system and the essential tools for using the Internet.

Instruction on the major programs within the Office suite is presented in units of four chapters each. Both the Core and Expert levels contain two units, which culminate with performance assessments to check your knowledge and skills. Each chapter contains the following sections:

- performance objectives that identify specifically what you are expected to learn
- instructional text that introduces and explains new concepts and features
- step-by-step, hands-on exercises following each section of instruction
- a chapter summary
- a knowledge self-check called Concepts Check
- skill assessment exercises called Skills Check

Exercises offered at the end of units provide writing and research opportunities that will strengthen your performance in other college courses as well as on the job. The final activities simulate interesting projects you could encounter in the workplace.

Benchmark Series Ancillaries

The Benchmark Series includes some important resources that will help you succeed in your computer applications courses:

Online Resource Center

Internet Resource Centers hosted by EMC/Paradigm provide additional material for students and teachers using the Benchmark books. Online you will find Web links, updates to textbooks, study tips, quizzes and assignments, and supplementary projects.

Class Connection

Available for both the WebCT and Blackboard e-learning platforms, EMC/Paradigm's Class Connection is a course management tool for traditional and distance learning. The Class Connection allows students to access the course syllabus and assignment schedule online, provides self-quizzes and study aids, and facilitates communication among students and instructors via e-mail and e-discussions.

MOUS CERTIFICATION

APPROVED COURSEWARE

What Does This Logo Mean?

It means this courseware has been approved by the Microsoft® Office User Specialist Program to be among the finest available for learning Microsoft PowerPoint 2002. It also means that upon completion of this courseware, you may be prepared to become a Microsoft Office User Specialist.

What Is a Microsoft Office User Specialist?

A Microsoft Office User Specialist is an individual who has certified his or her skills in one or more of the Microsoft Office desktop applications of Microsoft Word, Microsoft Excel, Microsoft PowerPoint®, Microsoft Outlook® or Microsoft Access, or in Microsoft Project. The Microsoft Office User Specialist Program typically offers certification exams at the "Core" and "Expert" skill levels. * The Microsoft Office User Specialist Program is the only Microsoft approved program in the world for certifying proficiency in Microsoft Office desktop applications and Microsoft Project. This certification can be a valuable asset in any job search or career advancement.

More Information

- To learn more about becoming a Microsoft Office User Specialist, visit www.mous.net.
- To purchase a Microsoft Office User Specialist certification exam, visit www.DesktopIQ.com.
- To learn about other Microsoft Office User Specialist approved courseware from EMC/Paradigm, visit www.emcp.com/college_division/MOUS_ready.php.

EMC/Paradigm Publishing is independent from Microsoft Corporation and not affiliated with Microsoft in any manner. This publication may be used in assisting students to prepare for a Microsoft office User Specialist Exam. Neither Microsoft, its designated review company, nor EMC/Paradigm Publishing warrants that use of this publication will ensure passing the relevant exam.

---

* The availability of Microsoft Office User Specialist certification exams varies by application, application version and language. Visit www.mous.net for exam availability.

Microsoft, the Microsoft Office User Specialist Logo, PowerPoint and Outlook are either registered trademarks or trademarks of Microsoft Corporation in the United States and/or other countries.

POWERPOINT

OFFICE XP

GETTING STARTED IN OFFICE XP

In this textbook, you will learn to operate several microcomputer application programs that combine to make an application "suite." This suite of programs is called Microsoft Office XP. The programs you will learn to operate are the *software*, which include instructions telling the computer what to do. Some of the software programs in the suite include a word processing program called *Word*, a spreadsheet program called *Excel*, a presentation program called *PowerPoint*, and a database program called *Access*.

Identifying Computer Hardware

The computer equipment you will use to operate the suite of programs is referred to as *hardware*. You will need access to a microcomputer system that should consist of the CPU, monitor, keyboard, printer, disk drives, and mouse. If you are not sure what equipment you will be operating, check with your instructor. The computer system displayed in figure G.1 consists of six components. Each component is discussed separately in the material that follows.

FIGURE

G.1 *Microcomputer System*

CPU

CPU stands for Central Processing Unit and is the intelligence of the computer. All the processing occurs in the CPU. Silicon chips, which contain miniaturized circuitry, are placed on boards that are plugged into slots within the CPU. Whenever an instruction is given to the computer, that instruction is processed through circuitry in the CPU.

Monitor

The monitor is a piece of equipment that looks like a television screen. It displays the information of a program and the text being input at the keyboard. The quality of display for monitors varies depending on the type of monitor and the type of resolution. Monitors can also vary in size—generally from 14-inch size up to 21-inch size or larger.

Keyboard

The keyboard is used to input information into the computer. Keyboards for microcomputers vary in the number and location of the keys. Microcomputers have the alphabetic and numeric keys in the same location as the keys on a typewriter. The symbol keys, however, may be placed in a variety of locations, depending on the manufacturer. In addition to letters, numbers, and symbols, most microcomputer keyboards contain function keys, arrow keys, and a numeric keypad. Figure G.2 shows an enhanced keyboard.

FIGURE

G.2 *Microcomputer Enhanced Keyboard*

The 12 keys at the top of the enhanced keyboard, labeled with the letter F followed by a number, are called *function keys*. These keys can be used to perform functions within each of the suite programs. To the right of the regular keys is a group of *special* or *dedicated keys*. These keys are labeled with specific functions that will be performed when you press the key. Below the special keys are arrow keys. These keys are used to move the insertion point in the document screen.

In the upper right corner of the keyboard are three mode indicator lights. When certain modes have been selected, a light appears on the keyboard. For example, if you press the Caps Lock key, which disables the lowercase alphabet, a light appears next to Caps Lock. Similarly, pressing the Num Lock key will disable the special functions on the numeric keypad, which is located at the right side of the keyboard.

Disk Drives

Depending on the computer system you are using, Microsoft Office XP is installed on a hard drive or as part of a network system. Whether you are using

Office on a hard drive or network system, you will need to have available a CD drive and a floppy disk drive. You will insert the CD (Compact Disk) that accompanies this textbook in the CD drive and then copy folders from the CD to a disk in the floppy disk drive. You will also save documents you complete at the computer to folders on your disk in the floppy drive.

Printer

When you create a document in Word, it is considered *soft copy*. If you want a *hard copy* of a document, you need to print it. To print documents you will need to access a printer, which will probably be either a laser printer or an ink-jet printer. A laser printer uses a laser beam combined with heat and pressure to print documents while an ink-jet printer prints a document by spraying a fine mist of ink on the page.

Mouse

Many functions in the suite of programs are designed to operate more efficiently with a *mouse*. A mouse is an input device that sits on a flat surface next to the computer. A mouse can be operated with the left or the right hand. Moving the mouse on the flat surface causes a corresponding mouse pointer to move on the screen. Figure G.1 shows an illustration of a mouse.

Using the Mouse

The programs in the Microsoft Office suite can be operated using a keyboard or they can be operated with the keyboard and a mouse. The mouse may have two or three buttons on top, which are tapped to execute specific functions and commands. To use the mouse, rest it on a flat surface or a mouse pad. Put your hand over it with your palm resting on top of the mouse and your wrist resting on the table surface. As you move the mouse on the flat surface, a corresponding pointer moves on the screen.

When using the mouse, there are four terms you should understand—point, click, double-click, and drag. When operating the mouse, you may need to *point* to a specific command, button, or icon. Point means to position the mouse pointer on the desired item. With the mouse pointer positioned on the desired item, you may need to *click* a button on the mouse. Click means quickly tapping a button on the mouse once. To complete two steps at one time, such as choosing and then executing a function, *double-click* a mouse button. Double-click means to tap the left mouse button twice in quick succession. The term *drag* means to press and hold the left mouse button, move the mouse pointer to a specific location, and then release the button.

Using the Mouse Pointer

The mouse pointer will change appearance depending on the function being performed or where the pointer is positioned. The mouse pointer may appear as one of the following images:

The mouse pointer appears as an I-beam (called the *I-beam pointer*) in the document screen and can be used to move the insertion point or select text.

The mouse pointer appears as an arrow pointing up and to the left (called the *arrow pointer*) when it is moved to the Title bar, Menu bar, or one of the toolbars at the top of the screen or when a dialog box is displayed. For example, to open a new document with the mouse, you would move the I-beam pointer to the File option on the Menu bar. When the I-beam pointer is moved to the Menu bar, it turns into an arrow pointer. To make a selection, position the tip of the arrow pointer on the File option, and then click the left mouse button. At the drop-down menu that displays, make selections by positioning the arrow pointer on the desired option, and then clicking the left mouse button.

The mouse pointer becomes a double-headed arrow (either pointing left and right, pointing up and down, or pointing diagonally) when performing certain functions such as changing the size of an object.

In certain situations, such as moving an object or image, the mouse pointer becomes a four-headed arrow. The four-headed arrow means that you can move the object left, right, up, or down.

When a request is being processed or when a program is being loaded, the mouse pointer may appear with an hourglass beside it. The hourglass image means "please wait." When the process is completed, the hourglass image is removed.

The mouse pointer displays as a hand with a pointing index finger in certain functions such as Help and indicates that more information is available about the item.

Choosing Commands

Once a program is open, several methods can be used in the program to choose commands. A command is an instruction that tells the program to do something. You can choose a command with one of the following methods:

- Click a toolbar button with the mouse
- Choose a command from a menu
- Use shortcut keys
- Use a shortcut menu

Choosing Commands on Toolbars

When a program such as Word or PowerPoint is open, several toolbars containing buttons for common tasks are available. In many of the suite programs, two toolbars are visible on the screen. One toolbar is called the Standard toolbar; the other is referred to as the Formatting toolbar. To choose a command from a toolbar, position the tip of the arrow pointer on a button, and then click the left mouse button. For example, to print the file currently displayed in the screen, position the tip of the arrow pointer on the Print button on the Standard toolbar, and then click the left mouse button.

Choosing Commands on the Menu Bar

Each of the suite programs contains a Menu bar that displays toward the top of the screen. This Menu bar contains a variety of options you can use to perform functions and commands on data. Functions are grouped logically into options, which display on the Menu bar. For example, features to work with files are grouped in the File option. Either the mouse or the keyboard can be used to make choices from the Menu bar or make a choice at a dialog box.

To use the mouse to make a choice from the Menu bar, move the I-beam pointer to the Menu bar. This causes the I-beam pointer to display as an arrow pointer. Position the tip of the arrow pointer on the desired option, and then click the left mouse button.

To use the keyboard, press the Alt key to make the Menu bar active. Options on the Menu bar display with an underline below one of the letters. To choose an option from the Menu bar, key the underlined letter of the desired option, or move the insertion point with the left or right arrow keys to the option desired, and then press Enter. This causes a drop-down menu to display.

For example, to display the File drop-down menu in Word as shown in figure G.3 using the mouse, position the arrow pointer on File on the Menu bar, and then click the left mouse button. To display the File drop-down menu with the keyboard, press the Alt key, and then key the letter F for File.

FIGURE

G.3 **Word File Drop-Down Menu**

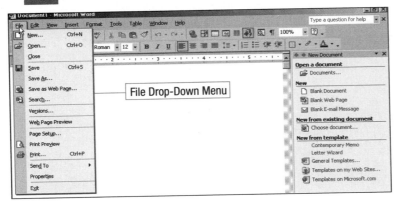

Choosing Commands from Drop-Down Menus

To choose a command from a drop-down menu with the mouse, position the arrow pointer on the desired option, and then click the left mouse button. At the drop-down menu that displays, move the arrow pointer down the menu to the desired option, and then click the left mouse button.

To make a selection from the drop-down menu with the keyboard, key the underlined letter of the desired option. Once the drop-down menu displays, you do not need to hold down the Alt key with the underlined letter. If you want to close a drop-down menu without making a choice, click in the screen outside the drop-down menu; or, press the Esc key twice.

If an option can be accessed by clicking a button on a toolbar, the button is displayed preceding the option in the drop-down menu. For example, buttons display before the New, Open Save, Save as Web Page, Search, Print Preview, and Print options at the File drop-down menu (see figure G.3).

Some menu options may be gray shaded (dimmed). When an option is dimmed, that option is currently not available. For example, if you choose the Table option on the Menu bar, the Table drop-down menu displays with dimmed options including Merge Cells, Split Cells, and Split Table.

Some menu options are preceded by a check mark. The check mark indicates that the option is currently active. To make an option inactive (turn it off) using the mouse, position the arrow pointer on the option, and then click the left mouse button. To make an option inactive (turn it off) with the keyboard, key the underlined letter of the option.

If an option from a drop-down menu displays followed by an ellipsis (...), a dialog box will display when that option is chosen. A dialog box provides a variety of options to let you specify how a command is to be carried out. For example, if you choose File and then Print from the PowerPoint Menu bar, the Print dialog box displays as shown in figure G.4.

FIGURE

G.4 *PowerPoint Print Dialog Box*

Or, if you choose Format and then Font from the Word Menu bar, the Font dialog box displays as shown in figure G.5.

FIGURE

G.5 *Word Font Dialog Box*

Some dialog boxes provide a set of options. These options are contained on separate tabs. For example, the Font dialog box shown in figure G.5 contains a tab at the top of the dialog box with the word Fo<u>n</u>t on it. Two other tabs display to the right of the Font tab. The tab that displays in the front is the active tab. To make a tab active using the mouse, position the arrow pointer on the desired tab, and then click the left mouse button. If you are using the keyboard, press Ctrl + Tab or press Alt + the underlined letter on the desired tab. For example, to change the tab to Character Spacing in the Font dialog box, click Character Spacing, or press Ctrl + Tab, or press Alt + R.

To choose options from a dialog box with the mouse, position the arrow pointer on the desired option, and then click the left mouse button. If you are using the keyboard, press the Tab key to move the insertion point forward from option to option. Press Shift + Tab to move the insertion point backward from option to option. You can also hold down the Alt key and then press the underlined letter of the desired option. When an option is selected, it displays either in reverse video (white letters on a dark background) or surrounded by a dashed box called a *marquee*.

A dialog box contains one or more of the following elements: text boxes, list boxes, check boxes, option buttons, spin boxes, and command buttons.

Text Boxes

Some options in a dialog box require text to be entered. For example, the boxes below the Fi<u>n</u>d what and Re<u>p</u>lace with options at the Excel Find and Replace dialog box shown in figure G.6 are text boxes. In a text box, you key text or edit existing text. Edit text in a text box in the same manner as normal text. Use the left and right arrow keys on the keyboard to move the insertion point without deleting text and use the Delete key or Backspace key to delete text.

FIGURE
G.6 **Excel Find and Replace Dialog Box**

List Boxes

Some dialog boxes such as the Access Open dialog box shown in figure G.7 may contain a list box. The list of files below the Look <u>i</u>n: option is contained in a list box. To make a selection from a list box with the mouse, move the arrow pointer to the desired option, and then click the left mouse button.

G.7 Access Open Dialog Box

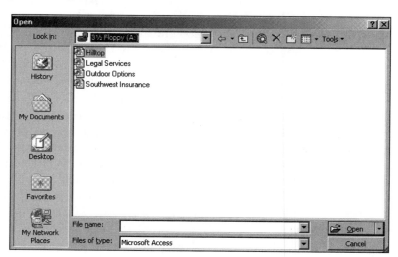

Some list boxes may contain a scroll bar. This scroll bar will display at the right side of the list box (a vertical scroll bar) or at the bottom of the list box (a horizontal scroll bar). Either a vertical scroll bar or a horizontal scroll bar can be used to move through the list if the list is longer than the box. To move down through a list on a vertical scroll bar, position the arrow pointer on the down scroll triangle and hold down the left mouse button. To scroll up through the list in a vertical scroll bar, position the arrow pointer on the up scroll triangle and hold down the left mouse button. You can also move the arrow pointer above the scroll box and click the left mouse button to scroll up the list or move the arrow pointer below the scroll box and click the left mouse button to move down the list. To move through a list with a horizontal scroll bar, click the left scroll triangle to scroll to the left of the list or click the right scroll triangle to scroll to the right of the list.

To make a selection from a list using the keyboard, move the insertion point into the box by holding down the Alt key and pressing the underlined letter of the desired option. Press the up and/or down arrow keys on the keyboard to move through the list.

In some dialog boxes where enough room is not available for a list box, lists of options are inserted in a drop-down list box. Options that contain a drop-down list box display with a down-pointing triangle. For example, the Underline style option at the Word Font dialog box shown in figure G.5 contains a drop-down list. To display the list, click the down-pointing triangle to the right of the Underline style option box. If you are using the keyboard, press Alt + U.

Check Boxes

Some dialog boxes contain options preceded by a box. A check mark may or may not appear in the box. The Word Font dialog box shown in figure G.5 displays a variety of check boxes within the Effects section. If a check mark appears in the box, the option is active (turned on). If there is no check mark in the check box, the option is inactive (turned off).

Any number of check boxes can be active. For example, in the Word Font dialog box, you can insert a check mark in any or all of the boxes in the Effects section and these options will be active.

To make a check box active or inactive with the mouse, position the tip of the arrow pointer in the check box, and then click the left mouse button. If you are using the keyboard, press Alt + the underlined letter of the desired option.

Option Buttons

In the PowerPoint Print dialog box shown in figure G.4, the options in the Print range section are preceded by option buttons. Only one option button can be selected at any time. When an option button is selected, a dark circle displays in the button.

To select an option button with the mouse, position the tip of the arrow pointer inside the option button, and then click the left mouse button. To make a selection with the keyboard, hold down the Alt key, and then press the underlined letter of the desired option.

Spin Boxes

Some options in a dialog box contain measurements or numbers that can be increased or decreased. These options are generally located in a spin box. For example, the Word Paragraph dialog box shown in figure G.8 contains spin boxes located after the Left, Right, Before, and After options. To increase a number in a spin box, position the tip of the arrow pointer on the up-pointing triangle to the right of the desired option, and then click the left mouse button. To decrease the number, click the down-pointing triangle. If you are using the keyboard, press Alt + the underlined letter of the desired option, and then press the up arrow key to increase the number or the down arrow key to decrease the number.

FIGURE

G.8 **Word Paragraph Dialog Box**

Command Buttons

In the Excel Find and Replace dialog box shown in figure G.6, the boxes along the bottom of the dialog box are called *command buttons*. A command button is used to execute or cancel a command. Some command buttons display with an ellipsis (...). A command button that displays with an ellipsis will open another dialog box. To choose a command button with the mouse, position the arrow pointer on the desired button, and then click the left mouse button. To choose a command button with the keyboard, press the Tab key until the desired command button contains the marquee, and then press the Enter key.

Choosing Commands with Shortcut Keys

At the left side of a drop-down menu is a list of options. At the right side, shortcut keys for specific options may display. For example, the shortcut keys to save a document are Ctrl + S and are displayed to the right of the Save option at the File drop-down menu shown in figure G.3. To use shortcut keys to choose a command, hold down the Ctrl key, key the letter for the command, and then release the Ctrl key.

Choosing Commands with Shortcut Menus

The software programs in the suite include menus that contain commands related to the item with which you are working. A shortcut menu appears right where you are working in the document. To display a shortcut menu, click the *right* mouse button or press Shift + F10.

For example, if the insertion point is positioned in a paragraph of text in a Word document, clicking the *right* mouse button or pressing Shift + F10 will cause the shortcut menu shown in figure G.9 to display in the document screen.

FIGURE

G.9 | *Word Shortcut Menu*

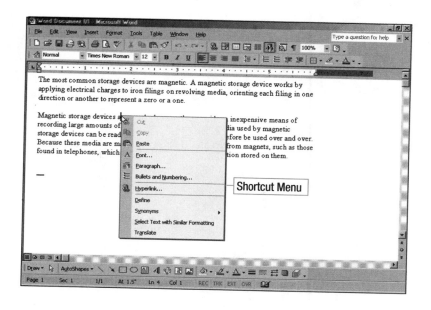

To select an option from a shortcut menu with the mouse, click the desired option. If you are using the keyboard, press the up or down arrow key until the desired option is selected, and then press the Enter key. To close a shortcut menu without choosing an option, click anywhere outside the shortcut menu or press the Esc key.

Working with Multiple Programs

As you learn the various programs in the Microsoft Office suite, you will notice how executing commands in each is very similar. For example, the steps to save, close, and print are virtually the same whether you are working in Word, Excel, or PowerPoint. This consistency between programs greatly enhances a user's ability to easily transfer knowledge learned in one program to another within the suite.

Another appeal of Microsoft Office is the ability to have more than one program open at the same time. For example, you can open Word, create a document, and then open Excel, create a spreadsheet, and copy the spreadsheet into Word.

When a program is open, the name of the program, followed by the file name, displays in a button on the Taskbar. When another program is opened, the program name and file name display in a button that is positioned to the right of the first program button. Figure G.10 shows the Taskbar with Word, Excel, and PowerPoint open. To move from one program to another, all you need to do is click the button on the Taskbar representing the desired program file.

FIGURE

G.10 *Taskbar with Word, Excel, and PowerPoint Open*

| 🏁 Start | 🗐 Word Document 01 - Micr... | 🗙 Microsoft Excel - Excel Wo... | 🗔 Microsoft PowerPoint... | 🔊🖳🕹🅰EN🖳 10:41 AM |

Setting Clicking Options

You can set clicking options for the Windows environment and specify either a double-click or single-click to open a program or file. Steps in this textbook assume that you will double-click to open a file or program. To change from single-click to open (point to select) to double-click to open (single-click to select), complete these steps:

1. At the Windows desktop, click the My Computer icon.
2. At the My Computer window, click Tools on the Menu bar, and then click Folder Options at the drop-down menu.
3. At the Folder Options dialog box with the General tab selected, click the Double-click to open an item (single-click to select) option located in the Click items as follows section.
4. Click the Apply button and then click OK.

Completing Computer Exercises

Some computer exercises in this textbook require that you open an existing file. Exercise files are saved on the CD that accompanies this textbook. The files you need for each chapter are saved in individual folders. Before beginning a chapter, copy the necessary folder from the CD to a preformatted data disk. After completing exercises in a chapter, delete the chapter folder before copying the next chapter folder. (Check with your instructor before deleting a folder.)

Copying a Folder

The CD that accompanies this textbook contains numerous files you use to complete some exercises and assessments in chapters. As you begin working in a chapter, copy the chapter folder from the CD to your disk. (Not every chapter contains a folder on the CD. For example, when completing exercises in the Access chapters, you will copy database files from the Database folder rather than individual chapter folders. This is to ensure that there is adequate space on your disk for saving files.) Copy the chapter folder from the CD to your disk using Windows Explorer by completing the following steps:

1. Insert the CD that accompanies this textbook in the CD drive.
2. Insert a formatted 3.5-inch disk in the disk drive.
3. At the Windows desktop, open Windows Explorer by clicking the Start button, pointing to Programs, pointing to Accessories, and then clicking Windows Explorer.
4. Double-click My Computer in the Folders pane.
5. Double-click the CD drive in the Folders pane (probably displays as OFFICEXP_BENCH followed by the drive letter).
6. Double-click the desired program folder name in the Contents pane. (For example, if you are copying a folder for a core Word chapter, double-click the *Word 2002 Core* folder in the Contents pane.)
7. Click once on the desired chapter subfolder name to select it.
8. Click the Copy To button on the toolbar.
9. At the Browse For Folder dialog box, click *3¹/₂ Floppy (A:)* in the list box and then click OK. (If *3¹/₂ Floppy (A:)* is not visible, click the plus symbol preceding *My Computer.*)
10. After the folder is copied to your disk, close Windows Explorer by clicking the Close button (contains an X) located in the upper right corner of Windows Explorer.

Deleting a Folder

Before copying a chapter folder onto your disk, delete any previous chapter folders. Do this in Windows Explorer by completing the following steps:

1. Insert your disk in the disk drive.
2. At the Windows desktop, click the Start button on the Taskbar, point to Programs, point to Accessories, and then click Windows Explorer.
3. In Windows Explorer, click the down-pointing triangle at the right side of the Address list box.
4. At the drop-down list that displays, click the drive where your disk is located.
5. Click the chapter folder in the list box.
6. Click the Delete button on the Windows Explorer toolbar.
7. At the message asking if you want to remove the folder and all its contents, click the Yes button.
8. At the message asking if you want to delete a read-only file, click the Yes to All button.
9. Close Windows Explorer by clicking the Close button located in the upper right corner of Windows Explorer.

OFFICE XP

USING WINDOWS 2000

A computer requires an operating system to provide necessary instructions on a multitude of processes including loading programs, managing data, directing the flow of information to peripheral equipment, and displaying information. Windows 2000 Professional is an operating system that provides functions of this type (along with much more) in a graphical environment. Windows is referred to as a *graphical user interface* (GUI—pronounced *gooey*) that provides a visual display of information with features such as icons (pictures) and buttons. In this introduction you will learn basic features of Windows 2000 Professional.

Before using one of the software programs in the Microsoft Office suite, you will need to start the operating system. To do this, turn on the computer. Depending on your computer equipment configuration, you may also need to turn on the monitor and printer. When the computer is turned on, the Windows 2000 operating system is automatically started and, after a few moments, the desktop will display as shown in figure W.1. (Your desktop may vary from what you see in figure W.1.)

FIGURE

W.1 *Windows 2000 Desktop*

Taskbar

Exploring the Desktop

When Windows 2000 is loaded, the main portion of the screen is called the *desktop*. Think of the desktop in Windows as the top of a desk in an office. A business person places necessary tools—such as pencils, pens, paper, files, calculator—on his or her desktop to perform functions. Like the tools that are located on a desk, the desktop contains tools for operating the computer. These tools are logically grouped and placed in dialog boxes or panels that can be displayed using one of the icons at the left side of the desktop.

The desktop contains a variety of icons and features for using your computer and software programs installed on the computer. The features available on the desktop are described in the following text.

Using Icons

Icons are visual symbols that represent programs, files, or folders. In figure W.2, the figure on the left shows an icon for the Microsoft program Internet Explorer and the figure on the right shows the Windows folder icon. To open a folder or start a program, you double-click the icon.

FIGURE

W.2 *Internet Explorer Icon and Windows Folder*

Using the Taskbar

The bar that displays at the bottom of the desktop (see figure W.1) is called the Taskbar. The Taskbar, shown in figure W.3, is divided into four areas: the Start button, the Quick Launch toolbar, the program button area, and the System tray.

FIGURE

W.3 *Windows 2000 Taskbar*

The Start button is located at the left side of the Taskbar. Use this button to start a program, use the Help feature, change settings, and open files. To display the options available with the Start button, position the arrow pointer on the Start button, and then click the left mouse button. This causes a pop-up menu to display, as shown in figure W.4.

FIGURE

W.4 *Start Button Pop-up Menu*

To choose an option from this pop-up menu, move the arrow pointer to the desired option (referred to as *pointing*), and then click the left mouse button. Pointing to options at the Start pop-up menu followed by a right-pointing triangle will cause a side menu to display with additional options.

When a program is open, a program button appears in the Taskbar. In the Taskbar shown in figure W.5, the Microsoft Word 2002 program is open. An icon representing Word displays in the program button area of the Taskbar.

FIGURE

W.5 *Windows Taskbar with Microsoft Word Open*

Start | Document1 - Mic... | 7:03 PM

Switching between Open Programs

To switch between open programs, click the program's button on the Taskbar. In figure W.6, three programs are open—Microsoft Word, Excel, and Publisher. Microsoft Excel is the active button. Clicking either the Microsoft Word or Microsoft Publisher button will activate that program.

FIGURE

W.6 *Taskbar with the Microsoft Excel Program Active*

Start | Document1 - Micro... | Microsoft Excel ... | (Unsaved Publicati... | 7:08 PM

Almost every program you open will appear on the Taskbar. (A few specialized tools may not.) Each button on the Taskbar gets a little smaller each time you open a program.

exercise 1

OPENING PROGRAMS AND SWITCHING BETWEEN PROGRAMS

1. Open Windows 2000. (To do this, turn on the computer and, if necessary, turn on the monitor and/or printer. Check with your instructor to determine if you need to complete additional steps.)
2. When the desktop displays, open Microsoft Word by completing the following steps:
   a. Position the arrow pointer on the Start button on the Taskbar and then click the left mouse button.
   b. At the Start pop-up menu, point to *Programs*. (This causes a side menu to display.)
   c. Drag the arrow pointer to *Microsoft Word* in the side menu and then click the left mouse button.
   d. When the Microsoft Word program is opened, notice that a button representing Word displays in the program button area of the Taskbar.
3. Open Microsoft Excel by completing the following steps:
   a. Position the arrow pointer on the Start button on the Taskbar and then click the left mouse button.
   b. At the Start pop-up menu, point to *Programs*.
   c. Drag the arrow pointer to *Microsoft Excel* in the side menu and then click the left mouse button.
   d. When the Microsoft Excel program is opened, notice that a button representing Excel displays in the program button area of the Taskbar to the right of the button representing Word.
4. Switch to the Word program by clicking the button on the Taskbar representing Word.
5. Switch to the Excel program by clicking the button on the Taskbar representing Excel.
6. Exit Excel by clicking <u>F</u>ile on the Excel Menu bar and then clicking E<u>x</u>it at the drop-down menu.
7. Click the button on the Taskbar representing Word.
8. Exit Word by clicking <u>F</u>ile on the Word Menu bar and then clicking E<u>x</u>it at the drop-down menu.

Exploring the System Tray

The System tray is the recessed area on the far right side of the Taskbar. The System tray contains a digital clock and specialized programs that run in the background. Position the arrow pointer over the current time on the Taskbar and today's date displays in a small yellow box as shown in figure W.7. (Your date will vary.)

FIGURE

W.7 *Current Time and Date in System Tray*

Double-click the current time displayed on the Taskbar and the Date/Time Properties dialog box displays as shown in figure W.8.

FIGURE

W.8 **Date/Time Properties Dialog Box**

Change the date with options in the Date section of the dialog box. For example, to change the month, click the down-pointing triangle at the right side of the list box containing the current month, and then click the desired month at the drop-down list. Change the year by clicking the up- or down-pointing triangle at the right side of the list box containing the current year until the desired year displays. To change the day, click the desired day in the monthly calendar that displays in the dialog box. To change the time, double-click either the hour, minute, or seconds and use the up and down arrows to adjust the time.

Using the Quick Launch Toolbar

The Quick Launch toolbar is positioned between the Start button and the program button area on the Taskbar. It contains icons for programs that can be launched with a single click, such as Internet Explorer. The appearance of the Quick Launch toolbar can vary considerably depending on your installation of Windows 2000. A typical installation is shown in figure W.9.

FIGURE

W.9 **Windows 2000 Taskbar Quick Launch Toolbar**

Quick Launch Toolbar

Setting Taskbar Properties

The default settings for the Taskbar display it at the bottom of the desktop with the time displayed. These default settings can be changed with options at the Taskbar and Start Menu Properties dialog box, shown in figure W.10. To display this dialog box, position the arrow pointer on any empty spot on the Taskbar, and then click the *right* mouse button. At the pop-up menu that displays, click *Properties*.

FIGURE

W.10 *Taskbar and Start Menu Properties Dialog Box*

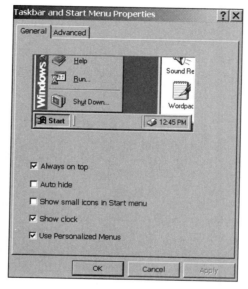

Each property is controlled by a check box. Property options containing a check mark are active. Click the option to remove the check mark and make the option inactive. If an option is inactive, clicking the option will insert a check mark in the check box and turn on the option (make it active). The Taskbar and Start Menu Properties dialog box contains these options:

Always on top: Keeps the Taskbar visible at all times. Check this if you want to see the Taskbar even when you are running programs.

Auto hide: Collapses the Taskbar into a thin line at the bottom of the screen. When you move the insertion point to the bottom of the screen, the Taskbar will display.

Show small icons in Start menu: Displays small icons in the Start menu. If unchecked, large icons are used (see figure W.11).

Show clock: Shows or hides the clock.

Use Personalized Menus: Keeps the Programs menu clean by hiding items you have not used recently. Access hidden programs by clicking the down-pointing triangle at the bottom of the Programs menu.

FIGURE

W.11 *Start Menu Showing Large and Small Icons*

Large Icons

Small Icons

---

exercise 2

CHANGING TASKBAR PROPERTIES

1. Make sure Windows 2000 is open and the desktop is displayed.
2. Change the size of the icons in the Start pop-up menu and remove the display of the clock by completing the following steps:
   a. Position the arrow pointer on any empty area on the Taskbar and then click the *right* mouse button.
   b. At the pop-up menu that displays, click *Properties*.
   c. At the Taskbar and Start Menu Properties dialog box, click *Show small icons in Start menu*. (This inserts a check mark in the check box.)
   d. Click *Show clock*. (This removes the check mark from the check box.)
   e. Click the Apply button.
   f. Click OK to close the dialog box.
3. Notice that the time no longer displays at the right side of the Taskbar. Click the Start button at the left side of the Taskbar and notice that the icons in the pop-up menu are smaller. Click on any empty spot on the desktop to remove the pop-up menu.
4. Return to the default settings for the Taskbar by completing the following steps:
   a. Position the arrow pointer on any empty area on the Taskbar and then click the *right* mouse button.
   b. At the pop-up menu that displays, click *Properties*.
   c. At the Taskbar and Start Menu Properties dialog box, click *Show small icons in Start menu*. (This removes the check mark from the check box.)
   d. Click *Show clock*. (This inserts a check mark in the check box.)
   e. Click the Apply button.
   f. Click OK to close the dialog box.

Setting Clicking Options

You can set clicking options for the Windows environment and specify either a double-click or single-click to open a program or file. Steps in this textbook assume that you will double-click to open a file or program. To change from single-click to open (point to select) to double-click to open (single-click to select), complete these steps:

1. At the Windows desktop, click the My Computer icon.
2. At the My Computer window, click Tools on the Menu bar, and then click Folder Options at the drop-down menu.
3. At the Folder Options dialog box with the General tab selected, click the Double-click to open an item (single-click to select) option located in the Click items as follows section.
4. Click the Apply button and then click OK.

Using Windows Explorer

Windows Explorer in Windows 2000 is a file management program. Use Windows Explorer to see the contents of every drive and folder attached to your computer. You can even look into drives and folders on a network.

Looking at the Windows Explorer Window

To open Windows Explorer, click the Start button on the Taskbar, point to *Programs*, point to *Accessories*, and then click *Windows Explorer*. This displays the Windows Explorer window similar to the one shown in figure W.12. (Your Windows Explorer window will vary from what you see in figure W.12.)

FIGURE

W.12 *Windows Explorer Window*

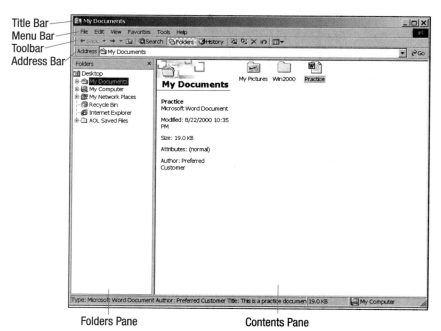

The left side of the Windows Explorer window is referred to as the Folders pane. (You can turn off the display of the Folders pane by clicking the Folders button on the toolbar.) The Folders pane shows special system folders and gives you a large view of your computer system. The right side of the Windows Explorer window is referred to as the Contents pane and displays the contents of the folder as well as related hyperlinks. (The related hyperlinks display as underlined blue text. Click a hyperlink and the hyperlinked folder displays in the Contents pane.)

Open Windows Explorer and the My Documents folder opens by default as shown in figure W.12. The Folders pane is based on a *hierarchy* with Desktop displayed at the top. As you can see from figure W.12, all the other icons are shown below the Desktop icon.

A folder may display preceded by a plus symbol. This plus symbol indicates that the folder contains additional folders (or drives). Double-click the folder name in the Folders pane and the contents of the folder display in the Folders pane as well as the Contents pane. You can also click the plus symbol and the contents of the folder display in the Folders pane but not the Contents pane. When the contents of a folder display, the plus symbol changes to a minus symbol. Click the minus symbol and the contents of the folder are hidden in the Folders pane. Double-click the My Computer folder name in the Folders pane and the Windows Explorer window displays as shown in figure W.13 (your window may vary slightly).

FIGURE

W.13 *Contents of My Computer*

Clicking the *Up* button on the toolbar moves Windows Explorer up the hierarchy. You can also click the Back button on the toolbar to move back to the previously displayed folder or drive. Figure W.14 identifies the buttons on the Windows Explorer toolbar.

FIGURE

W.14 *Windows Explorer Toolbar Buttons*

Copying, Moving, and Deleting Files/Folders in Windows Explorer

File and folder management activities can be performed in Windows Explorer. These activities include copying and moving files or folders from a folder or drive to another or deleting files or folders. Windows Explorer offers a variety of methods for copy, moving, and deleting files/folders. You can use buttons on the toolbar, drop-down menu options, or shortcut menu options. This section will provide you with the steps for copying, moving, and deleting files/folders using buttons on the toolbar.

To copy a file/folder to another folder or drive, select the file or folder by clicking it in the Contents pane and then clicking the Copy To button on the toolbar. At the Browse For Folder dialog box shown in figure W.15, click the desired folder or drive (you may need to click a plus symbol to display hidden folders) and then click OK. To move a file or folder to another folder or drive, select the file or folder and then click the Move To button on the toolbar. At the Browse For Folder dialog box, specify the location, and then click OK. Copying a file or folder leaves the file or folder in the original location and saves a copy at the new location while moving removes the file or folder from the original location and moves it to the new location.

FIGURE

W.15 *Browse For Folder Dialog Box*

A file or folder can be easily removed (deleted) from Windows Explorer. To delete a file or folder, click the file or folder and then click the Delete button on the toolbar. At the dialog box asking you to confirm the deletion, click the Yes button. A deleted file or folder is sent to the Recycle Bin. You will learn more about the Recycle Bin in the next section.

COPYING A FILE AND FOLDER AND DELETING A FILE

1. At the Windows 2000 desktop, open Windows Explorer by completing the following steps:
   a. Click the Start button located at the left side of the Taskbar.
   b. At the pop-up menu that displays, point to *Programs*, point to *Accessories*, and then click *Windows Explorer*.
2. Copy a file from the CD that accompanies this textbook to a disk in drive A by completing the following steps:
   a. Insert the CD that accompanies this textbook into the CD drive.
   b. Insert a formatted 3.5-inch disk in drive A.
   c. Double-click the My Computer folder name in the Folders pane.
   d. Double-click the name of the drive containing the CD in the Folders pane (probably displays as OFFICEXP_BENCH followed by a drive letter). (Make sure you double-click because you want the contents of the CD to display in the Folders pane as well as the Contents pane.)
   e. Double-click the *Windows* folder in the Contents pane.
   f. Click *Word Document 01* in the Contents pane to select it.
   g. Click the Copy To button on the toolbar.
   h. At the Browse For Folder dialog box, display the drives and folders in My Computer by double-clicking My Computer in the dialog box list box. (Skip this step if the drives and folders are already displayed.)
   i. Click *3¹/₂ Floppy (A:)* in the dialog box list box.
   j. Click OK.
3. Delete *Word Document 01* from drive A by completing the following steps:
   a. Scroll up the display in the Folders pane until *3¹/₂ Floppy (A:)* is visible and then double-click *3¹/₂ Floppy (A:)*.
   b. Click *Word Document 01* (all of the document name may not be visible) in the Contents pane to select it.
   c. Click the Delete button on the toolbar.
   d. At the message asking you to confirm the deletion, click the Yes button.
4. Copy the *Windows* folder from the CD drive to the disk in drive A by completing the following steps:
   a. Scroll down the display in the Folders pane until the drive containing the CD displays (this will probably display as OFFICEXP_BENCH followed by the letter of the CD drive) and then double-click the drive.
   b. Click the *Windows* folder in the Contents pane to select it.
   c. Click the Copy To button on the toolbar.
   d. At the Browse For Folder dialog box, click *3¹/₂ Floppy (A:)* in the list box.
   e. Click OK.
5. Close Windows Explorer by clicking File on the Menu bar and then clicking Close at the drop-down menu. (You can also close Windows Explorer by clicking the Close button [contains an X] located in the upper right corner of Windows Explorer.)

Selecting Files/Folders

More than one file or folder can be moved, copied, or deleted at one time. Before moving, copying, or deleting files/folders, select the desired files or folders. Selecting files/folders in Windows Explorer is easier when the display of the Files pane is changed to List or Details. To change the display, open Windows Explorer and then click View on the Menu bar. At the drop-down menu, click the List option or the Details option.

To move adjacent files/folders, click the first file or folder and then hold down the Shift key and click the last file or folder. This selects and highlights all files/folders from the first file/folder you clicked to the last file/folder you clicked. With the adjacent files/folders selected, click the Move To button on the toolbar and then specify the desired location at the Browse For Folder dialog box. To select nonadjacent files/folders, click the first file/folder to select it, hold down the Ctrl key and then click any other files/folders to be moved or copied.

exercise 4

COPYING AND DELETING FILES

1. At the Windows 2000 desktop, open Windows Explorer by clicking the Start button, pointing to *Programs*, pointing to *Accessories*, and then clicking *Windows Explorer*.
2. Copy files from the CD that accompanies this textbook to a disk in drive A by completing the following steps:
   a. Insert the CD that accompanies this textbook into the CD drive.
   b. Insert your disk in drive A.
   c. Double-click My Computer in the Folders pane.
   d. Double-click the CD drive in the Folders pane (probably displays as OFFICEXP_BENCH followed by the drive letter).
   e. Double-click the *Windows* folder in the Contents pane.
   f. Change the display to Details by clicking View on the Menu bar and then clicking Details.
   g. Position the arrow pointer on *Word Document 01* in the Contents pane and then click the left mouse button.
   h. Hold down the Shift key, click *Word Document 05*, and then release the Shift key. (This selects *Word Document 01, Word Document 02, Word Document 03, Word Document 04,* and *Word Document 05*.)
   i. Click the Copy To button on the toolbar.
   j. At the Browse For Folder dialog box, click *3¹/₂ Floppy (A:)* in the list box and then click OK.
3. Double-click *3¹/₂ Floppy (A:)* in the Folders pane to display the files saved on the disk in drive A. (You may need to scroll up the Folders pane to display *3¹/₂ Floppy (A:)*.)
4. Delete the files from drive A that you just copied by completing the following steps:
   a. Change the view by clicking View on the Menu bar and then clicking List.
   b. Position the arrow pointer on *Word Document 01* in the Contents pane and then click the left mouse button.
   c. Hold down the Shift key, click *Word Document 05*, and then release the Shift key. (This selects *Word Document 01, Word Document 02, Word Document 03, Word Document 04,* and *Word Document 05*.)
   d. Click the Delete button on the toolbar.
   e. At the message asking you to confirm the deletion, click the Yes button.
   f. At the message telling you that the document is a read-only file and asking if you want to delete it, click the Yes to All button.
5. Close Windows Explorer by clicking File and then Close, or clicking the Close button (contains an X) located in the upper right corner of Windows Explorer.

Manipulating and Creating Folders in Windows Explorer

Organize and group files in folders. To help you organize files, you can create folders in Windows Explorer. To do this, double-click in the Folders pane the drive or folder in which you want to create the new folder. Click File on the Menu bar, point to New, and then click Folder. This inserts a folder icon in the Contents pane and names the folder *New Folder* as shown in figure W.16. Key the desired name for the new folder and then press Enter.

FIGURE

W.16 *New Folder Icon in Windows Explorer*

CREATING A NEW FOLDER

1. At the Windows 2000 desktop, open Windows Explorer.
2. Create a new folder by completing the following steps:
   a. Insert your disk in drive A (this disk contains the *Windows* folder you copied in exercise 3).
   b. Double-click *3¹/₂ Floppy (A:)* in the Folders pane.
   c. Double-click the *Windows* folder in the Contents pane. (This opens the folder.)
   d. Click File on the Menu bar, point to New, and then click Folder.
   e. Key **Spell Check Files** and then press Enter. (This changes the name from *New Folder* to *Spell Check Files*.)
3. Copy *Word Spell Check 01, Word Spell Check 02, Word Spell Check 03*, and *Word Spell Check 04* into the Spell Check Files folder you just created by completing the following steps:
   a. Click View on the Menu bar and then click List.
   b. Click once on the file named *Word Spell Check 01* located in the Contents pane.
   c. Hold down the Shift key, click once on the file named *Word Spell Check 04*, and then release the Shift key. (This selects *Word Spell Check 01, Word Spell Check 02, Word Spell Check 03*, and *Word Spell Check 04*.)
   d. Click the Copy To button on the toolbar.
   e. At the Browse For Folder dialog box, double-click *3¹/₂ Floppy (A:)* in the list box.
   f. Double-click *Windows* (below *3¹/₂ Floppy (A:)*) in the list box.
   g. Click once on *Spell Check Files* in the list box (below *Windows*) and then click OK.
4. Display the files you just copied by double-clicking the Spell Check Files folder in the Contents pane.
5. Double-click *3¹/₂ Floppy (A:)* in the Folders pane. (This displays in the Contents pane the contents of the your disk.)

6. Delete the Spell Check Files folder and its contents by completing the following steps:
   a. Double-click the *Windows* folder in the Contents pane.
   b. Click the Spell Check Files folder in the Contents pane to select it.
   c. Click the Delete button on the toolbar.
   d. At the message asking you to confirm the deletion, click the Yes button.
   e. At the message telling you that the document is a read-only file and asking if you want to delete it, click the Yes to All button.
7. Close Windows Explorer by clicking File and then Close, or clicking the Close button (contains an X) located in the upper right corner of Windows Explorer.

Using the Recycle Bin

Deleting the wrong file can be a disaster but Windows 2000 helps protect your work with the Recycle Bin (see figure W.17). The Recycle Bin acts just like an office wastepaper basket; you can throw away unwanted files, but you can reach in and take paper out if you threw it away by accident.

FIGURE

W.17 *Recycle Bin Icon*

Deleting Files to the Recycle Bin

A file/folder or selected files/folders deleted from the hard drive are automatically sent to the Recycle Bin. Files/folders deleted from a disk are deleted permanently. (Recovery programs are available, however, that will help you recover deleted text. If you accidentally delete a file/folder from a disk, do not do anything more with the disk until you can run a recovery program.)

Another method for deleting a file is to drag the file to the Recycle Bin icon on the desktop. Drag a file icon to the Recycle Bin until the Recycle Bin icon is selected (displays with a blue background) and then release the mouse button. This drops the file you are dragging into the Recycle Bin.

Recovering Files from the Recycle Bin

If you accidentally delete a file to the Recycle Bin, it can be easily restored. To restore a file, double-click the Recycle Bin icon on the desktop. This opens the Recycle Bin window shown in figure W.18. (The contents of the Recycle Bin will vary.)

W.18 *Recycle Bin Window*

To restore a file, click the file you want restored, click File on the Menu bar, and then click Restore at the drop-down menu. The file is removed from the Recycle Bin and returned to its original location. You can also restore a file by positioning the arrow pointer on the file, clicking the *right* mouse button, and then clicking *Restore* at the pop-up menu.

DELETING FILES TO AND RECOVERING FILES FROM THE RECYCLE BIN

(Before completing this exercise, check with your instructor to determine if you can copy files to the hard drive.)

1. At the Windows 2000 desktop, open Windows Explorer.
2. Copy files from your disk in drive A to the My Documents folder on your hard drive by completing the following steps:
   a. Insert your disk in drive A (this disk contains the *Windows* folder).
   b. Double-click My Computer in the Folders pane.
   c. Double-click *3¹/₂ Floppy (A:)* in the Folders pane.
   d. Double-click the *Windows* folder in the Contents pane.
   e. Position the arrow pointer on *Word Spell Check 01* and then click the left mouse button.
   f. Hold down the Shift key, click *Word Spell Check 04*, and then release the Shift key.
   g. Click the Copy To button on the toolbar.
   h. At the Browse For Folder dialog box, click *My Documents* in the list box.
   i. Click OK.
3. Double-click My Documents in the Folders pane to display the files located in the folder. (The files you copied, *Word Spell Check 01* through *Word Spell Check 04*, will display in the Contents pane in alphabetical order.)
4. Delete *Word Spell Check 01* through *Word Spell Check 04* from the My Documents folder and send them to the Recycle Bin by completing the following steps:

a. Select *Word Spell Check 01* through *Word Spell Check 04* in the Contents pane. (If these files are not visible, you will need to scroll down the list of files.)

b. Click the Delete button on the toolbar.

c. At the message asking you to confirm the deletion, click the Yes button.

d. At the message telling you that the document is a read-only file and asking if you want to delete it, click the Yes to All button.

5. Close Windows Explorer.

6. At the desktop, display the contents of the Recycle Bin by double-clicking the Recycle Bin icon.

7. At the Recycle Bin window, restore *Word Spell Check 01* through *Word Spell Check 04* to the My Documents folder by completing the following steps:

a. Scroll to the end of the list of files.

b. When *Word Spell Check 01* through *Word Spell Check 04* display in the list box, select all four files.

c. With the files selected, click File on the Menu bar and then click Restore at the drop-down menu.

d. At the message asking you to confirm that you want to move the read-only file, click the Yes to All button.

8. Close the Recycle Bin window by clicking File on the Menu bar and then clicking Close at the drop-down menu.

9. Open Windows Explorer.

10. Make sure the My Documents folder is selected. (If it is not, select it by double-clicking My Documents in the Folders pane.)

11. Delete the files you restored by completing the following steps:

a. Select *Word Spell Check 01* through *Word Spell Check 04* in the Contents pane. (If these files are not visible, you will need to scroll down the list of files. These are the files you recovered from the Recycle Bin.)

b. Click the Delete button on the toolbar.

c. At the message asking you to confirm the deletion, click the Yes button.

d. At the message telling you that the document is a read-only file and asking if you want to delete it, click the Yes to All button.

12. Close Windows Explorer.

Emptying the Recycle Bin

Just like a wastepaper basket, the Recycle Bin can get full. To empty the Recycle Bin, position the arrow pointer on the Recycle Bin icon on the desktop and then click the *right* mouse button. At the pop-up menu that displays, click *Empty Recycle Bin*. At the message asking you to confirm the deletion, click the Yes button. You can also empty the Recycle Bin by double-clicking the Recycle Bin icon. At the Recycle Bin window that displays, click the Empty Recycle Bin button that displays at the left side of the window. At the message asking you to confirm the deletion, click the Yes button. (You can also empty the Recycle Bin by clicking File on the Menu bar and then clicking Empty Recycle Bin at the drop-down menu.)

Emptying the Recycle Bin deletes all files/folders. You can delete a specific file/folder from the Recycle Bin (rather than all files/folders). To do this, double-click the Recycle Bin icon on the desktop. At the Recycle Bin window, select the file/folder or files/folders to be deleted, and then click the Delete button on the toolbar. At the message asking you to confirm the deletion, click the Yes button.

(Before completing this exercise, check with your instructor to determine if you can delete files/folders from the Recycle Bin.)

1. At the Windows 2000 desktop, double-click the Recycle Bin icon.
2. At the Recycle Bin window, empty the contents of the Recycle Bin by completing the following steps:
   a. Click the Empty Recycle Bin button that displays at the left side of the window.
   b. At the message asking you to confirm the deletion, click the Yes button.
3. Close the Recycle Bin window by clicking File and then Close.

When the Recycle Bin is emptied the files cannot be recovered by the Recycle Bin or by Windows 2000. If you have to recover a file, you will need to use a file recovery program such as Norton Utilities. These utilities are separate programs, but might be worth their cost if you ever need them.

Customizing the Recycle Bin

The Recycle Bin settings can be customized at the Recycle Bin Properties dialog box. To display this dialog box, position the arrow pointer on the Recycle Bin icon on the desktop and then click the *right* mouse button. At the pop-up menu that displays, click *Properties*.

Using My Computer

Use the My Computer folder to display the contents of the floppy disk and hard disk, CD-ROM drive, mapped network drives and to open the Control Panel. To display the My Computer window shown in figure W.19, double-click the My Computer icon on the desktop.

FIGURE

W.19 *My Computer Window*

Using the My Computer window, you can navigate to the various drives and folders on your computer. You can also double-click on a file in the My Computer window and the program in which the file was created is opened (provided the program is located on your computer) as well as the file. You can copy, move, and delete folders and files in My Computer following the same steps you learned earlier in the *Using Windows Explorer* section. For example, to copy a file/folder, click the file or folder, and then click the Copy To button on the My Computer window toolbar. At the Browse For Folder dialog box, click the desired location in the list box, and then click OK.

Changing the My Computer Window Display

By default, the My Computer window displays objects in the window as large icons. With the Large Icons option selected at the View drop-down menu, the My Computer window should look something like the window shown in figure W.19.

Click the Small Icons option at the View drop-down menu and the icons in the My Computer window are reduced in size. Clicking the List option displays objects in the My Computer window in a list towards the left side of the window. Click the Details option at the View drop-down menu and a detailed view of each object displays in the My Computer window as shown in figure W.20.

FIGURE

W.20 **My Computer Window in Details View**

exercise **8**

| CHANGING THE DISPLAY AND COPYING AND DELETING A FILE IN MY COMPUTER |

(Before completing this exercise, check with your instructor to determine if you can copy files to the My Documents folder on the hard drive.)

1. At the Windows 2000 desktop, double-click the My Computer icon.
2. At the My Computer window, display folders and files in a list (rather than large icons) by clicking View and then List.
3. Insert your disk in drive A.
4. Copy a document from the *Windows* folder on the disk in drive A to the My Documents folder on the hard drive by completing the following steps:
   a. Double-click *3¹/₂ Floppy (A:)* in the My Computer list box.
   b. Double-click the *Windows* folder (this displays the documents in the folder).
   c. Change the display of the files in the *Windows* folder by clicking View on the Menu bar and then clicking Details.
   d. Click once on the document named *Word Document 01*.
   e. Click the Copy To button on the toolbar.
   f. At the Browse For Folder dialog box, click My Documents in the list box.
   g. Click OK.
5. Delete *Word Document 01* from the My Documents folder by completing the following steps:
   a. Click the down-pointing triangle at the right side of the Address bar located towards the top of the My Computer window (just below the toolbar).
   b. At the drop-down list that displays, click *My Documents*.
   c. Click *Word Document 01* to select it.
   d. Click the Delete button on the toolbar.
   e. At the message asking you to confirm the deletion, click the Yes button.
6. Close the My Computer window by clicking File on the Menu bar and then clicking Close or by clicking the Close button (displays with an X) located at the right side of the My Computer Title bar.

Creating a Shortcut

Shortcuts are specialized icons. They are very small files that point the operating system to the actual item, whether it is a file, a folder, or an application. For example, in figure W.21, the *Shortcut to Practice Document* icon represents a path to a specific file in the Word 2002 program. The icon is not the actual file but a path to the file. Double-click the shortcut icon and Windows opens the Word 2002 program and also opens the file named Practice Document.

FIGURE

| W.21 | *Practice Document Shortcut Icon*

Shortcuts provide quick and easy access to files or programs used every day without having to remember where the file is stored. One method for creating a shortcut is to display the My Computer window and then display the drive or folder where the file is located. Position the arrow pointer on the file, hold down the *right* mouse button, drag the outline of the file to the desktop, and then release the mouse button. At the pop-up menu that displays, click *Create Shortcut(s) Here*. This creates a shortcut icon on the desktop like the one shown in figure W.21.

A shortcut icon can be easily deleted from the desktop by dragging the shortcut icon to the Recycle Bin icon. This deletes the shortcut icon but does not delete the file to which the shortcut pointed.

exercise 9

CREATING A SHORTCUT

1. At the Windows 2000 desktop, double-click the My Computer icon.
2. Insert your disk in drive A.
3. At the My Computer window, double-click *3¹/₂ Floppy (A:)*.
4. Double-click the *Windows* folder.
5. Change the display of files to a list by clicking View on the Menu bar and then clicking List at the drop-down menu.
6. Create a shortcut to the file named *Word Letter 01* by completing the following steps:
   a. Position the arrow pointer on *Word Letter 01*.
   b. Hold down the *right* mouse button, drag the outline of the file to the desktop window, and then release the mouse button.
   c. At the pop-up menu that displays, click *Create Shortcut(s) Here*.
7. Close the My Computer window by clicking the Close button located in the upper right corner of the window.
8. Open Word 2002 and the file named *Word Letter 01* by double-clicking the Word Letter 01 shortcut icon on the desktop.
9. After viewing the file in Word, exit Word by clicking <u>F</u>ile on the Menu bar and then clicking E<u>x</u>it at the drop-down menu.
10. Delete the Word Letter 01 shortcut icon by completing the following steps:
    a. At the desktop, position the arrow pointer on the Word Letter 01 shortcut icon.
    b. Hold down the left mouse button, drag the icon on top of the Recycle Bin icon, and then release the mouse button.

Customizing the Desktop

The Windows 2000 operating environment is very customizable. You can change background patterns and colors and set screen savers directly from the desktop. To change display properties, position the arrow pointer on any empty location on the desktop and then click the *right* mouse button. At the pop-up menu that displays, click *Properties*. This displays the Display Properties dialog box with the Background tab selected as shown in figure W.22.

W.22 Display Properties Dialog Box with Background Tab Selected

Changing the Desktop Background

The desktop background is customized at the Display Properties dialog box with the Background tab selected. Add a wallpaper background to the Windows desktop with options in the dialog box list box. Click any wallpaper option in the list box and preview the results in the preview screen. Wallpaper can be centered, tiled or stretched. Choose the display by clicking the down-pointing triangle at the right side of the Picture Display list box and then clicking the desired display. Choose the Tile option and the wallpaper covers the entire screen with a repeated series of images. Choose Center and the wallpaper is one image set in the middle of the screen or choose the Stretch option and the image is stretched across the entire screen. You can use the Browse button to select an HTML document from the network for your desktop background.

Add a pattern to the desktop with options from the Pattern dialog box. Display this dialog box by clicking the Pattern button located towards the bottom right corner of the Display Properties dialog box. The Pattern button is available only when the Picture Display option is set for Center.

If you want, you can choose (None) for both the wallpaper and pattern. This leaves the desktop one solid color. When you are satisfied with the pattern and wallpaper choices, click OK to set the changes and close the Display Properties dialog box.

Adding a Screen Saver

If your computer sits idle for periods of time, consider adding a screen saver. If a screen sits idle for a long period of time, you run the risk of burning any images onto the screen. (Fortunately, monitor technology has improved and burning images on the screen is becoming less of a problem.) A screen saver is a pattern that changes constantly, thus eliminating the problem of an image staying on the screen too long.

To add a screen saver, display the Display Properties dialog box and then click the Screen Saver tab. This displays the dialog box as shown in figure W.23.

W.23 *Display Properties Dialog Box with Screen Saver Tab Selected*

Click this down-pointing triangle to display a list of installed screen savers.

Click the down-pointing triangle at the right side of the Screen Saver list box to display a list of installed screen savers. Click a screen saver and a preview displays in the monitor located toward the top of the dialog box. Click the Preview button and the dialog box is hidden and the screen saver displays on your monitor. Move the mouse or click a button on the mouse and the dialog box will reappear.

Click the Settings button to display additional options for customizing a screen saver. Protect the screen saver with a password by clicking the Password protected check box. If a check mark appears in this check box, you must enter the correct password to clear the screen saver and return to the desktop.

If your computer's hardware is Energy Star compatible, the *Energy saving features of monitor* section is enabled. Click the Power button and a dialog box displays with options for choosing a power scheme appropriate to the way you use your computer. The dialog box also includes options for specifying how long the computer can be left unused before the monitor and hard disk are turned off and the system goes to standby or hibernate mode.

Changing Colors

Click the Appearance tab at the Display Properties dialog box and the dialog box displays as shown in figure W.24. At this dialog box, you can change the desktop scheme. Schemes are predefined collections of colors that are used in windows, menus, title bars, and system fonts. Windows 2000 loads with the Windows Standard scheme. Click the down-pointing triangle at the right side of the Scheme list box to display a list of available schemes. When you choose a scheme, the results are previewed in the sample dialog boxes.

W.24 *Display Properties Dialog Box with Appearance Tab Selected*

Schemes set the appearance of the entire operating system. If you want to set the desktop to a unique color, but leave the rest of the scheme intact, specify options at the Item drop-down list. Click the down-pointing triangle at the right side of the Item list box and then click the specific object to which you want the scheme applied.

Displaying Web Pages on the Desktop

Click the Web tab and the Display Properties dialog box displays. Windows uses your Internet browser to display Web pages and other Internet files on your desktop. Using the tab requires a working Internet connection.

Changing Desktop Icons

Click the Effects tab and the Display Properties dialog box displays. Use options from this dialog box to change desktop icons from the default icons used by Windows. Select the icon you want to change, click the Change Icon button, and select a new icon from the Current icon list box in the Change Icon dialog box. Use the Browse button to select an icon of your own design.

Changing Settings

Click the Settings tab at the Display Properties dialog box and the dialog box displays as shown in figure W.25. At this dialog box, you can set color and screen resolution.

W.25 *Display Properties Dialog Box with Settings Tab Selected*

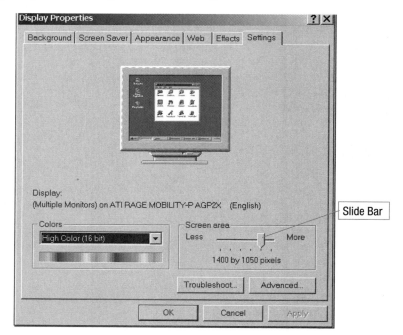

The Colors option determines how many colors are displayed on your monitor. The more colors that are shown, the more realistic the images will appear. However, a lot of computer memory is required to show thousands of colors. Your exact choice is determined by the specific hardware you are using. The Screen area slide bar sets the screen's resolution. The higher the number, the more you can fit onto your screen. Again, your actual values depend on your particular hardware. Clicking the Advanced button displays a dialog box with advanced display settings for changing font size.

exercise 10

CUSTOMIZING THE DESKTOP

(Before completing this exercise, check with your instructor to determine if you can customize the desktop.)

1. At the Windows 2000 desktop, display the Display Properties dialog box by positioning the arrow pointer on an empty location on the desktop, clicking the *right* mouse button, and then clicking *Properties* at the pop-up menu.
2. At the Display Properties dialog box, add wallpaper to the desktop by completing the following steps:
   a. Make sure the Background tab is selected. (If it is not, click the Background tab.)
   b. Click *Blue Lace 16* in the Wallpaper list box. (If this option is not available, choose another wallpaper.)
   c. Make sure Center is selected in the Picture Display list box.
   d. Click OK to close the dialog box.
3. After viewing the desktop with the Blue Lace 16 wallpaper, add a pattern to fill in the space around the wallpaper by completing the following steps:
   a. Display the Display Properties dialog box.

b. At the Display Properties dialog box with the Background tab selected, click the Pattern button. (This displays the Pattern dialog box.)

c. Click *Paisley* in the Pattern list box. (If *Paisley* is not visible, click the down-pointing triangle in the Pattern list box until *Paisley* displays.)

d. Click OK to close the Pattern dialog box, and then click OK to close the Display Properties dialog box.

4. After viewing the desktop with the Blue Lace 16 wallpaper and the Paisley pattern applied, add a screen saver by completing the following steps:

a. Display the Display Properties dialog box.

b. At the Display Properties dialog box, click the Screen Saver tab. (If a screen saver is already selected in the Screen Saver list box, make a note of this screen saver name.)

c. Click the down-pointing triangle at the right side of the Screen Saver list box.

d. At the drop-down list that displays, click a screen saver that interests you. (A preview of the screen saver displays in the screen located toward the top of the dialog box.)

e. Click a few other screen savers to see how they will display on the monitor.

f. With a screen saver selected, click OK. (This closes the dialog box.)

g. At the desktop the screen saver will display, by default, after the monitor has sat idle for 15 minutes.

5. Return all settings back to the default by completing the following steps:

a. Display the Display Properties dialog box.

b. Make sure the Background tab is selected.

c. Click *(None)* in the Wallpaper list box.

d. Click the Pattern button.

e. At the Pattern dialog box, click *(None)* in the Pattern list box.

f. Click OK to close the Pattern dialog box.

g. Click the Screen Saver tab.

h. At the Display Properties dialog box with the Screen Saver tab selected, click the down-pointing triangle at the right side of the Screen Saver list box, and then click *(None)*. (If a screen saver was selected before completing this exercise, return to that screen saver.)

i. Click OK to close the Display Properties dialog box.

Exploring Windows 2000 Help Files

Windows 2000 includes an on-screen reference guide providing information, explanations, and interactive help on learning Windows features. The on-screen reference guide, referred to as "Help," contains complex files with hypertext used to access additional information by clicking a word or phrase. The Help feature can interact with open programs to help guide you through difficult tasks.

Using Windows Help Files

Display the Help window by clicking the Start button on the Taskbar and then click Help at the pop-up menu. The pane at the left side of the window contains four tabs—Contents, Index, Search, and Favorites. Click the Contents tab and help topics display in the list box below the tabs with each option preceded by a book icon as shown in figure W.26. Click a book icon and a list of subtopics appears. Click a subtopic that interests you and information about the topic displays in the pane at the right side of the window.

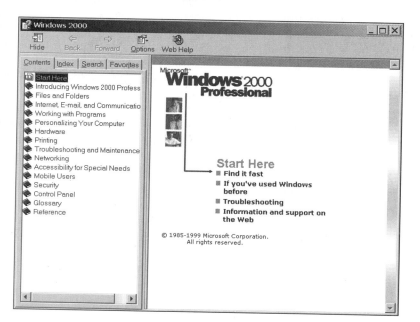

exercise **11**

USING THE HELP TOPICS OR WINDOWS HELP DIALOG BOX WITH THE CONTENTS TAB SELECTED

(Depending on the type of installation completed on Windows, some of the Help categories may not be available. If some of the Help categories in exercise 11 do not display, experiment with other categories that interest you.)

1. At the Windows 2000 desktop, use the Help feature to learn about new Windows 2000 features by completing the following steps:
    a. Click the Start button located at the left side of the Taskbar.
    b. At the pop-up menu that displays, click *Help*.
    c. At the Help window, click the Contents tab. (Skip this step if the Contents tab is already selected.)
    d. Click *Introducing Windows 2000 Professional* located in the list box in the pane at the left side of the window. (This causes the book icon preceding *Introducing Windows 2000 Professional* to display as an open book and a list of subtopics to display below *Introducing Windows 2000 Professional*.)
    e. Click *What's new?* and information about new Windows 2000 features displays in the pane at the right side of the window.
    f. Click *Easier to use* (located in the pane at the right side of the window) and then read the information that displays below the topic.
    g. Click the other topics in the pane at the right side of the window and read the information supplied.
2. Close the Help window by clicking the Close button (displays with an X) that displays in the upper right corner of the window.

Click the Index tab and the Help window displays as shown in figure W.27. Key the desired feature, keyword, term, etc., in the *Type in the keyword to find* text box. Help displays a list of topics matching or related to the keyed text. Using the Help window with the In̲dex tab selected is often easier than looking through the window with the C̲ontents tab selected.

F I G U R E

W.27 **Help Window with In̲dex Tab Selected**

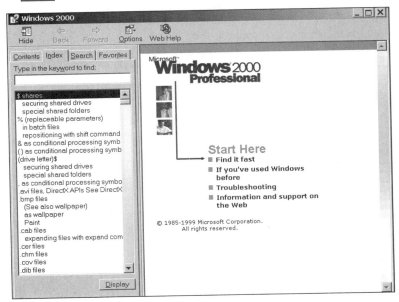

Use the Help window with the S̲earch tab selected to search for a specific word, term, or phrase. At the Help window with the S̲earch tab selected, as shown in figure W.28, key the desired word or phrase in the *Type in the keyw̲ord to find* list box and then press Enter or click the L̲ist Topics button.

F I G U R E

W.28 **Help Window with S̲earch Tab Selected**

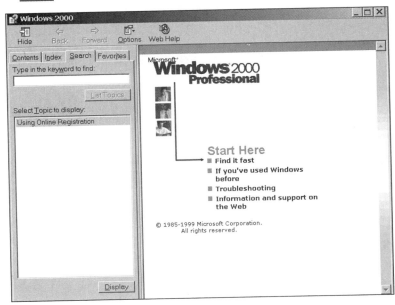

You can enter a word or phrase in the *Type in the keyword to find* list box. If you want to find help topics that contain a specific phrase, enclose the phrase in quotation marks. This tells Help to display only those topics that contain all the words in the phrase in the specific order.

If you repeatedly use a Help topic, you can add it to the Favorites tab. To do this, display the Help window and then display the desired topic. With the topic displayed in the pane at the right side of the window, click the Favorites tab. Click the <u>A</u>dd button and the topic name is added to the list box located in the pane at the left side of the window. The next time you want to display the Help topic, display the Help window, click the Favorites tab, and then double-click the desired topic.

exercise 12

USING THE HELP WINDOW WITH THE INDEX TAB AND THE SEARCH TAB SELECTED

1. At the Windows 2000 desktop, use the Help feature to learn about deleting files and folders to the Recycle Bin by completing the following steps:
   a. Click the Start button and then click *Help* at the pop-up menu.
   b. At the Help window, click the I<u>n</u>dex tab.
   c. With the insertion point positioned in the *Type in the key<u>w</u>ord to find* text box, key **deleting files**.
   d. At the list of topics that displays in the list box in the pane at the left side of the window, double-click the subtopic *Recycle Bin* that displays below the *deleting files* topic.
   e. At the Topics Found dialog box with the *Delete or restore files in the Recycle Bin* topic selected, click the Display button.
   f. Read the information that displays in the pane at the right side of the window.
   g. Click <u>Related Topics</u> that displays at the bottom of the pane at the right side of the window.
   h. At the pop-up list box that displays, click the *Remove items permanently when you delete them* topic.
   i. Read the information that displays in the pane at the right side of the window.
   j. Click the Close button (contains an X) that displays in the upper right corner of the Help window.
2. Use the Help feature to search for information on the Display Properties dialog box by completing the following steps:
   a. Click the Start button and then click *Help* at the pop-up menu.
   b. At the Help window, click the <u>S</u>earch tab.
   c. Key **"Display Properties dialog box"** in the *Type in the key<u>w</u>ord to find* text box. (Make sure you key the quotation marks.)
   d. Click the <u>L</u>ist Topics button.
   e. When a list of topics displays, double-click *Display overview*. (This displays the topic in the pane at the right side of the window with the phrase *Display Properties dialog box* selected.)
   f. Read the information that displays in the pane at the right side of the window.
   g. Select the text currently displayed in the *Type in the key<u>w</u>ord to find* text box and then key **Display Properties dialog box** (without the quotation marks).
   h. Press Enter or click the <u>L</u>ist Topics button.
   i. Notice the list of topics that displays is different than the list that displayed for the previous search. Double-click one of the topics in the list and notice that the topic displays with one or more of the words in the phrase selected.
   j. Close the Help window.

OFFICE **XP**

BROWSING THE INTERNET USING INTERNET EXPLORER

Microsoft Internet Explorer is a Web browser program with options and features for displaying sites as well as navigating and searching for information on the Internet. The *Internet* is a network of computers connected around the world. Users access the Internet for several purposes: to communicate using e-mail, to subscribe to news groups, to transfer files, to socialize with other users around the globe in "chat" rooms, and largely to access virtually any kind of information imaginable.

Using the Internet, people can access a phenomenal amount of information for private or public use. To use the Internet, three things are generally required—an Internet Service Provider (ISP), a program to browse the Web (called a *Web browser*), and a *search engine*. In this section, you will learn how to use the Internet Explorer Web browser to browse web sites, search for specific sites, and download a web page and image.

Browsing the Internet

You will use the Microsoft Internet Explorer Web browser to locate information on the Internet. Uniform Resource Locators, referred to as URLs, are the method used to identify locations on the Internet. The steps for browsing the Internet vary but generally include: opening Internet Explorer, keying the URL for the desired site, navigating the various pages of the site, printing web pages, and then closing Internet Explorer.

To launch Internet Explorer, double-click the Internet Explorer icon on the Windows desktop. Figure IE.1 identifies the elements of the Internet Explorer, version 5.5, window. The web page that displays in your Internet Explorer window may vary from what you see in Figure IE.1.

IE.1 *Internet Explorer Window*

Title Bar
Menu Bar
Toolbar
Address Bar

Vertical Scroll Bar

If you know the URL for the desired web site, click in the Address bar, key the URL, and then press Enter. In a few moments, the web site opening page displays in the Internet Explorer window. URLs (Uniform Resource Locators) are the method used to identify locations on the Internet. The format of a URL is *http://server-name.path*. The first part of the URL, *http* stands for HyperText Transfer Protocol, which is the protocol or language used to transfer data within the World Wide Web. The colon and slashes separate the protocol from the server name. The server name is the second component of the URL. For example, in the URL http://www.microsoft.com, the server name is *microsoft*. The last part of the URL specifies the domain to which the server belongs. For example, *.com* refers to "commercial" and establishes that the URL is a commercial company. Other examples of domains include *.edu* for "educational," *.gov* for "government," and *.mil* for "military."

exercise **1**

BROWSING THE INTERNET WITH INTERNET EXPLORER

1. Make sure you are connected to the Internet through an Internet Service Provider and that the Windows desktop displays. (Check with your instructor to determine if you need to complete steps for accessing the Internet.)
2. Launch Microsoft Internet Explorer by double-clicking the Internet Explorer icon located on the Windows desktop.
3. At the Internet Explorer window, explore the web site for Yosemite National Park by completing the following steps:
   a. Click in the Address bar, key **www.nps.gov/yose** and then press Enter.

Step
3a

b. Scroll down the web site home page for Yosemite National Park by clicking the down-pointing triangle on the vertical scroll bar located at the right side of the Internet Explorer window.

c. Print the web site home page by clicking the Print button located on the Internet Explorer toolbar.

4. Explore the web site for Glacier National Park by completing the following steps:

   a. Click in the Address bar, key **www.nps.gov/glac** and then press Enter.

   b. Print the web site home page by clicking the Print button located on the Internet Explorer toolbar.

5. Close Internet Explorer by clicking the Close button (contains an X) located in the upper right corner of the Internet Explorer window. (You can also close Internet Explorer by clicking File on the Internet Explorer Menu bar and then clicking Close at the drop-down menu.)

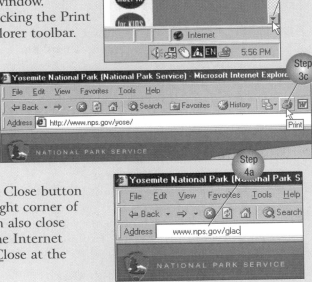

Navigating Using Hyperlinks

Most web pages contain "hyperlinks" that you click to connect to another page within the web site or to another site on the Internet. Hyperlinks may display in a web page as underlined text in a specific color or as images or icons. To use a hyperlink, position the mouse pointer on the desired hyperlink until the mouse pointer turns into a hand, and then click the left mouse button. Use hyperlinks to navigate within and between sites on the Internet. The Internet Explorer toolbar contains a Back button that, when clicked, will take you back to the previous web page. If you click the Back button and then want to go back to the previous page, click the Forward button. By clicking the Back button, you can back your way out of hyperlinks and return to the web site home page.

exercise 2

VISITING WEB SITES AND NAVIGATING USING HYPERLINKS

1. Make sure you are connected to the Internet and then double-click the Internet Explorer icon on the Windows desktop.

2. At the Internet Explorer window, display the White House web page and navigate in the page by completing the following steps:

   a. Click in the Address bar, key **whitehouse.gov** and then press Enter.

   b. At the White House home web page, position the mouse pointer on the *History* hyperlink located towards the left side of the window until the pointer turns into a hand, and then click the left mouse button. (If this hyperlink is not available, click another hyperlink that interests you.)

c. At the History web page, click the Back button.

d. At the White House home web page, click the Forward button to return to the History page.

e. Print the History page by clicking the Print button on the Internet Explorer toolbar.

3. Display the Amazon.com web site and navigate in the site by completing the following steps:

a. Click in the Address bar, key **www.amazon.com** and then press Enter.

b. At the Amazon.com home page, click a hyperlink related to books.

c. When a book web page displays, click the Print button on the Internet Explorer toolbar.

4. Close Internet Explorer by clicking the Close button (contains an X) located in the upper right corner of the Internet Explorer window.

Searching for Specific Sites

If you do not know the URL for a specific site or you want to find information on the Internet but do not know what site to visit, complete a search with a search engine. A search engine is a software program created to search quickly and easily for desired information. A variety of search engines are available on the Internet, each offering the opportunity to search for specific information. One method for searching for information is to click the Search button on the Internet Explorer toolbar. This displays a Search pane, as shown in figure IE.2 with options for completing a search. Another method for completing a search is to visit the web site home page for a search engine and use options at the site.

FIGURE

IE.2 *Internet Explorer Search Pane*

Search Pane

1. Make sure you are connected to the Internet and then double-click the Internet Explorer icon on the Windows desktop.

2. At the Internet Explorer window, search for sites on Bluegrass music by completing the following steps:

   a. Click the Search button on the Internet Explorer toolbar. (This displays the Search pane at the left side of the window.)

   b. Click in the search text box, key **Bluegrass music** and then click the search button.

   c. When a list of sites displays in the Search pane, click a site that interests you.

   d. When the web site home page displays, click the Print button.

3. Click the Search button on the Internet Explorer toolbar to remove the Search pane.

4. Use the Yahoo search engine to find sites on Bluegrass music by completing the following steps:

   a. Click in the Address bar, key **www.yahoo.com** and then press Enter.

   b. At the Yahoo web site, click in the Search text box, key **Bluegrass music** and then click the Search button (or press Enter). (Notice that the sites displayed vary from the sites displayed in the earlier search.)

   c. Click hyperlinks until a Web site displays that interests you.

   d. When the site displays, click the Print button on the Internet Explorer toolbar.

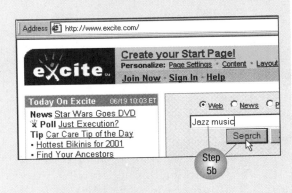

5. Use the Excite search engine to find sites on Jazz music by completing the following steps:

   a. Click in the Address bar, key **www.excite.com** and then press Enter.

   b. When the Excite web site home page displays, click in the Search text box, key **Jazz music** and then click the Search button.

   c. Click a site that interests you.

   d. When the web site home page displays, click the Print button on the Internet Explorer toolbar.

6. Close Internet Explorer.

Completing Advanced Searches for Specific Sites

The Internet contains a phenomenal amount of information. Depending on what you are searching for on the Internet and the search engine you use, some searches can result in several thousand "hits" (sites). Wading through a large number of sites can be very time consuming and counterproductive. Narrowing a search to very specific criteria can greatly reduce the number of hits for a search. To narrow a search, use the advanced search options offered by the search engine.

exercise 4

NARROWING A SEARCH

1. Make sure you are connected to the Internet and then double-click the Internet Explorer icon on the Windows desktop.
2. Search for sites on skydiving in Oregon by completing the following steps:

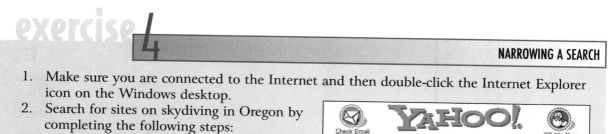

   a. Click in the Address bar and then key **www.yahoo.com**.
   b. At the Yahoo web site home page, click the *advanced search* hyperlink.
   c. At the Search Options page, click in the search text box and then key **skydiving in Oregon**.
   d. Click the *An exact phrase match* option in the *Select a search method* section. (This limits the search to any web sites that contain the exact phrase "skydiving in Oregon.")
   e. Click the *Web Sites* option in the *Select a search area* section. (Clicking this option tells Yahoo to display only web sites that contain the exact phrase and not Yahoo categories.)
   f. Click the Search button.
   g. When the list of web sites displays, click a hyperlink that interests you.
   h. Click the Print button on the Internet Explorer toolbar to print the web page.
   i. Click the Back button on the Internet Explorer toolbar until the Yahoo Search Options page displays.
3. Search for specific sites on tandem skydiving and static line skydiving in Oregon by completing the following steps:
   a. Select the text currently displayed in the search text box and then key **skydiving Oregon tandem static line**.
   b. Click the *Matches on all words (AND)* option in the *Select a search method* section. (Clicking this option tells Yahoo to find web sites that contain all of the words keyed in the Search text box.)
   c. Make sure *Web Sites* is selected in the *Select a search area* section.
   d. Click the Search button.
   e. When the list of web sites displays, click a hyperlink that interests you, and then print the web page.
4. Close Internet Explorer.

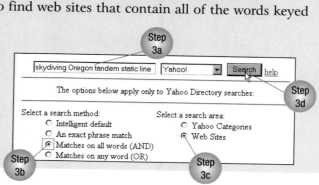

POWERPOINT

UNIT 1: CREATING AND FORMATTING POWERPOINT PRESENTATIONS

Preparing a PowerPoint Presentation

Modifying a Presentation and Using Help

Formatting Slides

Adding Visual Appeal and Animation to Presentations

MICROSOFT® POWERPOINT 2002

BENCHMARK MOUS SKILLS-UNIT 1

Reference No.	Skill	Pages
PP2002-1	**Creating Presentations**	
PP2002-1-1	Create presentations (manually and using automated tools)	
	Create a presentation using a design template	4-13
	Create a presentation using the AutoContent Wizard	22-23
	Create a presentation with the Blank Presentation template	69-71
PP2002-1-2	Add slides to and delete slides from presentations	
	Insert and delete slides	41, 43-45
	Copy and rearrange slides	42-45
PP2002-1-3	Modify headers and footers in the Slide Master	
	Insert headers and footers	74-76
	Insert text in the Footer area of the Slide Master	75-76
PP2002-2	**Inserting and Modifying Text**	
PP2002-2-2	Insert, format, and modify text	
	Insert, delete, find, and replace text in slides	33-36
	Cut, copy, and paste text in slides	36-41
	Format text in a slide	57-63
PP2002-3	**Inserting and Modifying Visual Elements**	
PP2002-3-1	Add tables, charts, clip art, and bitmap images to slides	
	Draw, select, delete, move, copy, size, and format objects	85-91
	Insert, size, move, delete, and format images in a presentation	91-98
	Add bitmapped graphics to a slide	98-99
PP2002-3-2	Customize slide backgrounds	
	Change slide color scheme and background color	65-68
	Change design template	68-69
PP2002-4	**Modifying Presentation Formats**	
PP2002-4-1	Apply formats to presentations	
	Format text in a slide	57-63
	Format with a Slide Master	60-63
	Apply more than one design template to a presentation	64-65
	Format and customize slide color scheme	65-68
	Change the design template	68-69
	Apply formatting with Format Painter	69-71
PP2002-4-2	Apply animation schemes	99-102
PP2002-4-3	Apply slide transitions	18-20
PP2002-4-4	Customize slide formats	
	Change slide color scheme and background color	65-68
	Change design template	68-69
PP2002-4-6	Manage a Slide Master	60-63
PP2002-4-8	Rearrange slides	41-45
PP2002-4-9	Modify slide layout	
	Rearrange text in slides	36-41
	Rearrange object boxes in slides	38-41
PP2002-5	**Printing Presentations**	
PP2002-5-1	Preview and print slides, outlines, handouts, and speaker notes	
	Print a presentation	9, 13, 17, 25, 70
	View a presentation	13-14, 16-18
	Add and print speaker notes	77-78
PP2002-6	**Working with Data from Other Sources**	
PP2002-6-2	Add sound and video to slides	
	Add sound to slides	18-20
PP2002-7	**Managing and Delivering Presentations**	
PP2002-7-2	Deliver presentations	
	Running a slide show	14-18
	Run a slide show automatically	20-21

PREPARING A POWERPOINT PRESENTATION

PERFORMANCE OBJECTIVES

Upon successful completion of chapter 1, you will be able to:
- **Plan a PowerPoint presentation**
- **Create a PowerPoint presentation**
- **Print a PowerPoint presentation**
- **Save, open, and close a presentation**
- **View a presentation**
- **Run a presentation**
- **Add transitions and sound effects to a presentation**
- **Run a slide show automatically**
- **Prepare a presentation in Outline view**
- **Delete a presentation**

PowerPoint Chapter 01

During a presentation, the person doing the presenting may use visual aids to strengthen the impact of the message as well as help organize the presentation. Visual aids may include transparencies, slides, photographs, or an on-screen presentation. With Microsoft's PowerPoint program, you can easily create visual aids for a presentation and then print copies of the aids as well as run the presentation. PowerPoint is a presentation graphics program that you can use to organize and present information.

PowerPoint provides a variety of output capabilities for presentations. A presentation prepared in PowerPoint can be run directly on the computer. In addition, black and white overheads can be created by printing slides on transparencies; or, color transparencies can be created if you have access to a color printer. Slides can be created in PowerPoint and then sent to a film processing company to be converted to 35mm slides. Also, printouts of slides can be made for use as speaker's notes, audience handouts, or outline pages.

Planning a Presentation

With PowerPoint, you can create slides for an on-screen presentation, or for an overhead or slide projector. You can also print handouts of the presentation, print an outline, or print the entire presentation. When planning a presentation, first define the purpose of the presentation. Is the intent to inform? educate? sell? motivate? and/or entertain? Additionally, consider the audience who will be listening to and watching the presentation. Determine the content of the presentation and also the medium that will be used to convey the message. Will a computer be used to display the slides of a presentation or will overhead transparencies be created from the slides? Some basic guidelines to consider when preparing the content of the presentation include:

- **Determine the main purpose of the presentation.** Do not try to cover too many topics—this may strain the audience's attention or cause confusion. Identifying the main point of the presentation will help you stay focused and convey a clear message to the audience.
- **Determine the output.** Is the presentation going to be presented in PowerPoint? Will slides be used? Or will black and white or color transparencies be made for an overhead? To help decide the type of output needed, consider the availability of equipment, the size of the room where the presentation will be made, and the number of people who will be attending the presentation.
- **Show one idea per slide.** Each slide in a presentation should convey only one main idea. Too many thoughts or ideas on a slide may confuse the audience and cause you to stray from the purpose of the slide. Determine the specific message you want to convey to the audience and then outline the message to organize ideas.
- **Maintain a consistent layout.** A consistent layout and color scheme for slides in a presentation will create continuity and cohesiveness. Do not get carried away by using too many colors and too many pictures or other graphic elements.
- **Keep slides easy to read and uncluttered.** Keep slides simple and easy for the audience to read. Keep words and other items such as bullets to a minimum. If the presentation is done with 35mm slides, consider using a dark background color for slides. Use a light background color when creating overhead transparencies.
- **Determine other outputs needed.** Will you be providing audience members with handouts? If so, will these handouts consist of a printing of each slide? an outline of the presentation? a printing of each slide with space for taking notes?

[handwritten margin note: 35mm Slide use Dark background use light BG when creating overhead transparencies]

Creating a PowerPoint Presentation

PowerPoint provides several methods for creating a presentation. You can use PowerPoint's AutoContent Wizard, which asks questions and then chooses a presentation layout based on your answers. You can also create a presentation using predesigned templates. PowerPoint's templates provide a variety of formatting options for slides. If you want to apply your own formatting to slides, you can choose a blank presentation. The steps you follow to create a presentation will vary depending on the method you choose, but will probably follow these basic steps:

1. Open PowerPoint.
2. Choose the desired slide layout.
3. Choose a design template.
4. Key the text for each slide, adding additional elements as needed such as graphic images.

5. Save the presentation.
6. Print the presentation as slides, handouts, notes pages, or an outline.
7. Run the presentation.
8. Close the presentation.
9. Exit PowerPoint.

Understanding the PowerPoint Window

When you choose the specific type of presentation you want to create, you are presented with the PowerPoint window in the Normal view. What displays in the window will vary depending on the type of presentation you are creating. However, the PowerPoint window contains some consistent elements as shown in figure 1.1. The PowerPoint window elements are described following the figure.

In figure 1.1, the Standard and Formatting toolbars are displayed as two separate toolbars. When you start PowerPoint, the Standard and Formatting toolbars may appear together on the same row. In this case, you will notice two buttons on the toolbar containing a double right-pointing arrow and a down-pointing triangle. These are the Toolbar Options buttons and are used to access the Standard and Formatting toolbar buttons that are not visible. The Toolbar Options button approximately halfway across the toolbar provides access to additional Standard toolbar buttons, while the Toolbar Options button at the right side of the toolbar provides access to additional Formatting toolbar buttons. Click the down-pointing triangle on the Toolbar Options button to display a palette of additional buttons.

Toolbar
Options

To set up PowerPoint so that the Standard and Formatting toolbars are separate as shown in figure 1.1, click the Toolbar Options button (either one), and then click Show Buttons on Two Rows at the drop-down list.

FIGURE

1.1 *PowerPoint Window*

The PowerPoint window contains many elements that are similar to other Microsoft Office programs such as Word and Excel. For example, the PowerPoint window, like the Word window, contains a Title bar, Menu bar, Standard and Formatting toolbars, scroll bars, and a Status bar. The elements of the PowerPoint window include:

- **Title bar:** This bar displays the program name, a presentation title, a control menu, the Close button, and the Minimize and Restore buttons for resizing the window.
- **Menu bar:** PowerPoint commands are grouped into options that display on the Menu bar. For example, options for formatting slides can be found at the Format drop-down menu.
- **Standard toolbar:** This toolbar contains buttons for the most frequently used commands in PowerPoint such as cutting, copying, and pasting text; inserting hyperlinks, tables, and charts; and changing the zoom display.
- **Formatting toolbar:** Frequently used commands for formatting a PowerPoint presentation are grouped onto the Formatting toolbar. This toolbar contains options such as changing typeface and size, increasing and decreasing type size, adding typestyles such as bold and italics, changing paragraph alignment, and adding animation effects.
- **Drawing toolbar:** With buttons on the Drawing toolbar, you can draw objects such as lines, arcs, and shapes. Buttons on this toolbar also contain options for adding attributes to objects, such as color, shading, and shadow.
- **Outline/Slides pane:** The pane at the left side of the screen contains two tabs—Outline and Slides. With the Outline tab selected, the contents of a presentation display in the pane. With the Slides tab selected, a slide miniature displays in the pane.
- **Slide pane:** The slide pane is where slides are created and displayed. Here you can see how text looks on each slide and add elements such as clip art images, hyperlinks, and animation effects.
- **Notes pane:** Add notes to a presentation in the Notes pane.
- **Vertical scroll bar:** Use the vertical scroll bar to display specific slides in a presentation. The small box located on the vertical scroll bar is called the *elevator*. Drag the elevator on the vertical scroll bar and a yellow box displays specifying the slide number within the presentation. Use the elevator to move quickly to a specific slide.
- **Horizontal scroll bar:** The Outline/Slides pane contains a horizontal scroll bar you can use to shift text left or right in the pane.
- **View toolbar:** The View toolbar, located at the left side of the horizontal scroll bar, contains buttons for changing the presentation view. For example, you can view individual slides, view several slides at once, view slide information as an outline, and also run the presentation.
- **Status bar:** Messages about PowerPoint features display in the Status bar, which is located toward the bottom of the PowerPoint window. The Status bar also displays information about the view.

PowerPoint, like other Microsoft Office programs, provides ScreenTips for buttons on toolbars. Position the arrow pointer on a button on any of the PowerPoint toolbars, and a ScreenTip displays (after approximately one second) for the button.

POWERPOINT

Creating a Presentation Using a Design Template

PowerPoint provides a variety of design templates you can use when creating slides for a presentation. These design templates include formatting such as color, background, fonts, and so on. To choose a template, click the Slide Design button on the Formatting toolbar. This displays the available templates in the Slide Design Task Pane that displays at the right side of the screen as shown in figure 1.2. Position the mouse pointer on a thumbnail of a template and the name of the template displays in a yellow box.

After choosing the desired template, choose a slide layout. PowerPoint provides a number of slide layouts you can display by clicking Format on the Menu bar and then clicking Slide Layout. This displays the available layouts in the Slide Layout Task Pane shown in figure 1.3. You can also display layouts by clicking the Other Task Panes button (displays with a down-pointing triangle) located in the upper right corner of the current task pane and then clicking Slide Layout at the drop-down list.

After choosing a slide layout, key the desired text and/or insert the desired elements in the slide. To create another slide, click the New Slide button on the Formatting toolbar, click the desired layout in the Slide Layout Task Pane, and then key the text in the slide or insert the desired elements.

When all slides have been completed, save the presentation by clicking the Save button on the Standard toolbar. At the Save As dialog box, key a name for the presentation and then click the Save button or press Enter.

Slide Design

HINT

Design templates provided by PowerPoint were designed by professional graphic artists who understand the use of color, space, and design.

New Slide

Save

FIGURE

1.2 *Slide Design Task Pane*

HINT

Use the Blank Presentation template if you want complete control over the presentation design.

1.3 *Slide Layout Task Pane*

Slide Layout Task Pane

Displaying and Maneuvering in Task Panes

As you use various PowerPoint features, a task pane may display at the right side of the screen. The name of the task pane varies depending on the feature. For example, when you click the Slide Design button on the Formatting toolbar, the Slide Design Task Pane displays. If you click Format on the Menu bar and then click Slide Layout, the Slide Layout Task Pane displays. A task pane presents features to help you easily identify and use more of the program.

You can maneuver within various task panes by clicking the Back button (contains a left-pointing arrow) and/or the Forward button (contains a right-pointing arrow) that display at the top of the task pane. You can also maneuver within various task panes by clicking the Other Task Panes button (contains a down-pointing triangle) and then clicking the desired task pane at the drop-down list.

You can control whether the display of the task pane is on or off by clicking View and then Task Pane. You can also close the task pane by clicking the Close button (contains an *X*) located in the upper right corner of the task pane.

The task pane can be docked and undocked. By default, the task pane is docked at the right side of the screen. Move (undock) the task pane by positioning the mouse pointer on the task pane title bar, holding down the left mouse button, and then dragging the task pane to the desired location. If you move the task pane (undock it), you can dock it back at the right side of the screen by double-clicking the task pane title bar.

Inserting a New Slide

Create a new slide in a presentation by clicking the New Slide button on the Formatting toolbar. This displays the Slide Layout Task Pane at the right side of the screen. Click the desired layout in the Slide Layout Task Pane and then insert the desired data in the slide. The new slide is inserted after the selected slide.

Choosing a Slide Layout

A variety of slide layout options are available at the Slide Layout Task Pane. This task pane displays when you click Format and then Slide Layout or click the New Slide button on the Formatting toolbar. Position the mouse pointer on a slide layout and the name of the layout displays in a yellow box.

When you position the mouse pointer on a slide layout, the name of the layout displays along with a down-pointing triangle at the right side of the layout. Click this triangle and a drop-down list displays with options for applying the layout to selected slides, reapplying a master style, or inserting a new slide.

The slide layouts in the Slide Layout Task Pane contain placeholders. A placeholder is a location on the slide where information is entered or inserted. For example, many slides contain a title placeholder. Click in this placeholder and then key the title of the slide. When text is entered into a placeholder, the placeholder turns into a text object.

HINT
Slide layouts make arranging elements in a slide easier.

HINT
Scroll down the Apply slide layout list box to view additional slide layouts.

PLACEHOLDER = location on slide where info is entered

Printing a Presentation

A presentation can be printed in a variety of formats. You can print each slide on a separate piece of paper; print each slide at the top of the page, leaving the bottom of the page for notes; print up to six slides or a specific number of slides on a single piece of paper; or print the slide titles and topics in outline form. Use the Print what option at the Print dialog box to specify what you want printed.

To display the Print dialog box, shown in figure 1.4, click File and then Print. At the Print dialog box, click the down-pointing triangle at the right side of the Print what text box, and then click the desired printing format.

HINT
Printing a hard copy of your presentation helps reinforce your message.

FIGURE

1.4 *Print Dialog Box*

different ways to print

Click this down-pointing triangle to display a list of printing options.

Expanding Drop-Down Menus

When you open PowerPoint, the menus display a limited selection of basic commands called *first rank options*. At the bottom of each menu is a down-pointing double arrow. Click this double arrow to expand the drop-down menu and display additional options, known as *second rank options*. Or, allow the mouse pointer to rest on the menu option for approximately five seconds and the menu will expand to show all options. Second rank options display with a lighter gray background.

As you create and edit presentations, the commands you use most often are stored as personalized options and display on the drop-down menus when you select them. Expand the menu if an option you require does not appear on the menu. Second rank options become first rank options after you use them once.

To disable the personalized menu feature and display all menu options, click Tools and then Customize. At the Customize dialog box, click the Options tab. Click the Always show full menus option to insert a check mark in the check box and then click the Close button to close the dialog box.

The instructions in this book assume that the personalized menu feature has been disabled. If the computer you are using has this feature enabled, you may need to expand the drop-down menus to find the required options.

Saving a Presentation

After creating a presentation, save it by clicking File and then Save or by clicking the Save button on the Standard toolbar. This displays the Save As dialog box. By default, a PowerPoint presentation is saved to the *My Documents* folder. To save a presentation onto your data disk, you will need to change the active folder. To change to a data disk that is located in drive A, click the down-pointing triangle at the right of the Save in text box, and then click *3½ Floppy (A:)*. After changing the default folder, key the presentation document name in the File name text box, and then click the Save button or press Enter.

Closing a Presentation

After creating, viewing, and/or printing a presentation, close the presentation. To do this, click the Close button at the right side of the Menu bar or click File and then Close. If any changes were made to the presentation that were not saved, you will be asked if you want to save the changes.

Completing Computer Exercises

At the end of sections within chapters and at the end of chapters, you will be completing hands-on exercises at the computer. These exercises will provide you with the opportunity to practice the presented functions and commands. The skill assessment exercises at the end of each chapter include general directions. If you do not remember how to perform a particular function, refer to the text in the chapter.

POWERPOINT

Copying Presentations

In some exercises in each chapter, you will be opening a presentation provided with this textbook. Before beginning each chapter, copy the chapter folder from the CD that accompanies this textbook to a floppy disk (or other folder). Steps on how to copy a folder from the CD to your floppy disk are printed on the inside of the back cover of this textbook.

Changing the Default Folder

In this chapter and the other chapters in this textbook, you will be saving presentations onto a disk (or other folder). To save presentations to and open presentations from the chapter folder on your disk, you will need to specify the chapter folder on your disk as the default folder. Once you specify the chapter folder on your disk, PowerPoint uses this as the default folder until you exit the PowerPoint program. The next time you open PowerPoint, you will again need to specify the chapter folder on your disk as the default folder.

Change the default folder at the Open dialog box or the Save As dialog box. To change the folder to the *PowerPoint Chapter 01* folder on the disk in drive A at the Open dialog box, you would complete the following steps:

1. Click the Open button on the Standard toolbar (the second button from the left); or click File and then Open.
2. At the Open dialog box, click the down-pointing triangle at the right side of the Look in option box.
3. From the drop-down list that displays, click *3¹/₂ Floppy (A:)*.
4. Double-click *PowerPoint Chapter 01* that displays in the list box.
5. Click the Cancel button in the lower right corner of the dialog box.

exercise

CREATING AND PRINTING A PRESENTATION

1. Copy the *PowerPoint Chapter 01* folder from the CD that accompanies this textbook to your disk. For steps on how to copy the folder, please refer to the steps that are printed on the inside of the back cover of this textbook.
2. Prepare a presentation on the steps for planning a publication by completing the following steps:
    a. At the PowerPoint window, click the Slide Design button on the Formatting toolbar. (This displays the Slide Design Task Pane at the right side of the screen.)
    b. Scroll down the list of design templates in the Apply a design template list box until the Digital Dots template displays. (Position the mouse pointer on a template and, after approximately one second, the name of the template displays in a yellow box. The design templates are listed in alphabetical order.)
    c. Click once on the Digital Dots template. (This applies the design template to the slide in the Slide pane with the Title Slide layout selected.)
    d. Display slide layout options by clicking Format and then Slide Layout. (This displays the Slide Layout Task Pane.)

Step 2c

e. Click the Title Only slide layout at the Slide Layout Task Pane. (Position the mouse pointer on a layout and after approximately one second the name of the layout displays in a yellow box.)

f. Click anywhere in the text *Click to add title* and then key **ELECTRONIC DESIGN**.

g. Click the New Slide button on the Formatting toolbar. (This causes a new slide to display in the Slide pane.)

h. Click the Title Slide layout in the Slide Layout Task Pane. (The Title Slide layout is probably the first layout from the left in the top row.)

i. At the slide, click anywhere in the text *Click to add title* and then key **Guidelines for Using Color**.

j. Click anywhere in the text *Click to add subtitle* and then key **Limit your use of color to two or three colors, including the color of the paper.**

k. Click the New Slide button.

l. Click the Title Slide layout (probably the first layout from the left in the top row) in the Apply slide layout list box in the Slide Layout Task Pane.

m. Complete steps similar to those in 2g through 2j to create the following slides:

Slide 3	Title	=	**Guidelines for Using Color**
	Subtitle	=	**Do not let color overpower the words.**
Slide 4	Title	=	**Guidelines for Using Color**
	Subtitle	=	**Use color to identify consistent elements.**
Slide 5	Title	=	**Guidelines for Using Color**
	Subtitle	=	**Do not set text in light colors because the text is too hard to read.**
Slide 6	Title	=	**Guidelines for Using Color**
	Subtitle	=	**Use color to communicate, not decorate.**

n. Click in the slide outside the selected area. (This should deselect the box containing the subtitle.)

3. Save the presentation by completing the following steps:

a. Click the Save button on the Standard toolbar.

b. At the Save As dialog box, click the down-pointing triangle to the right of the Save in text box, and then click *3½ Floppy (A:)*.

c. Double-click the *PowerPoint Chapter 01* folder.

d. Select the text in the File name text box, key **Color Guidelines Presentation**, and then press Enter or click Save. (*PowerPoint Chapter 01* is now the default folder until you exit PowerPoint.)

4. Print all six slides on the same page by completing the following steps:

   a. Click File and then Print.
   b. At the Print dialog box, click the down-pointing triangle to the right of the Print what option, and then click *Handouts* from the drop-down list.
   c. Make sure the number 6 displays in the Slides per page text box in the Handouts section of the dialog box.
   d. Click OK.

5. Close Color Guidelines Presentation by clicking File and then Close.

Opening a Presentation

A saved presentation can be opened at the Open dialog box. To display this dialog box, click File and then Open or click the Open button on the Standard toolbar. At the Open dialog box, double-click the desired presentation in the list box.

Open

Viewing a Presentation

PowerPoint provides a variety of viewing options for a presentation. The presentation view can be changed with options from the View drop-down menu or with viewing buttons that display on the View toolbar, shown in figure 1.5, located at the left side of the horizontal scroll bar. The viewing choices include:

- **Normal View:** This is the default view and displays three panes— outline/slides, slide, and notes. With these three panes, you can work with all features in one place. This view is also referred to as tri-pane view.
- **Slide Sorter View:** Choosing the Slide Sorter view displays all slides in the presentation in slide miniatures. In this view, you can easily add, move, rearrange, and delete slides.
- **Notes Page View:** Change to the Notes Page view and an individual slide displays on a page with any added notes displayed below the slide.
- **Slide Show View:** Use the Slide Show view to run a presentation. When you choose this view, the slide fills the entire screen.

HINT
Key and edit text in individual slides in Normal view.

HINT
Quickly and easily reorganize slides in Slide Sorter view.

FIGURE

1.5 *View Toolbar*

Change the view using either buttons on the View toolbar or options from the View drop-down menu. To use the View toolbar, click the desired button. (The View toolbar does not contain a button for changing to the Notes Page view.) To use the View option on the Menu bar, click View, and then click the desired view from the drop-down menu. The View drop-down menu contains the Notes Page option. At the Notes Page view, the slide displays along with a space below the slide for inserting text. Click the text *Click to add text* that displays in the box below the slide and then key the desired note. When running the presentation, you can display any notes attached to a slide.

In the Normal view, change slides by clicking the Previous Slide or Next Slide buttons located at the bottom of the vertical scroll bar. You can also change to a different slide by using the mouse pointer on the scroll box (called the *elevator*) on the vertical scroll bar. To do this, position the mouse pointer on the elevator, hold down the left mouse button, drag up or down until a yellow box displays with the desired slide number, and then release the mouse button. The keyboard can also be used to change to a different slide. Press the Page Down key to display the next slide in the presentation or press the Page Up key to display the previous slide in the presentation.

Previous Slide

Next Slide

HINT

In addition to the Next Slide and Previous Slide buttons, you can use the Page Up and Page Down keys to move from one slide to another.

Running a Slide Show

Slides created in PowerPoint can be converted to 35mm slides or transparencies, or the computer screen can provide the output. An on-screen presentation saves the expense of producing slides, requires no projection equipment, and lets you use the computer's color capability. Several methods are available for running a slide show. You can run the slide show manually (you determine when to advance to the next slide), advance slides automatically, or set up a slide show to run continuously for demonstration purposes.

If you want to run a slide show manually, open the presentation, and then click the Slide Show button on the View toolbar or click View and then Slide Show. To control movement through slides in a slide show, refer to figure 1.6.

Slide Show

1.6 Commands for Controlling Slide Show

To do this	Perform this action
Show next slide	Click left mouse button; or press one of the following keys: spacebar, N, right arrow, down arrow, or Page Down
Show previous slide	Click right mouse button and then click desired direction at the pop-up menu; or press one of the following keys: Backspace, P, left arrow, up arrow, or Page Up
Show specific slide	Key slide number and then press Enter
Toggle mouse on or off	Key A or equal sign (=)
Switch between black screen and current slide	Key B or period (.)
Switch between white screen and current slide	Key W or comma (,)
End slide show and return to PowerPoint	Press one of the following keys: Esc, hyphen (-), or Ctrl + Break

Starting the Slide Show on any Slide

Click the Slide Show button on the View toolbar and the presentation begins with the currently active slide. To begin a slide show on any slide, make the desired slide active and then click the Slide Show button. If you want to begin the presentation with the first slide, make sure it is the active slide before clicking the Slide Show button.

Using the Pen during a Presentation

If you move the mouse when running a presentation, the *Slide Show* menu icon displays in the lower left corner of the slide. Click this icon and a pop-up menu displays as shown in figure 1.7. With options at this pop-up menu, you can perform such actions as navigating within the presentation, keying speaker notes, displaying a pen, changing the screen display, getting help, and ending the presentation.

Emphasize major points or draw the attention of the audience to specific items in a slide during a presentation using the pen. To use the pen on a slide, run the presentation, and when the desired slide displays, move the mouse to display the *Slide Show* menu icon and then click the icon. At the pop-up menu that displays, point to Pointer Options, and then click Pen. This removes the pop-up menu and displays the mouse pointer as a pen. Use the pen to draw attention to specific items in the slide. If you want to draw a straight horizontal or vertical line with the pen, hold down the Shift key while drawing. Change the color of the pen by clicking the Slide Show menu icon, pointing to Pointer Options, pointing to Pen Color, and then clicking the desired color at the side menu.

If you want to erase the marks you made with the pen, click the *Slide Show* menu icon, point to S<u>c</u>reen, and then click <u>E</u>rase Pen. The <u>E</u>rase Pen option is available only when the pen is selected. When you are finished with the pen, click the *Slide Show* menu icon, point to P<u>o</u>inter Options, and then click A<u>u</u>tomatic.

FIGURE

1.7 *Slide Show Menu Icon Pop-Up Menu*

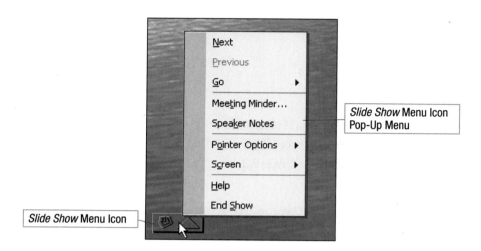

exercise **2**

VIEWING, PRINTING, AND RUNNING A PRESENTATION

1. Open the Planning Presentation located in the *PowerPoint Chapter 01* folder on your disk by completing the following steps:
   a. At the PowerPoint window, click the Open button on the Standard toolbar.
   b. At the Open dialog box, make sure *PowerPoint Chapter 01* on your disk is the default folder, and then double-click *Planning Presentation* in the list box.

2. With Planning Presentation open, change the views by completing the following steps:
   a. Click the Next Slide button located at the bottom of the vertical scroll bar until Slide 6 is visible.
   b. Position the mouse pointer on the elevator (the scroll box) located on the vertical scroll bar, hold down the left mouse button, drag the elevator to the top of the vertical scroll bar until a yellow box displays with Slide 1 and the title of the slide, and then release the mouse button.
   c. Change to the Notes Page view by clicking <u>V</u>iew on the Menu bar and then clicking Notes <u>P</u>age at the drop-down list.
   d. Use the elevator on the vertical scroll bar to display Slide 6.

e. Change to the Slide Sorter view by clicking the Slide Sorter View button on the View toolbar.

f. Double-click Slide 1. (This displays Slide 1 in Normal view.)

3. Print the presentation in Outline view by completing the following steps:
   a. Choose File and then Print.
   b. At the Print dialog box, change the Print what option to *Outline View*.
   c. Click OK or press Enter.

4. Run the slide presentation on the screen by completing the following steps:
   a. Make sure Slide 1 displays in the Slide pane.
   b. Click the Slide Show button on the View toolbar. (Slide 1 fills the entire screen.)
   c. After viewing Slide 1, click the left mouse button. (This causes Slide 2 to display.)
   d. Continue viewing and then clicking the left mouse button until all six slides have been viewed.
   e. At the black screen with the message *End of slide show, click to exit.*, click the left mouse button.

5. Run the presentation beginning with Slide 3 by completing the following steps:
   a. Click the Slide Sorter View button on the View toolbar.
   b. Double-click Slide 3. (This displays Slide 3 in Normal view.)
   c. Click the Slide Show button on the View toolbar.
   d. After viewing Slide 3, click the left mouse button.
   e. Continue viewing slides until the black screen displays. At this screen, click the left mouse button.

6. Run the presentation and use the pen to highlight specific words in the slides by completing the following steps:
   a. Drag the elevator to the top of the vertical scroll bar. (This displays Slide 1 in the Slide pane.)
   b. Click the Slide Show button on the View toolbar.
   c. When Slide 1 displays on the screen, click the left mouse button. (This displays Slide 2.)
   d. With Slide 2 displayed, use the pen to underline a word by completing the following steps:
      1) Move the mouse to display the *Slide Show* menu icon.
      2) Click the *Slide Show* menu icon, point to Pointer Options, and then click Pen.
      3) Using the mouse, draw a circle around the text below *STEP 1*.
      4) Hold down the Shift key and then use the mouse to draw a horizontal line below the word *identify*.
      5) Erase the pen markings by clicking the *Slide Show* menu icon, pointing to Screen, and then clicking Erase Pen.
      6) Change the color of the pen by clicking the *Slide Show* menu icon, pointing to Pointer Options, pointing to Pen Color, and then clicking Yellow.
      7) Hold down the Shift key and use the mouse to draw a yellow line below the word *identify*.

8) Turn off the pen by clicking the *Slide Show* menu icon, pointing to Pointer Options, and then clicking Automatic.

e. Click the left mouse button until Slide 5 displays (this slide contains STEP 4) and then use the pen to underline in yellow the word *after*.

f. Turn off the display of the pen.

g. Click the left mouse button to display Slide 6 (this slide contains STEP 5) and use the pen to underline in yellow the word *effective*.

h. Turn off the display of the pen.

i. Click the left mouse button and then, at the black screen, click the left mouse button again.

7. Close Planning Presentation.

HINT

Make a presentation more appealing by adding effects such as sound and transitions.

Adding Transition and Sound Effects

Slide
Transition

Interesting transitions and sounds can be applied to a presentation. A transition is how one slide is removed from the screen during a presentation and the next slide is displayed. Interesting transitions can be added such as blinds, boxes, checkerboards, covers, random bars, stripes, and wipes. To add transitions and sounds, open a presentation, and then display the Slide Transition Task Pane shown in figure 1.8 by clicking Slide Show and then Slide Transition. You can also display this task pane by changing to the Slide Sorter view and then clicking the Slide Transition button on the Slide Sorter toolbar. The Slide Sorter toolbar displays at the right side of the Standard toolbar in Slide Sorter view. If the Slide Transition button is not visible, click the Toolbar Options button (contains two right-pointing arrows and a down-pointing triangle) that displays at the right side of the toolbar, and then click Transition at the drop-down list.

FIGURE

1.8 *Slide Transition Task Pane*

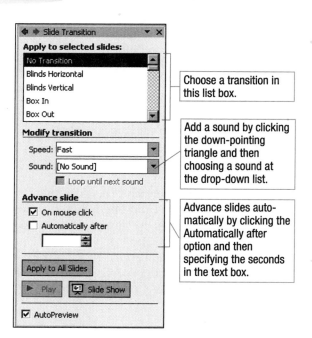

To add a transition effect, click the desired transition in the *Apply to selected slides* list box located in the Slide Transition Task Pane. When you click the desired transition, the transition effect displays in the slide in Normal view or in the selected slide miniature in Slide Sorter view. You can also display the transition effect by clicking the Play button located toward the bottom of the Slide Transition Task Pane. When a transition is added to a slide, a transition icon displays below the slide number in the Outline/Slides pane in Normal view or below the slide in Slide Sorter view.

As a slide is removed from the screen and another slide is displayed, a sound can be added. To add a sound, click the down-pointing triangle to the right of the Sound option box located in the *Modify transition* section of the Slide Transition Task Pane, and then click the desired sound at the drop-down list. You can choose from a list of sounds such as applause, bomb, breeze, camera, and much more.

Transition and sound effects apply only to the currently displayed slide in Normal view or the selected slide in Slide Sorter view. If you want transition and sound to affect all slides in Normal view, click the Apply to All Slides button located toward the bottom of the Slide Transition Task Pane. In Slide Sorter view, select all slides by clicking Edit and then Select All or by pressing Ctrl + A, and then apply the desired transition and/or sound.

exercise 3

ADDING TRANSITIONS AND SOUNDS TO A PRESENTATION

1. At the PowerPoint window, click the Open button on the Standard toolbar.
2. At the Open dialog box, make sure the *PowerPoint Chapter 01* folder on your disk is the active folder, and then double-click *Planning Presentation* in the list box.
3. Save the presentation with Save As and name it Planning Pres with Transitions by completing the following steps:
   a. Click File and then Save As.
   b. At the Save As dialog box, key **Planning Pres with Transitions** in the File name text box.
   c. Click Save or press Enter.
4. Add transition and sound effects by completing the following steps:
   a. Click Slide Show on the Menu bar and then click Slide Transition.
   b. At the Slide Transition Task Pane, click *Blinds Horizontal* in the Apply to selected slides list box.
   c. Click the down-pointing triangle at the right side of the Sound option box in the Modify transition section of the Slide Transition Task Pane and then click *Camera* at the drop-down list. (You will need to scroll down the list to display *Camera*.)
   d. Click the Apply to All Slides button located toward the bottom of the Slide Transition Task Pane.

5. Run the presentation by clicking the Slide Show button on the View toolbar and then clicking the left mouse button to advance each slide. (When the presentation is done and the black screen displays with the message *End of slide show, click to exit.*, click the left mouse button or press the Esc key.)
6. Click the Save button on the Standard toolbar to save the presentation with the same name (Planning Pres with Transitions).
7. Close Planning Pres with Transitions.

Running a Slide Show Automatically

Slides in a slide show can be advanced automatically after a specific number of seconds with options in the *Advance slide* section of the Slide Transition Task Pane. To automatically advance slides, click in the Automatically after check box and then insert the desired number of seconds in the text box. Change the time in the text box by clicking the up- or down-pointing triangle at the right side of the text box or by selecting any text in the text box and then keying the desired time. If you want the transition time to affect all slides in the presentation, click the Apply to All Slides button. In Slide Sorter view, the transition time displays below each affected slide.

To automatically run the presentation, make sure the first slide is selected, and then click the Slide Show button located toward the bottom of the task pane. (You can also click the Slide Show button on the View toolbar.) The first slide displays for the specified amount of time and then the next slide automatically displays.

In some situations, such as at a trade show or convention, you may want to prepare a self-running presentation. A self-running presentation is set up on a continuous loop and does not require someone to run the presentation. To design a self-running presentation, choose options at the Set Up Show dialog box shown in figure 1.9. To display this dialog box, open a presentation, click Slide Show, and then click Set Up Show.

FIGURE

1.9 *Set Up Show Dialog Box*

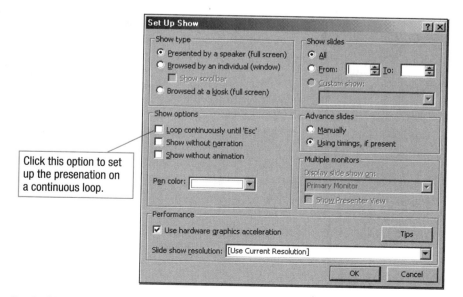

Click this option to set up the presenation on a continuous loop.

Click the Loop continuously until 'Esc' option and the presentation runs over and over again until the Esc key is pressed. With other options in the Show type section of the Set Up Show dialog, you can specify what a presentation shows when running. In the Advance slides section of the dialog box, specify whether the slides will be advanced manually or automatically. Use options in the Slides section to specify whether options are to be applied to all slides or specific slides within the presentation.

exercise 4

PREPARING A SELF-RUNNING PRESENTATION

1. Open History of Computers 1980s. (This presentation is located in *PowerPoint Chapter 01* folder on your disk.)
2. Save the presentation with Save As in the *PowerPoint Chapter 01* folder on your disk and name it Self-Running History.
3. Add transition and sound effects and specify a time for automatically advancing slides by completing the following steps:
   a. Change to the Slide Sorter view.
   b. Click Slide Show and then Slide Transition.
   c. Select all slides by clicking Edit and then Select All. (You can also select all slides by pressing Ctrl + A.)
   d. At the Slide Transition Task Pane, click in the Automatically after option check box in the Advance Slide section. (This inserts a check mark.)
   e. Click the up-pointing triangle at the right side of the time box until *00:05* displays.
   f. Add a transition effect by clicking *Box Out* in the Apply to selected slides list box.
   g. Add a sound effect by clicking the down-pointing triangle to the right of the Sound option box in the Modify transition section of the task pane and then clicking *Laser* at the drop-down list.
4. Set up the presentation to run continuously by completing the following steps:
   a. Click Slide Show and then Set Up Show.
   b. At the Set Up Show dialog box, click in the Loop continuously until 'Esc' option check box to insert a check mark. (Make sure All is selected in the Show slides section and Using timings, if present is selected in the Advance slides section.)
   c. Click OK to close the dialog box.
5. Click Slide 1 to select it and then run the presentation continuously by clicking the Slide Show button in the Slide Transition Task Pane.
6. After viewing the presentation at least twice, press the Esc key on the keyboard.
7. Save the presentation again with the same name (Self-Running History).
8. Close Self-Running History.

Planning a Presentation with the AutoContent Wizard

PowerPoint contains an AutoContent Wizard that will help you in the planning and organizing of a presentation. You respond to certain questions from the wizard and, based on your responses, you are presented with slides containing information on how to organize the presentation. For example, suppose you are an employee of an investment firm and have been asked to prepare a presentation on a variable annuity fund. You can use the AutoContent Wizard for help on how to organize this presentation. You will be doing this in exercise 5. The wizard provides additional information on other types of presentations. Consider printing the information for these other presentations.

exercise 5

GETTING HELP FROM THE AUTOCONTENT WIZARD

1. Prepare slides for helping organize a presentation to market and sell a service by completing the following steps:
   a. Make sure the task pane displays. (If not, click <u>V</u>iew and then Tas<u>k</u> Pane.)
   b. Click the Other Task Panes button (contains a down-pointing triangle) located toward the top of the task pane and then click *New Presentation* at the drop-down list.
   c. Click the <u>*From AutoContent Wizard*</u> hyperlink located in the New section of the New Presentation Task Pane.
   d. At the AutoContent Wizard Start dialog box, click the <u>N</u>ext> button that displays toward the bottom right side of the dialog box.
   e. At the AutoContent Wizard Presentation type dialog box, click the gray button containing <u>S</u>ales/Marketing, click *Product/Services Overview* in the list box, and then click the <u>N</u>ext> button.

Step 1c

   f. At the AutoContent Wizard Presentation style dialog box, make sure the *On-<u>s</u>creen presentation* option is selected, and then click the <u>N</u>ext> button.
   g. At the AutoContent Wizard Presentation options dialog box, make the following changes:
      1) Click inside the <u>P</u>resentation title text box and then key **McCormack Funds**.
      2) Press the Tab key. (This moves the insertion point to the <u>F</u>ooter text box.)
      3) Key **Variable Annuity Fund**.
      4) Click the <u>N</u>ext> button.

Step 1e

Step 1g1

Step 1g3

   h. At the AutoContent Wizard Finish dialog box, click the <u>F</u>inish button.
2. Save the presentation by completing the following steps:
   a. Click the Save button on the Standard toolbar.
   b. At the Save As dialog box, make sure *PowerPoint Chapter 01* is the default folder, key **Selling Presentation** in the File <u>n</u>ame text box, and then press Enter or click <u>S</u>ave.

3. Print the information on the slides provided by the wizard in Outline View by completing the following steps:
    a. Choose File and then Print.
    b. At the Print dialog box, click the down-pointing triangle to the right of the Print what option, and then click *Outline View* at the drop-down list.
    c. Click OK.
4. Run the presentation. (Read the information on each slide provided by the wizard.)
5. Close Selling Presentation. (If a dialog box displays asking if you want to save the changes, click Yes.)

Preparing a Presentation in the Outline/Slides Pane

In exercise 1, you created a slide presentation using a PowerPoint template. With this method, a slide with formatting applied was presented in the Slide pane where you entered specific text. You can also enter text on a slide in the Outline/Slides pane with the Outline tab selected. Consider turning on the display of the Outlining toolbar when using the Outline/Slides pane to create slides. Turn on the Outlining toolbar by clicking View, pointing to Toolbars, and then clicking *Outlining*. The Outlining toolbar displays along the left side of the Outline/Slides pane. The buttons on the Outlining toolbar are described in figure 1.10.

FIGURE

1.10 *Outlining Toolbar Buttons*

Click this button	Named	To do this
←	Promote	Move insertion point along with any text to the previous tab stop to the left
→	Demote	Move insertion point along with any text to the next tab stop to the right
↑	Move Up	Move insertion point along with any text up to the previous line
↓	Move Down	Move insertion point along with any text down to the next line
−	Collapse	Display only the titles of the slides
+	Expand	Display all levels of the slides
↑≡	Collapse All	Display only the titles of the slides
↓≡	Expand All	Display titles and body text for all slides (also available on the Standard toolbar)
📑	Summary Slide	Create a summary slide of presentation based on titles of slides you select
ᴬA	Show Formatting	Display all character formatting (also available on the Standard toolbar)

Demote

Promote

To create a slide in the Outline/Slides pane, click in the pane and then key the text. Press the Tab key or click the Demote button on the Outlining toolbar to move the insertion point to the next tab stop. This moves the insertion point and also changes the formatting. The formatting will vary depending on the design template you chose in the Slide Design Task Pane. Press Shift + Tab or click the Promote button on the Outlining toolbar to move the insertion point to the previous tab stop and change the formatting. Moving the insertion point back to the left margin will begin another slide. Slides are numbered at the left side of the screen and are followed by a slide icon.

exercise **6**

PREPARING A PRESENTATION IN THE OUTLINE/SLIDES PANE

1. Create a presentation in the Outline/Slides pane by completing the following steps:
   a. With PowerPoint open and a blank screen displayed, click the New button on the Standard toolbar (first button from the left).
   b. Click Format and then Slide Design.
   c. Click *Cascade* in the Apply a design template list box. (You will need to scroll down the list to display this design template. Position the arrow pointer on a design template to display the name. The design templates are listed in alphabetical order.)
   d. Display the Outlining toolbar by clicking View, pointing to Toolbars, and then clicking *Outlining*.
   e. Click the Outline tab in the Outline/Slides pane.
   f. Click immediately right of the Slide 1 icon in the Outline/Slides pane, key the first slide title shown in figure 1.11 *(Computer Technology)*, and then press Enter.
   g. Key the second slide title shown in figure 1.11 *(The Motherboard)* and then press Enter.
   h. Click the Demote button on the Outlining toolbar or press Tab, key the text after the first bullet in figure 1.11 *(Buses)*, and then press Enter.
   i. Continue keying the text as it displays in figure 1.11. Click the Demote button or press Tab to move the insertion point to the next tab stop. Click the Promote button or press Shift + Tab to move the insertion back to a previous tab stop.
   j. Click the Collapse All button on the Outlining toolbar. (This displays only the title of each slide.)
   k. Click the Expand All button on the Outlining toolbar.
2. Save the presentation by completing the following steps:
   a. Click the Save button on the Standard toolbar.

    b. At the Save As dialog box, make sure the *PowerPoint Chapter 01* folder on your disk is the active folder.

    c. Key **Technology Presentation** in the File name text box and then press Enter.

3. View the slides by clicking the Slide Sorter View button on the View toolbar.

4. Print the four slides as notes pages by displaying the Print dialog box and then changing the Print what option to *Notes Pages*.

5. Close Technology Presentation.

FIGURE

1.11 **Exercise 6**

1 Computer Technology
2 The Motherboard
   • Buses
   • System clock
   • Microprocessor
   • ROM and RAM
   • Power supply
   • Ports
   • Expansion slots
3 Input Devices
   • Keyboard
   • Mouse
   • Trackball
   • Touch pad and touch screen
   • Pen and tablet
   • Joystick
   • Scanner
4 Output Devices
   • Monitor
   • Printer
     - Dot matrix
     - Laser
     - Ink jet
   • Speakers

(Handwritten annotations: "S-TAB Promote", "TAB Demote", "3")

Deleting a Presentation

File management tasks in PowerPoint can be performed at the Open or Save As dialog box. To delete a PowerPoint presentation, display the Open dialog box, click the presentation you want deleted, and then click the Delete button on the dialog box toolbar. At the Confirm File Delete dialog box asking if you are sure you want to delete the document, click the Yes button.

Delete

1. Delete a presentation from the *PowerPoint Chapter 01* folder on your disk by completing the following steps:
   a. With PowerPoint open, display the Open dialog box by clicking the Open button on the Standard toolbar.
   b. At the Open dialog box, make sure the *PowerPoint Chapter 01* folder on your disk is the active folder.
   c. Click Selling Presentation in the list box to select it.
   d. Click the Delete button on the dialog box toolbar.
   e. At the dialog box asking if you are sure you want to delete the presentation, click <u>Y</u>es.
   f. At the Open dialog box, delete Self-Running History Presentation by completing steps similar to those in 1c through 1e.
2. Close the Open dialog box.

CHAPTER summary

➤ PowerPoint is a software program you can use to create slides for an on-screen presentation or for an overhead or slide projector. In PowerPoint, you can print handouts of the presentation, print an outline, or print the entire presentation.

➤ Before creating a presentation in PowerPoint, plan the presentation by defining the purpose and determining the content and medium.

➤ The PowerPoint window contains the following elements: Title bar, Menu bar, Standard toolbar, Formatting toolbar, Drawing toolbar, Outline/Slides pane, Slide pane, Notes pane, scroll bars, View toolbar, and Status bar.

➤ PowerPoint includes a variety of preformatted design templates you can use for creating a presentation. Click the Slide Design button on the Formatting toolbar and the Slide Design Task Pane displays with design templates.

➤ Choose a slide layout at the Slide Layout Task Pane. Display this task pane by clicking F<u>o</u>rmat on the Menu bar and then clicking Slide <u>L</u>ayout. Slide layouts contain placeholders, which are locations on the slide where information is entered or inserted.

➤ Click the New Slide button on the Formatting toolbar to insert a new slide in a presentation.

➤ With options at the Print dialog box, you can print presentations with each slide on a separate piece of paper; each slide at the top of the page, leaving room for notes; all or a specific number of slides on a single piece of paper; or slide titles and topics in outline form.

➤ Save a presentation by clicking the Save button on the Formatting toolbar, keying a name for the presentation, and then pressing Enter or clicking the Save button.

➤ Close a PowerPoint presentation document by clicking File and then Close or by clicking the Close button at the right side of the Menu bar.

➤ Create a new folder with the Create New Folder button on the Open dialog box toolbar.

➤ Open a presentation by clicking the Open button on the Standard toolbar and then double-clicking the desired presentation at the Open dialog box.

➤ View a presentation in one of the following four views: Normal view, which is the default and displays three panes—outline/slides, slide, and notes; Slide Sorter view, which displays all slides in the presentation in slide miniatures; Notes Page view, which displays an individual slide with any added notes displayed below the slide; and Slide Show view, which runs the presentation.

➤ A slide show can be run manually, where you determine when to advance to the next slide; automatically, where PowerPoint advances the slides; or continuously, for demonstration purposes.

➤ Use the pen during a presentation to emphasize major points or draw the attention of the audience to specific items on a slide. Change the mouse pointer to a pen by clicking the *Slide Show* menu icon, pointing to Pointer Options, and then clicking Pen.

➤ Enhance a presentation by adding transitions (how one slide is removed from the screen and replaced with the next slide) and sound. Add transitions and sound to a presentation with options at the Slide Transition Task Pane.

➤ In Slide Sorter view, select all slides by clicking Edit and then Select All or by pressing Ctrl + A.

➤ Use options at the Slide Transition Task Pane to automatically advance slides after a specific number of sections when running a presentation.

➤ Create a self-running presentation with options at the Set Up Show dialog box.

➤ Use PowerPoint's AutoContent Wizard to help in the planning and organizing of a presentation.

➤ You can enter text on a slide in the Outline/Slides pane. Use buttons on the Outlining toolbar to promote, demote, move up, or move down text on the slide and collapse and expand text on slides.

➤ Delete a presentation at the Open dialog box by clicking the presentation file name and then clicking the Delete button on the dialog box toolbar. Click Yes at the Confirm File Delete dialog box.

COMMANDS review

Command	Mouse
Open PowerPoint	Click Start button on Taskbar, point to *Programs*, click *Microsoft PowerPoint*
Display Slide Design Task Pane	Click Slide Design button on Formatting toolbar
Display Slide Layout Task Pane	Click F_ormat and then Slide L_ayout
Insert a new slide	Click the New Slide button on Formatting toolbar
Display Print dialog box	Click F_ile and then P_rint
Display Save As dialog box	Click Save button on Standard toolbar or click F_ile, S_ave
Close a presentation	Click F_ile and then C_lose
Display Open dialog box	Click Open button on Standard toolbar or click F_ile and then O_pen
Run presentation	Click Slide Show button on View toolbar or click Slide Show button in Slide Transition Task Pane
Display Slide Transition Task Pane	Click Slide Transition button on Slide Sorter toolbar or click Sli_de Show and then Slide T_ransition
Display Set Up Show dialog box	Click Sli_de Show and then S_et Up Show
Begin AutoContent Wizard	Click *From AutoContent Wizard* hyperlink in the New Presentation Task Pane
Display Outlining toolbar	Click V_iew, point to T_oolbars, and then click *Outlining*

CONCEPTS check

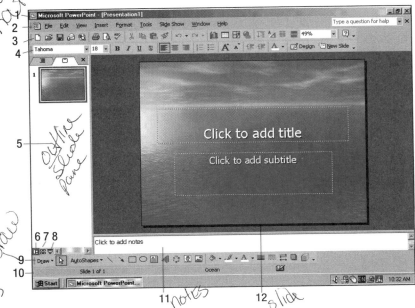

Handwritten annotations on image: title, menu, standard, format, Outline Slide Pane, draw, status, notes, slide

Identifying: Look at the PowerPoint screen shown above. This screen contains numbers with lines pointing to specific items. On a blank sheet of paper, write the name of the item that corresponds with each number in the PowerPoint screen.

Completion: On a blank sheet of paper, indicate the correct term, symbol, or command.

1. Click this button on the View toolbar to run a presentation.
2. Click this button on the View toolbar to display all slides in the presentation in slide miniatures.
3. While running a presentation, click this button on the mouse to display the previous slide.
4. If a presentation contains six slides, click this option at the Print what drop-down menu at the Print dialog box to print all of the slides on the same page.
5. This term refers to how one slide is removed from the screen and replaced with the next slide.
6. To display the Slide Transition Task Pane, click this option on the Menu bar, and then click Slide Transition.
7. Click this button on the Outlining toolbar to move the insertion point to the next tab stop.
8. Click this button on the Outlining toolbar to move the insertion point to the previous tab stop.

SKILLS check

Assessment 1

1. Create a presentation with the text shown in figure 1.12 by completing the following steps:
    a. With PowerPoint open, click the New button on the Standard toolbar (first button from the left).
    b. Click the Slide Design button on the Formatting toolbar.
    c. Click the Watermark design template in the Apply a design template list box. (You will need to scroll to the end of the list box to display this template.)
    d. Display the Slide Layout Task Pane by clicking Format and then Slide Layout.
    e. At the slide, click anywhere in the text *Click to add title*, and then key **DEDUCTIBLE INCOME**.
    f. Click anywhere in the text *Click to add subtitle* and then key **Exceptions to Deductible Income**.
    g. Click the New Slide button located on the Formatting toolbar.
    h. Click the Title Slide layout in the Slide Layout Task Pane and then create the second slide with the text shown in figure 1.12.
    i. Create the remaining slides as shown in figure 1.12 by completing steps similar to those in 1g and 1h.
2. Save the presentation in the *PowerPoint Chapter 01* folder on your disk and name the presentation Deductible Presentation.
3. Run the presentation.
4. Print all of the slides on one page.
5. Close Deductible Presentation.

FIGURE

1.12 *Assessment 1*

Slide 1	Title	=	DEDUCTIBLE INCOME
	Subtitle	=	Exceptions to Deductible Income
Slide 2	Title	=	EXCEPTION 1
	Subtitle	=	Any cost of living increase if increase becomes effective while disabled.
Slide 3	Title	=	EXCEPTION 2
	Subtitle	=	Reimbursement for hospital, medical, or surgical expense.
Slide 4	Title	=	EXCEPTION 3
	Subtitle	=	Reasonable attorney's fees incurred in connection with a claim for deductible income.

POWERPOINT

Slide 5	Title	=	EXCEPTION 4
	Subtitle	=	Benefits from any individual disability insurance policy.
Slide 6	Title	=	EXCEPTION 5
	Subtitle	=	Group credit or mortgage disability insurance benefits.

Assessment 2

1. Open Deductible Presentation.
2. Save the presentation with Save As in the *PowerPoint Chapter 01* folder on your disk and name the presentation Enhanced Deductible Presentation.
3. Make the following changes to the presentation:
   a. Add the transition *Split Vertical Out* to all slides in the presentation.
   b. Add the cash register sound to all slides in the presentation.
4. Save the presentation again with the same name (Enhanced Deductible Presentation).
5. Run the presentation.
6. Close Enhanced Deductible Presentation.

Assessment 3

1. Create a presentation with the text shown in figure 1.13. You determine the design template for the presentation and the layout for each slide. *(Hint: Use the Title Slide layout for the first slide and the Title and Text layout for the remaining slides.)*
2. Save the completed presentation in the *PowerPoint Chapter 01* folder on your disk and name it Newsletter Presentation.
3. Print Newsletter Presentation as an outline.
4. Print Newsletter Presentation as individual slides.
5. Close Newsletter Presentation.

FIGURE

1.13 *Assessment 3*

Slide 1	Title	=	PREPARING A COMPANY NEWSLETTER
	Subtitle	=	Planning and Designing the Layout
Slide 2	Title	=	Planning a Newsletter
	Bullets	=	• If a scanner is available, use pictures of different people from your organization in each issue.
			• Distribute contributor sheets soliciting information from employees.
			• Keep the focus of the newsletter on issues of interest to employees.

Slide 3	Title	=	Planning a Newsletter
	Bullets	=	• Make sure the focus is on various levels of employment; do not focus on top management only.
			• Conduct regular surveys to see if your newsletter provides a needed source of information.

Slide 4	Title	=	Designing a Newsletter
	Bullets	=	• Maintain consistent elements from issue to issue such as:
			- Column layout
			- Nameplate formatting and location
			- Formatting of headlines
			- Use of color

Slide 5	Title	=	Designing a Newsletter
	Bullets	=	• Consider the following elements when designing a newsletter:
			- Focus
			- Balance
			- White space
			- Directional flow

Slide 6	Title	=	Creating a Newsletter Layout
	Bullets	=	• Choose paper size
			• Choose paper weight
			• Determine margins
			• Specify column layout

Assessment 4

1. Open Newsletter Presentation.
2. Save the presentation with Save As in the *PowerPoint Chapter 01* folder on your disk and name the presentation Enhanced Newsletter Presentation.
3. Make the following changes to the presentation:
   a. Add a transition of your choosing to each slide.
   b. Add a sound of your choosing to each slide.
   c. Specify that all slides advance automatically after five seconds.
   d. Set up the presentation as continuous.
4. Save the presentation again with the same name (Enhanced Newsletter Presentation).
5. Run the presentation.
6. Close Enhanced Newsletter Presentation.

MODIFYING A PRESENTATION AND USING HELP

PERFORMANCE OBJECTIVES

Upon successful completion of chapter 2, you will be able to:
- **Insert and delete text in slides**
- **Find and replace text in slides**
- **Rearrange text and object boxes in slides**
- **Complete a spelling check**
- **Insert, copy, delete, and rearrange slides in a presentation**
- **Copy slides between presentations**
- **Preview a presentation**

PowerPoint Chapter 02

In this chapter, you will learn to edit text and slides in a PowerPoint presentation, including inserting, deleting, finding, replacing, and rearranging text within slides and inserting, copying, deleting, and rearranging slides within a presentation. The features of the Standard toolbar are described, and you will also learn about PowerPoint's preview and Help tools.

Editing Slides

You can edit text in slides in a PowerPoint presentation with much of the same functionality as in other Microsoft applications. For example, you can insert text into a slide or delete text from a slide. You can also search for specific text and replace it with other text; cut, copy, and paste text within and between slides; and complete a spelling check.

Inserting and Deleting Text in Slides

To insert or delete text in an individual slide, open the presentation, edit the text as needed, and then save the presentation again. If you want to delete more than an individual character, consider selecting the text first. Several methods can be used for selecting text as shown in figure 2.1.

2.1 *Selecting Text*

To do this	Perform this action
Select text mouse pointer passes through	Click and drag mouse
Select entire word	Double-click word
Select entire paragraph	Triple-click anywhere in paragraph
Select entire sentence	Ctrl + click anywhere in sentence
Select all text in selected object box	Click Edit, Select All or press Ctrl + A

Finding and Replacing Text in Slides

HINT

Press Ctrl + F to display the Find dialog box.

Use the find feature to look for specific text in slides in a presentation and use the find and replace feature to look for specific text in slides in a presentation and replace with other text. Begin a find by clicking Edit and then Find. This displays the Find dialog box shown in figure 2.2. In the Find what text box, key the text you want to find and then click the Find Next button. Continue clicking this button until a message displays telling you that the search is complete. At this message, click OK.

2.2 *Find Dialog Box*

In this text box, key the text for which you are searching.

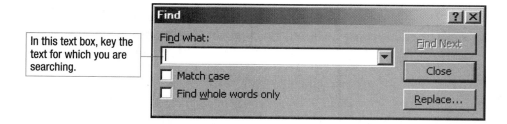

HINT

Press Ctrl + H to display the Replace dialog box.

Use options at the Replace dialog box shown in figure 2.3 to search for text and replace with other text. Display this dialog box by clicking Edit and then Replace. Key the text you want to find in the Find what text box, press the Tab key, and then key the replacement text in the Replace with text box. Click the Find Next button to find the next occurrence of the text or click the Replace All button to replace all occurrences in the presentation.

2.3 *Replace Dialog Box*

(Note: Before completing computer exercises, delete the PowerPoint Chapter 01 *folder on your disk. Next, copy to your disk the* PowerPoint Chapter 02 *subfolder from the* PowerPoint 2002 *folder on the CD that accompanies this textbook and then make* PowerPoint Chapter 02 *the active folder.)*

exercise 1

INSERTING, DELETING, FINDING AND REPLACING TEXT IN SLIDES

1. Open PowerPoint and then open Planning Presentation from the *PowerPoint Chapter 02* folder on your disk.
2. Save the presentation with Save As into the *PowerPoint Chapter 02* folder on your disk and name the presentation Edited Planning Presentation.
3. Delete and insert text in slides by completing the following steps:
    a. In the Normal view, click the Next Slide button located at the bottom of the vertical scroll bar until Slide 5 displays.
    b. Edit Slide 5 by completing the following steps:
        1) Position the I-beam pointer on the sentence below *STEP 4* and then click the left mouse button. (This inserts a frame around the text.)
        2) Edit the sentence so it reads *Decide what steps you want readers to take after reading the message.* (Use deleting and inserting commands to edit this sentence.)
    c. Click the Next Slide button to display Slide 6.
    d. Edit Slide 6 in the Outline/Slides pane by completing the following steps:
        1) Click the Outline tab in the Outline/Slides pane.
        2) Click in the sentence below *STEP 5* and then edit the sentence so it reads *Collect and assess examples of effective designs*.
        3) Click the Slides tab.
4. Find all occurrences of *Planning* in the presentation and replace with *Preparing* by completing the following steps:

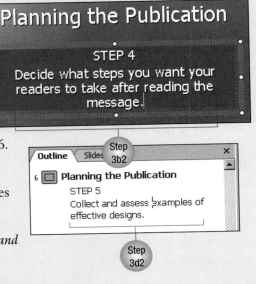

a. Display Slide 1 in the Slide pane.
b. Click Edit and then Replace.
c. At the Replace dialog box, key **Planning** in the Find what text box.
d. Press the Tab key.
e. Key **Preparing** in the Replace with text box.
f. Click the Replace All button.
g. At the message telling you that five replacements were made, click OK.
h. Click the Close button to close the Replace dialog box.

5. Find all occurrences of *Publication* and replace with *Newsletter* by completing steps similar to those in step 4.

6. Save the presentation again with the same name (Edited Planning Presentation).

7. Print the six slides on one page. (Change the Print what option at the Print dialog box to *Handouts*.)

8. Close Edited Planning Presentation.

Rearranging Text in Slides

Cut

Paste

Copy

With buttons on the Standard toolbar or options on the Menu bar, you can cut, copy, delete, and/or paste text in slides. For example, to move text in a slide, click once in the object box containing the text to be moved, select the text, and then click the Cut button on the Standard toolbar. Position the insertion point where you want the text inserted and then click the Paste button on the Standard toolbar. You can also move text from one slide to another by selecting the text, clicking the Cut button, displaying the slide where you want the text inserted, and then clicking the Paste button. To copy text in or between slides, complete similar steps. Select the text to be copied, click the Copy button on the Standard toolbar, move the insertion point to the position where the text is to be copied, and then click the Paste button.

The Standard toolbar contains the Cut, Copy, and Paste buttons along with other buttons to access commonly used features in PowerPoint. The buttons on the Standard toolbar are described in figure 2.4.

FIGURE

2.4 *PowerPoint Standard Toolbar Buttons*

Click this button	Named	To do this
	New	Display a new, blank presentation based on the default template
	Open	Display the Open dialog box to choose a previously saved presentation file
	Save	Save the current presentation with the same name; or, save a presentation at the Save As dialog box

E-mail	Send a slide presentation as an e-mail attachment or use the current slide text as the e-mail message
Search	Search for files meeting specific criteria
Print	Print the presentation currently open
Print Preview	Display presentation as it will appear when printed
Spelling	Complete a spelling check on the text in the current presentation
Cut	Remove selected text or object to the Clipboard
Copy	Insert a copy of selected text or object in the Clipboard
Paste	Insert the contents of the Clipboard into the current slide
Format Painter	Copy formatting from selected text or object and apply it to another
Undo	Undo the most recent action
Redo	Redo (or repeat) the most recent action
Insert Chart	Embed a graph in a slide using specified data
Insert Table	Insert a blank table with number of rows and columns you specify
Tables and Borders	Display the Tables and Borders toolbar containing buttons for drawing and customizing a table
Insert Hyperlink	Insert or edit a hyperlink
Expand All	Display all levels of the slides
Show Formatting	Display all character formatting as it will appear on the slide
Show/Hide Grid	Display or hide gridlines on a slide to help align objects
Color/Grayscale	Display a drop-down menu with options for displaying the presentation in color, grayscale, or pure black and white
Zoom	Increase or decrease the display of a presentation
Microsoft PowerPoint Help	Display Microsoft PowerPoint Help window with options for displaying information on PowerPoint functions and features

Rearranging Text in the Outline/Slides Pane

You can use the mouse to move text in the Outline/Slides pane with the Outline tab selected. To do this, position the mouse pointer on the slide icon or bullet at the left side of the text, until the arrow pointer turns into a four-headed arrow. Hold down the left mouse button, drag the arrow pointer (a thin horizontal line displays) to the desired location, and then release the mouse button.

If you position the arrow pointer on the slide icon and then hold down the left mouse button, all of the text in the slide is selected. If you position the arrow pointer on the bullet and then hold down the left mouse button, all text following that bullet is selected.

HINT
Press Ctrl + Shift + Tab to switch between the Outline and Slides tabs in the Outline/Slides pane.

Dragging selected text with the mouse moves the selected text to a new location in the presentation. You can also copy selected text. To do this, click the slide icon or click the bullet to select the desired text. Position the arrow pointer in the selected text, hold down the Ctrl key, and then the left mouse button. Drag the arrow pointer (displays with a light gray box and a plus sign attached) to the desired location, release the mouse button, and then release the Ctrl key.

Rearranging Object Boxes in a Slide

Text in a slide is positioned inside an object box. An entire selected object box can be moved easily in a slide. To do this, click once in the object box (outside any text) to select it (white sizing handles should display around the box). If white sizing handles do not display around the box, position the arrow pointer on the border of the box (small gray lines), and then click the left mouse button. Position the arrow pointer on the border around the object box until the arrow pointer displays with a four-headed arrow attached. Hold down the left mouse button, drag the outline of the box to the desired position, and then release the mouse button.

Dragging a selected box with the mouse moves the box. You can also copy a selected box. To do this, hold down the Ctrl key while dragging the box with the mouse. When the outline of the box is in the desired position, release the mouse button, and then release the Ctrl key.

Delete a placeholder by clicking in the placeholder once to select it (border around the placeholder displays as diagonal lines), clicking on the border of the placeholder (border changes to dots) and then pressing the Delete key.

Sizing an Object Box

HINT

Change the size of a select object box by dragging a corner or side sizing handle.

Click an object box in a slide and sizing handles display around the box. Use these sizing handles to increase or decrease the size of the box. To increase or decrease the size, position the arrow pointer on one of the white sizing handles until the arrow pointer turns into a double-headed arrow. Hold down the left mouse button, drag the outline of the box in to decrease the size or drag the outline out to increase the size, and then release the mouse button. You can increase or decrease the size of the box at the same time by using the sizing handles that display in each corner of the selected box.

Completing a Spelling Check

HINT

You can press F7 to begin spell checking a presentation.

Spelling

When you create a presentation, consider performing a spelling check on text in slides. PowerPoint's spelling check feature compares words in a presentation with words in its dictionary. If a match is found the word is passed over. If a match is not found, the spelling checker selects the word and offers replacement suggestions. To perform a spelling check on a PowerPoint presentation, click the Spelling button on the Standard toolbar. Change or ignore selected text as required.

(Note: By default, not all PowerPoint design templates are installed. Before completing exercise 2, make sure the additional design templates are installed. [You can begin the installation by scrolling to the end of the Apply a design template list box and then clicking the option for installing additional templates.])

POWERPOINT

1. Create the slides for a presentation as shown in figure 2.5 by completing the following steps:
   a. At a blank PowerPoint screen, click the New button on the Standard toolbar.
   b. Click the Slide Design button on the Formatting toolbar.
   c. Click *Cascade* in the Apply a design template list box in the Slide Design Task Pane.

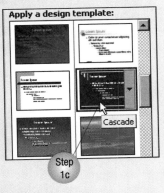

Apply a design template:

Cascade

Step 1c

   d. At the slide, key the text for the first slide shown in figure 2.5 by completing the following steps:
      1) Click anywhere in the text *Click to add title* and then key **Telecommunications System**.
      2) Click anywhere in the text *Click to add subtitle* and then key **Factors for Evaluating the Effectiveness of a Telecommunications System**.
   e. Click the New Slide button on the Formatting toolbar. (This displays a new slide with the Title and Text slide layout selected.)
   f. At the slide, key the text shown in the second slide in figure 2.5 by completing the following steps:
      1) Click anywhere in the text *Click to add title* and then key **COST**.
      2) Click anywhere in the text *Click to add text* and then key the text after the first bullet in the second slide in figure 2.5 (the text that begins *How does the cost of a new system compare...*).
      3) Key the text following the remaining bullets.
   g. Click the New Slide button.
   h. Continue creating the remaining slides in figure 2.5 by completing steps similar to those in 1e and 1f.
2. When all six slides have been created, make Slide 1 the active slide, and then perform a spelling check by clicking the Spelling button on the Standard toolbar. Change or ignore as required during the spelling check.
3. Save the presentation into the *PowerPoint Chapter 02* folder on your disk and name the presentation Telecommunications Presentation.
4. Print the six slides on one page.
5. Move and copy text within and between slides by completing the following steps:
   a. Make sure you are in Normal view.
   b. Click the Outline tab in the Outline/Slides pane.
   c. Move the first bulleted item in Slide 6 to the end of the list by completing the following steps:
      1) Scroll down the Outline/Slides pane until all of the Slide 6 text displays in the pane.
      2) Position the mouse pointer on the first bullet below *EASE OF USE* until it turns into a four-headed arrow.
      3) Hold down the left mouse button, drag the arrow pointer down until a thin horizontal line displays below the last bulleted item, and then release the mouse button.
      4) Click the Slides tab in the Outline/Slides pane.
   d. Copy a bulleted item from Slide 3 (*EFFICIENCY*) to Slide 5 (*TIME*) by completing the following steps:

Outline Slides

6 EASE OF USE
   • Will a reduction in company efficiency occur during the transition?
   • Will the new system improve employee productivity?
   • How long before user feel comfortable with new system?

Step 5c3

Bullet

1) Display Slide 3 in the Slide pane.
2) Click anywhere in the bulleted text. (This selects the object box containing the text.)
3) Position the mouse pointer on the last square bullet in Slide 3 until it turns into a four-headed arrow and then click the left mouse button. (This selects the text after the bullet.) [Step 5d3]
4) With the text selected, click the Copy button on the Standard toolbar.
5) Display Slide 5 in the Slide pane.
6) Position the I-beam pointer immediately after the question mark in the second bulleted item in Slide 5 and then click the left mouse button.
7) Press the Enter key. (This moves the insertion point down to the next line.)
8) Click the Paste button on the Standard toolbar. (This pastes the item and also inserts a bullet below the pasted item.)
9) Press the Backspace key twice to remove the extra bullet.

e. Move and size an object box in a slide by completing the following steps:
1) Display Slide 1 in the Slide pane.
2) Click anywhere in the subtitle text *Factors for Evaluating the Effectiveness of a Telecommunications System*. (This selects the object box containing the text.)
3) Position the arrow pointer on the border of the object box until the pointer turns into a four-headed arrow.
4) Hold down the left mouse button, drag the object box to the left as shown at the right, and then release the mouse button.
5) Increase the width of the box by completing the following steps:
   a) Position the mouse pointer on the middle sizing handle (white circle) at the right side of the object box until the pointer turns into a double-headed arrow pointing left and right.
   b) Hold down the left mouse button, drag to the right so the right edge of the object box is approximately positioned at the end of the white line at the bottom of the slide, and then release the mouse button.
   c) Drag the box down and position it as shown at the right.
   d) Click outside the object box to deselect it.

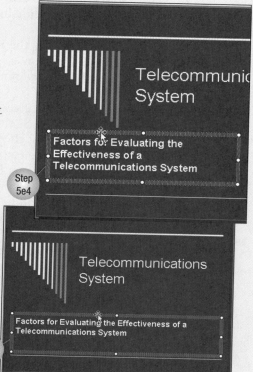

6. Add a transition and sound of your choosing to all slides.
7. Save the document again with the same name (Telecommunications Presentation).
8. Run the presentation.
9. Print the presentation in Outline view.
10. Close Telecommunications Presentation.

2.5 *Exercise 2*

Slide 1	Title	=	Telecommunications System
	Subtitle	=	Factors for Evaluating the Effectiveness of a Telecommunications System
Slide 2	Title	=	COST
	Bullets	=	• How does the cost of a new system compare with the cost of the current system?
			• What is the cost of maintaining the current system?
			• What will be the training costs of a new system?
Slide 3	Title	=	EFFICIENCY
	Bullets	=	• How does the efficiency of the current system compare with a paper-based system?
			• What is the time frame for implementing a new system?
			• Will improved efficiency translate into lowered personnel costs?
Slide 4	Title	=	QUALITY
	Bullets	=	• How does the current system rank in terms of usefulness?
			• What is the current quality of transmission?
			• Is the current system effective in producing the required internal and external documents?
Slide 5	Title	=	TIME
	Bullets	=	• How quickly can information be delivered?
			• What is the estimated training time for a new system?
			• What is the time frame for implementing a new system?
Slide 6	Title	=	EASE OF USE
	Bullets	=	• Will a reduction in company efficiency occur during the transition?
			• Will the new system improve employee productivity?
			• How long before users feel comfortable with a new system?

Organizing Slides

As you edit a presentation, you may need to reorganize slides and insert a new slide or delete an existing slide. Change to the Slide Sorter view to perform some reorganization activities such as moving, copying, and deleting slides.

Inserting and Deleting Slides

Delete a slide from a presentation by changing to the Slide Sorter view, clicking the slide you want to delete to select it, and then pressing the Delete key on the keyboard. You can also delete a slide in Normal view with the Slides tab selected in the Outline/Slides pane. To do this, click the slide miniature in the Outline/Slides pane, and then press the Delete key.

Insert a new slide in a presentation in the Normal view or the Slide Sorter view. To add a slide to a presentation in Normal view, click the New Slide button

HINT
Press Ctrl + M to insert a new slide.

on the Formatting toolbar, click the desired slide layout in the Slide Layout Task Pane, and then key the text in the slide. To add a slide to a presentation in Slide Sorter view, click the slide that will immediately precede the new slide, click Insert, and then click New Slide. Double-click the new blank slide (this displays the slide in Normal view), click the desired slide layout in the Slide Layout Task Pane, and then key the text in the slide.

Copying a Slide

Slides in some presentations may contain similar text, objects, and formatting. Rather than create a new slide, consider copying a slide. To do this, display the presentation in either Slide Sorter view or in Normal view with the Slides tab selected in the Outline/Slides pane. Position the arrow pointer in the slide, hold down the Ctrl key and then the left mouse button. Drag to the location where you want the slide copied, release the mouse button, and then release the Ctrl key.

Copying a Slide between Presentations

You can copy slides within a presentation as well as between presentations. To copy a slide, click the slide you want to copy (either in Slide Sorter view or in Normal view with the Slides tab selected in the Outline/Slides pane) and then click the Copy button on the Standard toolbar. Open the presentation into which the slide is to be copied (in either Slide Sorter view or Normal view with the Slides tab selected in the Outline/Slides pane). Click in the location where you want the slide positioned and then click the Paste button. The copied slide will take on the template design of the presentation into which it is copied.

Rearranging Slides

Rearrange slides in the Slide Sorter view or in Normal view with the Slides tab selected in the Outline/Slides pane. To do this, position the arrow pointer on the slide to be moved, hold down the left mouse button, drag the arrow pointer (with a square attached) to the desired position, and then release the mouse button.

Previewing a Presentation

Print Preview

Before printing a presentation, consider previewing the presentation. To do this, click the Print Preview button on the Standard toolbar or click File and then Print Preview. This displays the active slide in the Print Preview window as it will appear when printed. Figure 2.6 displays the Planning Presentation in Print Preview. The display of your slide in Print Preview may vary depending on the selected printer. (For example, if you have a color printer selected, the slide displays in color in Print Preview. If you have a black and white laser printer selected, the slide displays as you see in figure 2.6.) Use options on the Print Preview toolbar to display the next or previous slide, display the Print dialog box, specify how you want the presentation printed, change the zoom (percentage of display), choose an orientation (portrait or landscape), and close Print Preview.

POWERPOINT

2.6 Presentation in Print Preview

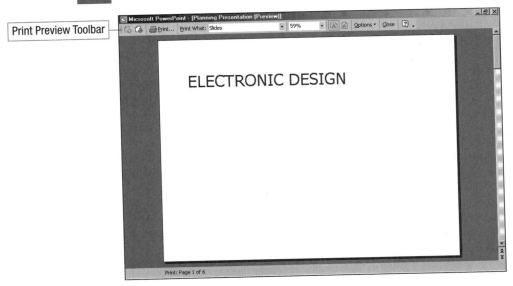

Print Preview Toolbar

Previewing with the Color/Grayscale Button

Along with Print Preview, you can view your presentation in color, grayscale, or black and white with options from the Color/Grayscale button on the Standard toolbar. Click the Color/Grayscale button and a drop-down list displays with three options—Color, Grayscale, and Pure Black and White. Click the Color option to display your presentation. (This is the default setting.) Click the Grayscale option and the presentation displays in black and white and the Grayscale View shortcut menu displays. Click the Setting option on the Grayscale View shortcut menu and options display for changing the appearance of objects on the slides in the presentation. Click the Pure Black and White option and most objects in slides display in either black or white. The display of objects depends on the options you select with the Setting option on the Grayscale View shortcut menu.

Color/Grayscale

exercise 3

INSERTING, COPYING, AND REARRANGING SLIDES

1. Open Planning Presentation.
2. Save the presentation with Save As into the *PowerPoint Chapter 02* folder on your disk and name the presentation Rearranged Planning Presentation.
3. Add a new slide to the presentation by completing the following steps:
   a. In Normal view, click the Next Slide button to display Slide 2 in the Slide pane.
   b. Click the New Slide button on the Formatting toolbar. (This displays a new blank slide in the Slide pane and also displays the Slide Layout Task Pane.)
   c. Click the Title Slide layout in the Slide Layout Task Pane.
   d. Click anywhere in the text *Click to add title* and then key **Preparing the Newsletter**.
   e. Click anywhere in the text *Click to add subtitle* and then key the following:
      1) Key **STEP 3** and then press Enter.
      2) Key **Determine the available budget for the publication.**

4. Add another new slide by completing the following steps:
   a. Click the Slide Sorter View button on the View toolbar.
   b. Click Slide 4 to select it.
   c. Click Insert on the Menu bar and then click New Slide at the drop-down menu.
   d. Double-click the new slide. (This changes the view from Slide Sorter view to Normal view.)
   e. Click the Title Slide layout in the Slide Layout Task Pane.
   f. Click anywhere in the text *Click to add title* and then key **Preparing the Newsletter**.
   g. Click anywhere in the text *Click to add subtitle* and then key the following:
      1) Key **STEP 5** and then press Enter.
      2) Key **Specify the layout of elements to be included in the newsletter.**

5. Delete Slide 2 by completing the following steps:
   a. Click the Slide Sorter View button on the View toolbar.
   b. Click Slide 2 to select it.
   c. Press the Delete key.
6. Move Slide 3 after Slide 5 by completing the following steps:
   a. In Slide Sorter view, position the mouse pointer in Slide 3, and then hold down the left mouse button.
   b. Drag the arrow pointer (with the gray square attached) between Slides 5 and 6 (a vertical black line displays between the slides) and then release the mouse button.
7. Complete steps similar to those in step 6 to move Slide 7 between Slides 2 and 3.
8. Edit each slide so the step numbers are in sequential order.
9. Copy slides from a different presentation into the Rearranged Planning Presentation by completing the following steps:
   a. Change to the Slide Sorter view.
   b. Open Company Newsletter located in the *PowerPoint Chapter 02* folder on your disk.
   c. With the Company Newsletter presentation open, change to the Slide Sorter view.
   d. Click Slide 2, hold down the Shift key, and then click Slide 3. (This selects both slides.)
   e. Click the Copy button on the Standard toolbar.
   f. Click the button on the Taskbar representing Rearranged Planning Presentation.
   g. Click to the right of the last slide in the presentation and then click the Paste button on the Standard toolbar.
10. Apply a transition and sound of your choosing to all slides in the presentation.
11. Save the presentation again with the same name (Rearranged Planning Presentation).
12. Run the presentation.
13. Preview and then print the presentation by completing the following steps:
   a. Click the Print Preview button on the Standard toolbar.

b. At the Print Preview window (with the first slide displayed), display the next slide by clicking the Next Page button on the Print Preview toolbar.

c. Continue clicking the Next Page button until the last slide displays in the presentation.

d. Click the down-pointing triangle to the right of the Print What button on the Print Preview toolbar and then click *Handouts (9 slides per page)* at the drop-down list.

e. Click the Print button on the Print Preview toolbar.

f. At the Print dialog box, click OK.

g. Click the Close button to close Print Preview.

14. Change to the Normal view and then display the presentation in grayscale by completing the following steps:

a. Click the Color/Grayscale button on the Standard toolbar.

b. At the drop-down list that displays, click the Grayscale option. (This displays the slide in grayscale and also displays the Grayscale View shortcut menu.)

c. Click the Setting option on the Grayscale View shortcut menu.

d. At the drop-down list that displays, click Light Grayscale. (Notice the changes to the slide.)

e. Click the Setting option on the Grayscale View shortcut menu and then click Inverse Grayscale at the drop-down list. (Notice the changes to the slide.)

f. Experiment with a few other options from the Setting drop-down list.

g. Click the Close Grayscale View option to turn off the display of the Grayscale View shortcut menu.

15. Close Rearranged Planning Presentation without saving the changes.

16. Close Company Newsletter.

Using Help

PowerPoint's Help feature is an on-screen reference manual containing information about all PowerPoint features and commands. PowerPoint's Help feature is similar to the Windows Help feature and the Help features in Word, Excel, and Access. Get help using the Ask a Question button on the Menu bar, the Help Topics window, or from the Office Assistant.

Ask a Question

Getting Help Using the Ask a Question Button

Click the text inside the Ask a Question button located at the right side of the Menu bar (this removes the text), key a help question, and then press Enter. A list of topics matching keywords in your question displays below the Ask a Question button. Click the desired topic and a Help window displays with information about the topic.

exercise 4

GETTING HELP USING THE ASK A QUESTION BUTTON

1. At a blank PowerPoint screen, click the text inside the Ask a Question button located at the right side of the Menu bar.
2. Key **How do I choose a design template?**.
3. Press the Enter key.
4. From the list of topics that displays below the Ask a Question button, click the *Create a presentation using a design template* option.
5. When the Help window displays, read the information contained in the window, and then click the Close button (contains an *X*) located in the upper right corner of the Help window.

Help

Auto Tile

Show

Back

Forward

Print

Options

Displaying the Microsoft PowerPoint Help Window

Keying a question in the Ask a Question button and then pressing Enter displays the Microsoft PowerPoint Help window. You can also display this Help window by clicking the Microsoft PowerPoint Help button on the Standard toolbar, or by clicking Help and then Microsoft PowerPoint Help.

Using Buttons at the Help Window

The Help window contains a toolbar with buttons. Click the Auto Tile button and all open windows are tiled so each window displays next to each other. Click the Auto Tile button again and it changes to the Untile button. Click the Show button to expand the window and display three tabs—Contents, Answer Wizard, and Index. If you move to various help items, click the Back button to return to the previous window. Click the Forward button to move forward to a help item. Click the Print button to send the Help information to the printer. Click the Options button and a drop-down menu displays with many of the same features as the buttons. For example, there is a Show Tabs option that will expand the window, and Back and Forward options that do the same thing as the Back and Forward buttons. Additional options include Home, Stop, Refresh, Internet Options, and Print.

Using Options at the Expanded Help Window

The Help window toolbar contains a Show button. Click the Show button and the window expands as shown in figure 2.7. Three tabs display in the expanded dialog box—Contents, Answer Wizard, and Index.

POWERPOINT

2.7 *Expanded Microsoft PowerPoint Help Window*

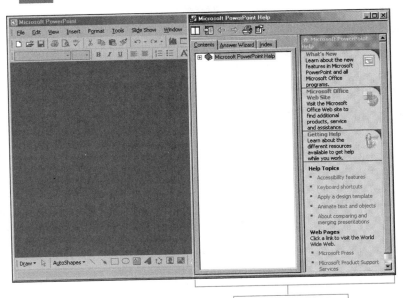

Expanded Help Window

Select the <u>C</u>ontents tab at the expanded window and *Microsoft PowerPoint Help* displays in the <u>C</u>ontents list box. Click the plus symbol preceding this option and a variety of categories display preceded by closed book icons. Most of these categories contain additional categories. To display these additional categories, double-click a category. This causes the closed book icon to change to an open book icon and the additional categories to display below the selected category.

Click the <u>A</u>nswer Wizard tab and a text box displays preceded by the question *What would you like to do?* Key your question in the text box and then click the <u>S</u>earch button. This displays a list of categories in the Select <u>t</u>opic to display list box. Click a topic in the list box, and information about the topic displays at the right side of the window.

With the <u>I</u>ndex tab selected, enter a keyword in the <u>T</u>ype keywords list box, and then click the <u>S</u>earch button. Topics related to the keyword display in the <u>C</u>hoose a topic list box. Click a topic in this list box and information about that topic displays at the right side of the dialog box. You can also scroll through the Or choose <u>k</u>eywords list box to display the desired topic. The topics in this list box are alphabetized.

In some situations, the Help window will display a list of topics. If you want to expand the topics and display all of the information related to each topic, click the *Show All* hyperlink located in the upper right corner of the Help window. (The *Show All* hyperlink changes to the *Hide All* hyperlink.)

HINT

Press F1 to open the
Microsoft PowerPoint
Help window.

1. Use the Help feature with the <u>C</u>ontents tab selected to find information on creating presentations by completing the following steps:
   a. Click the Microsoft PowerPoint Help button on the Standard toolbar.
   b. At the Help window, click the Show button to expand the window. (Skip this step if the window is already expanded.)
   c. Click the <u>C</u>ontents tab. (Skip this step if the <u>C</u>ontents tab is already selected.)
   d. Double-click *Microsoft PowerPoint Help* in the <u>C</u>ontents list box.
   e. Double-click *Creating Presentations* in the <u>C</u>ontents list box. (This displays subcategories below *Creating Presentations*.)
   f. Double-click *About creating presentations* in the <u>C</u>ontents list box.
   g. Read the information that displays at the right side of the Help window.
   h. Click several other subcategories that interest you and read the information about the subcategory.

2. Use the Help feature with the <u>A</u>nswer Wizard tab selected to search for information on adding a sound effect by completing the following steps:
   a. Click the <u>A</u>nswer Wizard tab.
   b. Key **How do I apply a sound effect?** in the <u>W</u>hat would you like to do? text box and then click the <u>S</u>earch button.
   c. Read the information on music and sound that displays at the right side of the Help window.
   d. Click the *Add music or sound effects to a slide* in the Select <u>t</u>opic to display list box.
   e. Click the *Show All* hyperlink located in the upper right corner of the Help window.
   f. Read the information that displays in the Help window.

3. Use the Help feature with the <u>I</u>ndex tab selected to search for information on slide layouts by completing the following steps:
   a. Click the <u>I</u>ndex tab.
   b. Key **layout** in the <u>T</u>ype keywords text box and then click the <u>S</u>earch button. (PowerPoint adds a semicolon at the right side of *layout*.)
   c. Click *About layouts* that displays in the <u>C</u>hoose a topic list box.
   d. Read the information that displays at the right side of the window.

4. Click the Close button (contains an *X*) that displays in the upper right corner of the Help window.

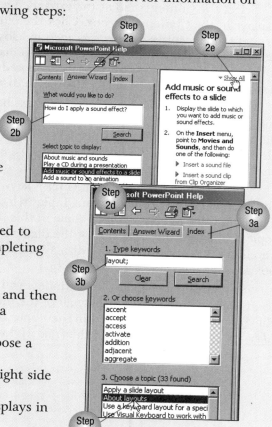

POWERPOINT

Getting Help from the Office Assistant

The Office Assistant provides information about specific topics. Display the Office Assistant by clicking Help and then Show the Office Assistant. To get help, click the Office Assistant and a help box displays above the assistant as shown in figure 2.8. Key a question about a specific feature in the text box and then click the Search button. The Office Assistant displays a list of related topics. At this list, click the desired topic and information displays in the Help window. After reading the information, click the Close button (contains an X) located in the upper right corner of the Help window.

FIGURE

2.8 *Office Assistant Help Box*

To turn off the display of the Office Assistant, click Help and then Hide the Office Assistant. This only hides the assistant. If you click Help and then Microsoft PowerPoint Help, the Office Assistant will display again. To permanently turn off the display of the Office Assistant, click the Office Assistant to display the Help box and then click the Options button. At the Office Assistant dialog box, click in the Use the Office Assistant check box to remove the check mark, and then click OK.

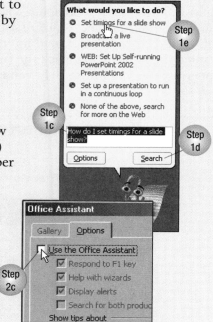

1. At the blank PowerPoint screen, use the Office Assistant to read information about setting timings for a slide show by completing the following steps:
   a. Click <u>H</u>elp and then Show the <u>O</u>ffice Assistant.
   b. Click the Office Assistant.
   c. Key **How do I set timings for a slide show?**.
   d. Click the <u>S</u>earch button.
   e. At the list that displays in the yellow box, click *Set timings for a slide show*. (When you position the arrow pointer on the topic, the pointer turns into a hand.)
   f. Click the *Show All* hyperlink located toward the upper right corner of the Help window.
   g. Read the information about setting timings for a slide show and then print the information by clicking the Print button on the Microsoft PowerPoint Help window toolbar and then clicking OK at the Print dialog box.
   h. Click the Close button (contains an *X*) located in the upper right corner of the Microsoft PowerPoint Help window.
2. Turn off the display of the Office Assistant permanently by completing the following steps:
   a. Click the Office Assistant. (This displays the Help box above the assistant.)
   b. Click the <u>O</u>ptions button.
   c. At the Office Assistant dialog box, click in the <u>U</u>se the Office Assistant check box to remove the check mark.
   d. Click OK.

CHAPTERsummary

➤ You can insert and/or delete text in an individual slide in a presentation. Click the object box containing the text you want to insert and/or delete. Select text you want to delete using options described in figure 2.1.

➤ Use the find feature to look for specific text in slides in a presentation and use the find and replace feature to search for specific text and replace with other text.

➤ Use Cut, Copy, and Paste buttons on the Standard toolbar to rearrange text in and between slides.

➤ You can use the mouse to move text within and between slides in the Outline/Slides pane with the Outline tab selected.

➤ Text in a slide is positioned in an object box. Move this object box by clicking the box to select it, positioning the mouse pointer on the border until the pointer turns into a four-headed arrow. Hold down the left mouse button, drag the outline of the box to the desired position, and then release the mouse button.

➤ Use the sizing handles that display around a selected object box to increase and/or decrease the size of the box.

➤ Click the Spelling button on the Standard toolbar to complete a spelling check on text in slides.

➤ Delete a slide in Slide Sorter view or in Normal view with the Slides tab selected in the Outline/Slides pane by clicking the slide and then pressing the Delete key.

➤ Insert a new slide in Normal view by clicking the New Slide button on the Formatting toolbar. Insert a new slide in Slide Sorter view by clicking Insert and then New Slide.

➤ Copy a selected slide clicking the slide, holding down the Ctrl key, dragging the outline of the slide to the new location, and then releasing the mouse button and the Ctrl key.

➤ You can copy slides within a presentation as well as between presentations.

➤ Rearrange slides within a presentation in Slide Sorter view or in Normal view with the Slides tab selected in the Outline/Slides pane.

➤ To see how a presentation will appear when printed, display the presentation in Print Preview. Use buttons on the Print Preview toolbar to display various slides, specify how you want the presentation printed, change the zoom display, and choose an orientation.

➤ View a presentation in color, grayscale, or black and white with options on the Color/Grayscale button on the Standard toolbar.

➤ PowerPoint's Help feature is an on-screen reference manual containing information about all PowerPoint features and commands.

➤ Get help by keying a question in the Ask a Question button located at the right side of the Menu bar.

➤ Display the Help window by clicking Help and then Microsoft PowerPoint Help.

➤ Click the Show button to expand the Help window. The expanded Microsoft PowerPoint Help window displays with three tabs—Contents, Answer Wizard, and Index.

➤ Display the Office Assistant by clicking Help and then Show the Office Assistant. Turn off the display of the assistant by clicking Help and then Hide the Office Assistant. Turn off the display of the Office Assistant permanently by clicking the Office Assistant and then clicking the Options button. At the Office Assistant dialog box, click the Use the Office Assistant option to remove the check mark, and then click OK.

COMMANDS review

Command	Mouse/Keyboard
Display Find dialog box	Click Edit, Find
Display Replace dialog box	Click Edit, Replace
Start a spelling check	Click Spelling button on Standard toolbar
Display presentation in Print Preview	Click Print Preview button on Standard toolbar; or click File, Print Preview
Display Color/Grayscale options	Click Color/Grayscale button on Standard toolbar
Display Microsoft PowerPoint Help window	Click Microsoft PowerPoint Help button on Standard toolbar; or click Help, Microsoft PowerPoint Help
Display Office Assistant dialog box	Click Office Assistant, click Options button

CONCEPTS check

Completion: On a blank sheet of paper, indicate the correct term, symbol, or command.

1. Perform this action with the mouse to select an entire word.
2. Display the Replace dialog box by clicking this option on the Menu bar and then clicking <u>R</u>eplace.
3. Copy a slide by holding down this key while dragging the slide.
4. Click an object box and these display around the box.
5. Click this button on the Standard toolbar to begin a spelling check.
6. Click this button on the Standard toolbar to display a drop-down list with options for displaying the presentation in color, grayscale, or black and white.
7. The Ask a Question button is located at the right side of this.
8. Click this button on the Microsoft PowerPoint Help window toolbar to expand the window.
9. Click this hyperlink located in the upper right corner of the Help window to expand the topics and display all of the information related to each topic.

SKILLS check

Assessment 1

1. Create a presentation with the text shown in figure 2.9. You determine the design template and the slide layout.
2. After creating the presentation, complete a spelling check.
3. Save the presentation into the *PowerPoint Chapter 02* folder on your disk and name the presentation Trends Presentation.
4. Add a transition and sound of your choosing to each slide.
5. Run the presentation.
6. Print the slides as handouts with six slides per page.
7. Close Trends Presentation.

2.9 Assessment 1

Slide 1	Title	=	TRENDS IN TELECOMMUNICATIONS
	Subtitle	=	Current and Future Trends
Slide 2	Title	=	Trend 1
	Subtitle	=	Continued movement toward the deregulation of telecommunications services
Slide 3	Title	=	Trend 2
	Subtitle	=	Continued expansion and enhancement of local and wide area networks
Slide 4	Title	=	Trend 3
	Subtitle	=	Movement toward integrated services digital networks
Slide 5	Title	=	Trend 4
	Subtitle	=	Movement toward standardization of data communication protocols
Slide 6	Title	=	Trend 5
	Subtitle	=	Increased use of wireless radio-based technology
Slide 7	Title	=	Trend 6
	Subtitle	=	Continued growth of photonics (fiber optics)
Slide 8	Title	=	Trend 7
	Subtitle	=	Expansion of video teleconferencing
Slide 9	Title	=	Trend 8
	Subtitle	=	Increased power in electronic workstations
Slide 10	Title	=	Trend 9
	Subtitle	=	More sophisticated software
Slide 11	Title	=	Trend 10
	Subtitle	=	Continued growth of voice processing
Slide 12	Title	=	Trend 11
	Subtitle	=	Greater use of optical storage technologies

Assessment 2

1. Open Trends Presentation.
2. Save the presentation with Save As into the *PowerPoint Chapter 02* folder on your disk and name the presentation Edited Trends Presentation.
3. Make the following edits to the presentation:
   a. Display the presentation in Slide Sorter view.
   b. Move Slide 2 between Slide 5 and Slide 6.
   c. Move Slide 10 between Slide 7 and 8.
   d. Renumber the trend numbers in the titles to reflect the correct order.
   e. Display Slide 4 in Slide view, delete the subtitle text, and then key **Multimedia in integrated systems**.
   f. Display Slide 8 in Slide view, delete the subtitle text, and then key **Information as a strategic resource**.
4. Save the presentation again with the same name (Edited Trends Presentation).

5. Run the presentation.
6. Print the presentation as handouts with six slides per page.
7. Close Edited Trends Presentation.

Assessment 3

1. Create the presentation shown in figure 2.10 using a design template of your choosing.
2. When the slides are completed, run a spelling check on the presentation.
3. Save the presentation into the *PowerPoint Chapter 02* folder on your disk and name the presentation EDP Presentation.
4. Run the presentation.
5. Print all four slides on one page.
6. Close EDP Presentation.

F I G U R E

| 2.10 | *Assessment 3* |

Slide 1	Title	=	Electronic Design and Production
	Subtitle	=	Designing a Document
Slide 2	Title	=	Creating Balance
	Bullets	=	• Symmetrical balance—Balancing similar elements equally on a page (centered alignment) of the document
			• Asymmetrical balance—Balancing contrasting elements on a page of the document
Slide 3	Title	=	Creating Focus
	Bullets	=	• Creating focus with titles, headings, and subheads in a document
			• Creating focus with graphic elements in a document
			- Clip art
			- Watermarks
			- Illustrations
			- Photographs
			- Charts
			- Graphs
Slide 4	Title	=	Providing Proportion
	Bullets	=	• Evaluating proportions in a document
			• Sizing graphic elements in a document
			• Using white space in a document

Assessment 4

1. Open EDP Presentation.
2. Save the presentation with Save As into the *PowerPoint Chapter 02* folder on your disk and name the presentation Revised EDP Pres.
3. Make the following changes to the presentation:
   a. Change to Slide Sorter view and then move Slide 3 between Slides 1 and 2.
   b. Move Slide 4 between Slides 2 and 3.
   c. Search for the word *document* and replace it with the word *brochure*.
   d. Add a transition and sound of your choosing to each slide.
4. Save the presentation again with the same name (Revised EDP Pres).
5. Run the presentation.
6. Print all four slides on one page.
7. Close Revised EDP Pres.

Assessment 5

1. A presentation created in PowerPoint can be sent to Word as an outline or as a handout. This might be useful if you want to format or enhance the presentation using Word tools and features. Use PowerPoint's Help feature to learn about how to send slide images to Word. *(Hint: To get started, display the Microsoft PowerPoint Help window with the Answer Wizard tab selected, key* **How do I send slide images to Word?**, *and then click the Search button. At the list of choices that displays, click* Send slides to Word.*)*
2. After reading the Help information, open EDP Presentation and then send it to Word. (At the Send to Microsoft Word dialog box, you choose the layout.)
3. When the document displays in Word, print the document.
4. Close the Word document without saving it and then exit Word.

6.9

4.5

FORMATTING SLIDES

PERFORMANCE OBJECTIVES

Upon successful completion of chapter 3, you will be able to:
- Format slides in a presentation
- Format a slide master and title master in a presentation
- Change slide color schemes, backgrounds, and design templates
- Create a presentation with the Blank Presentation template
- Format slides with Format Painter
- Format slides with bullets and numbers
- Insert the date and time, a header and footer, and page numbering in slides
- Create, format, and print speaker notes

PowerPoint Chapter 03

PowerPoint provides design templates that apply specific formatting to slides. You can further customize slides in a presentation by applying your own formatting. If you want formatting changes to affect all slides in a presentation, make the changes at the slide master. In this chapter, you will learn how to make formatting changes to slides, make formatting changes at a slide master, use the Format Painter to apply formatting, and insert headers and footers and speaker notes in slides.

Slide Master

Formatting a Presentation

PowerPoint provides a variety of design templates you can use to create a presentation. These templates contain formatting provided by the program. In some situations, the formatting provided by the template will be appropriate; in other situations you will want to change or enhance the formatting of a slide. Formatting can be applied to specific text in a slide or formatting can be applied to an object box.

Formatting Text in a Slide

Text formatting can include a variety of options such as changing fonts, changing font color, and changing paragraph alignment. The steps to change the formatting of a slide vary depending on the type of formatting desired. For example, to

HINT

Align text in slides with the alignment buttons (Align Left, Center, Align Right) on the Formatting toolbar.

change the font of text in a slide, you would select the text first, and then change to the desired font. To change the alignment of a paragraph of text, you would position the insertion point on any character in the paragraph, and then choose the desired alignment.

The Formatting toolbar contains several buttons for applying formatting to text in a slide. The buttons, button names, and a description of what each button accomplishes is shown in figure 3.1.

FIGURE

3.1 *PowerPoint Formatting Toolbar Buttons*

Click this button	Named	To do this
Arial	Font	Change selected text to a different font
28	Font Size	Change selected text to a different font size
B	Bold	Add or remove bolding to or from selected text
I	Italic	Add or remove italics to or from selected text
U	Underline	Add or remove underlining to or from selected text
S	Shadow	Add or remove a shadow to or from selected text
Align Left	Align Left	Left align text
Center	Center	Center align text
Align Right	Align Right	Right align text
Numbering	Numbering	Add or remove numbering to or from selected text
Bullets	Bullets	Add or remove bullets to or from selected text
A	Increase Font Size	Increase font size of selected text to the next available larger size
A	Decrease Font Size	Decrease font size of selected text to the next available smaller size
Decrease Indent	Decrease Indent	Move text to the previous tab stop (level)
Increase Indent	Increase Indent	Move text to the next tab stop (level)
A	Font Color	Change the font color of selected text
Design	Slide Design	Display slide design templates in the Slide Design Task Pane
New Slide	New Slide	Insert a new slide in a presentation

Choosing a Font

Design templates apply a font to text in slides. You may want to change this default to some other font for such reasons as changing the mood of a presentation, enhancing the visual appeal of slides, and increasing the readability of the text in slides. Change the font with the Font and Font Size buttons on the Formatting toolbar or at the Font dialog box. Display the Font dialog box shown in figure 3.2 by clicking Format and then Font. Use options at the Font dialog box to choose a font, font style, font size, and to apply special effects to text in slides such as Shadow, Emboss, Superscript, and Subscript.

Fonts may be decorative or plain and generally fall into one of two categories—*serif* or *sans serif*. A serif is a small line at the end of a character stroke. A serif font is easier to read and is generally used for large amounts of text. A sans serif font does not have serifs (*sans* is French for *without*) and is generally used for titles and headings.

Font

Font Size

HINT

Font, font size, style, and color of text are defined by the design template applied to the slides in the presentation.

F I G U R E

3.2 **Font Dialog Box**

HINT

Limit the number of fonts used in a slide to two.

Increasing/Decreasing Spacing Before/After Paragraphs

If you want control over line spacing in text or the amount of spacing before or after paragraphs of text, use options from the Line Spacing dialog box shown in figure 3.3. Display this dialog box by clicking Format and then Line Spacing. Change line spacing by increasing or decreasing the number in the Line spacing text box. Increase or decrease spacing before a paragraph by keying the desired line spacing measurement in the Before paragraph text box. Key a line spacing measurement in the After paragraph text box to control the amount of spacing after paragraphs. By default, the measurement used is Line spacing. This can be changed to *Points* by clicking the down-pointing triangle after the option box containing the word *Lines* and then clicking *Points* at the drop-down list.

HINT

If text in paragraphs fills more than one line, increase or decrease spacing between paragraphs with the Before paragraph or After paragraph option rather than the Line spacing option.

3.3 *Line Spacing Dialog Box*

Formatting with a Slide Master

If you use a PowerPoint design template, you may choose to use the formatting provided by the template, or you may want to customize the formatting. If you customize formatting in a presentation, PowerPoint's slide master can be very helpful in reducing the steps needed to format all slides in a presentation. If you know in advance that you want to change the formatting of slides, display the slide master in Slide Master view, make the changes needed, and then create the presentation. If the presentation is already created, edit the presentation in a slide master. Any changes made to a slide master will affect all slides in the presentation.

A slide master is added to a presentation when a design template is applied. Generally, a template contains a slide master as well as a title master. Changes made to a title master affect all slides with the Title Slide layout applied. Changes made to a slide master affect all other slides in a presentation.

To format a slide and/or title master, change to the Slide Master view. To do this, position the insertion point on the Normal View button on the View toolbar, hold down the Shift key (this causes the Normal View button to change to the Slide Master View button), and then click the left mouse button. You can also click View, point to Master, and then click Slide Master. This displays a slide master in the Slide pane as shown in figure 3.4. A slide-title master pair also display as slide miniatures at the left side of the window and a Slide Master View toolbar displays. Position the mouse pointer on the slide miniature and the name of the miniature displays in a yellow box above the miniature. Click the desired slide master miniature and then apply specific formatting to the slide master in the Slide pane. Switch between the slide-title master pair by clicking the desired miniature. When all changes have been made to the slide and title masters, click the Close Master View button on the Slide Master View toolbar; or, click the Normal View button on the View toolbar.

FIGURE

3.4 *Slide Master View*

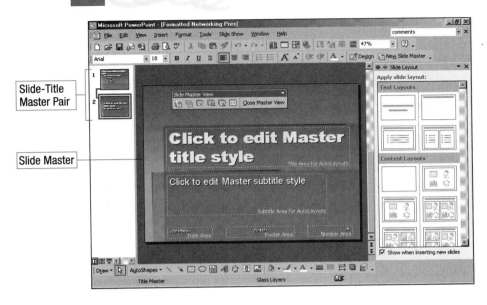

Slide-Title Master Pair

Slide Master

(Note: Before completing computer exercises, delete the PowerPoint Chapter 02 folder on your disk. Next, copy to your disk the PowerPoint Chapter 03 subfolder from the PowerPoint 2002 folder on the CD that accompanies this textbook and then make PowerPoint Chapter 03 the active folder.)

FORMATTING TEXT IN A PRESENTATION USING A SLIDE MASTER

1. Open Networking Presentation from the *PowerPoint Chapter 03* folder on your disk.
2. Save the presentation with Save As into the *PowerPoint Chapter 03* folder on your disk and name the presentation Formatted Networking Pres.
3. Add a slide by completing the following steps:
   a. Display Slide 4 in the Slide pane.
   b. Click the New Slide button on the Formatting toolbar.
   c. Click the Title Slide layout in the Slide Layout Task Pane.
   d. Click in the text *Click to add title* and then key **Designing a Network**.
   e. Click in the text *Click to add subtitle* and then key **Creating and Implementing the Network**.
4. Format the presentation using the slide master and the title master by completing the following steps:
   a. Display Slide 1 in Normal view.
   b. Position the arrow pointer on the Normal View button on the View toolbar, hold down the Shift key (the Normal View button turns into the Slide Master View button), and then click the left mouse button.

   Step 4b

   c. With the Glass Layers Title Master slide miniature selected at the left side of the window and the title master slide displayed in the Slide pane, complete the following steps:

1) Click anywhere in the *Click to edit Master title style*. (This selects the text in the object box.)
2) Click F̲ormat and then F̲ont.
3) At the Font dialog box, click *Bookman Old Style* in the F̲ont list box. (You will need to scroll up the list of typefaces to display Bookman Old Style. If this typeface is not available, choose a similar serif typeface.)
4) Click *48* in the S̲ize list box. (You may need to scroll up this list box to display *48*.)
5) Click the down-pointing triangle at the right of the C̲olor option box.
6) At the color drop-down menu, click the white color (second color from the left).
7) Click OK to close the Font dialog box.
8) Click anywhere in the text *Click to edit Master subtitle style*. (This selects the text in the object box.)
9) Click the down-pointing triangle at the right side of the Font button on the Formatting toolbar and then click *Bookman Old Style* at the drop-down list.
10) Click the down-pointing triangle at the right side of the Font Size button on the Formatting toolbar and then click *28* at the drop-down list.

d. Click the Glass Layers Slide Master miniature (the top miniature) located at the left side of the window.
e. Change the font and color of the text after bullets by completing the following steps:
   1) Click anywhere in the text *Click to edit Master title style*.
   2) Change the font to 48-point Bookman Old Style and the font color to white by completing steps similar to those in 4c2 through 4c7.
   3) Click anywhere in the text *Click to edit Master text styles*. (This selects the text after the first bullet.)
   4) Click F̲ormat and then F̲ont.
   5) At the Font dialog box, click *Bookman Old Style* in the F̲ont list box.
   6) Click the down-pointing triangle at the right of the C̲olor option box.
   7) Click the M̲ore Colors option that displays at the bottom of the drop-down menu.
   8) At the Colors dialog box with the Standard tab selected, click the light blue color shown at the right.
   9) Click OK to close the Colors dialog box.
   10) Click OK to close the Font dialog box.

f. Click the Close Master View button on the Slide Master View toolbar. (This displays Slide 1 with the formatting applied.)

g. Click the Slide Sorter View button on the View toolbar to see how the slides display with the new formatting.

5. Center the text in the title object box and move the object box by completing the following steps:

  a. At the Slide Sorter view, double-click Slide 1.

  b. Click anywhere in the text *Click to add subtitle*. (This selects the object box containing the text.

  c. Position the mouse pointer (displays with a four-headed arrow attached) on the border of the object box and then click the left mouse button.

  d. Press the Delete key. (This deletes the object box from the slide.)

  e. Click in the object box containing the text *NETWORKING*. (This selects the object box.)

  f. Click the Center button on the Formatting toolbar. (This centers the text horizontally in the object box.)

  g. With the object box still selected, position the arrow pointer on the object box border until a four-headed arrow displays attached to the arrow pointer.

  h. Hold down the left mouse button, drag the outline of the object box until it is centered horizontally and vertically on the slide, and then release the mouse button.

6. Decrease the line spacing between paragraphs for the text in Slide 2 by completing the following steps:

  a. Click the Next Slide button to display Slide 2.

  b. Click in the object box containing the bulleted text.

  c. Select the bulleted paragraphs of text.

  d. Click Format and then Line Spacing.

  e. At the Line Spacing dialog box, click the down-pointing triangle at the right of the Line spacing text box (contains the number *1*) until *0.9* displays in the text box.

  f. Click OK to close the dialog box.

  g. Deselect the text.

7. Add a transition and sound of your choosing to each slide.

8. Save the presentation again with the same name (Formatted Networking Pres).

9. Run the presentation.

10. Print the presentation as handouts with all slides printed on one page.

11. Close Formatted Networking Pres.

Applying More than One Design Template to a Presentation

Each design template applies specific formatting to slides. You can apply more than one design template to slides in a presentation. To do this, select the specific slides and then choose the desired design template. The design template is applied only to the selected slides. If you apply more than one design template to a presentation, multiple slide masters will display in the Slide Master view. For example, if two design templates are applied to a presentation, two slide-title master pairs will display—one pair for each design template. Use these slide-title master pairs to specify the formatting for each design template.

exercise 2

APPLYING MORE THAN ONE TEMPLATE TO A PRESENTATION

1. Open Planning Presentation.
2. Save the presentation into the *PowerPoint Chapter 03* folder on your disk and name the presentation Formatted Planning Pres.
3. Copy slides from the Company Newsletter presentation into the current presentation by completing the following steps:
   a. Make sure Normal view is selected and the Slides tab is selected in the Outline/Slides pane.
   b. Open Company Newsletter located in the *PowerPoint Chapter 03* folder on your disk.
   c. With the Company Newsletter presentation open, make sure the Slides tab is selected in the Outline/Slides pane.
   d. Click Slide 2 in the Outline/Slides pane, hold down the Shift key, and then click Slide 3. (This selects both slides.)
   e. Click the Copy button on the Standard toolbar.
   f. Click the button on the Taskbar representing Formatted Planning Pres.
   g. Click below Slide 6 in the Outline/Slides pane.
   h. Click the Paste button on the Standard toolbar. (The pasted slides take on the design template of the current presentation.)
   i. Click the button on the Taskbar representing Company Newsletter and then close Company Newsletter. (Make sure Formatted Planning Pres displays on the screen.)
4. Apply a different design template to the pasted slides by completing the following steps:
   a. With Slide 7 and Slide 8 selected in the Outline/Slides pane, click the Slide Design button on the Formatting toolbar.
   b. Click the *Radial* slide design in the Apply a design template list box. (You will need to scroll down the list to display this template.)
5. Format the slides using the slide-title master pairs by completing the following steps:
   a. Hold down the Shift key and then click the Normal View button (the button name changes to Slide Master View with the Shift key down).
   b. Click the Ocean Title Master slide miniature located at the left side of the window (second slide miniature from the top).

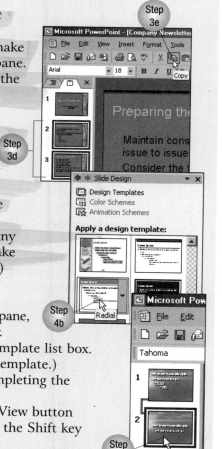

Step 3e

Step 3d

Step 4b

Step 5b

c. Click anywhere in the text *Click to edit Master subtitle style*. (This selects the text.)

d. Change the font by completing the following steps:
1) Click Format and then Font.
2) At the Font dialog box, click *Times New Roman* in the Font list box.
3) Click *Bold* in the Font style list box.
4) Click *36* in the Size list box.
5) Click the down-pointing triangle at the right of the Color option and then click More Colors options at the drop-down list.
6) At the Colors dialog box with the Standard tab selected, click a light blue color of your choosing and then click OK.
7) Click OK to close the Font dialog box.

Step 5e

e. Click the Radial Slide Master slide miniature located at the left side of the window (third slide miniature from the top).

f. Select the first and second bulleted text (this is the text *Click to edit Master text style* and *Second level*).

g. Change the font by completing the following steps:
1) Click Format and then Font.
2) At the Font dialog box, click *Times New Roman* in the Font list box. (You will need to scroll down this list to display *Times New Roman*.)
3) Click *Bold* in the Font style list box.
4) Click the down-pointing triangle at the right of the Color option and then click the blue color that is the last color at the right.
5) Click OK to close the Font dialog box.

Step 5g4

h. Click the Normal View button on the View toolbar.

6. Add a transition and sound of your choosing to all slides in the presentation.
7. Save the presentation again with the same name (Formatted Planning Pres).
8. Run the presentation.
9. Print the presentation as handouts with nine slides per page.
10. Close Formatted Planning Pres.

Formatting the Slide Color Scheme

PowerPoint design templates provide interesting and varied formatting effects and save time when preparing a presentation. Some of the formatting applied to slides by the design template can be formatted. For example, the color scheme and background of slides can be changed.

A design template includes a default color scheme consisting of eight colors. Colors are chosen for the background, accents, text, fills, shadows, title text, and hyperlinks. Additional color schemes are available for design templates. To choose another color scheme for a design template, display the Slide Design Task Pane. Click the *Color Schemes* hyperlink located toward the top of the task pane and then click the designed scheme. Figure 3.5 shows the Slide Design Task Pane with color schemes displayed for the Glass Layers design template used for the Networking Presentation.

3.5 *Slide Design Task Pane with Color Schemes Displayed*

Color schemes for Glass Layers slide design.

Click this hyperlink to display the Edit Color Scheme dialog box.

Customizing the Color Scheme

Customize a color scheme by clicking the *Edit Color Schemes* hyperlink located toward the bottom of the task pane. This displays the Edit Color Scheme dialog box similar to the one shown in figure 3.6. Click an option in the Scheme colors section and then click the Change Color button. At the dialog box that displays, choose the desired color, and then click OK.

3.6 *Edit Color Scheme Dialog Box*

Change color for a specific item by clicking the box preceding the desired item in this section and then clicking the Change Color button. At the dialog box that displays, choose the desired color.

Changing Background Color

Background color can be changed with options at the Edit Color Scheme dialog box or at the Background dialog box shown in figure 3.7. Display this dialog box by clicking Format and then Background. At the Background dialog box, click the down-pointing triangle at the right of the Background fill option box and then click the desired color at the drop-down list. Click the Apply button to apply the background color to the active slide or click Apply to All to apply the background color to all slides.

HINT
Create a custom fill for the slide background with options at the Fill Effects dialog box.

FIGURE

3.7 *Background Dialog Box*

Click this down-pointing triangle to display a list of color choices.

exercise 3

FORMATTING SLIDE COLOR SCHEMES

1. Open Networking Presentation.
2. Save the presentation with Save As into the *PowerPoint Chapter 03* folder on your disk and name the presentation Customized Networking Pres.
3. Change the color scheme by completing the following steps:
   a. With the presentation displayed in Normal view, click the Slide Design button on the Formatting toolbar.
   b. Click the *Color Schemes* hyperlink located toward the top of the task pane.
   c. Click the last color scheme option in the bottom row (the color scheme at the right).
4. Print the presentation as handouts with four slides per page.
5. Customize the slide color scheme by completing the following steps:
   a. Click the *Edit Color Schemes* hyperlink located toward the bottom of the Slide Design Task Pane.
   b. At the Edit Color Scheme dialog box, click the box next to *Text and lines* in the Scheme colors section.
   c. Click the Change Color button.

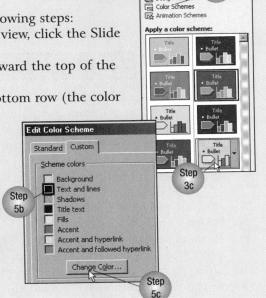

Step 3b

Step 3c

Step 5b

Step 5c

d. At the Text and Line Color dialog box, click a medium blue color of your choosing and then click OK.
e. At the Edit Color Scheme dialog box, click the box next to *Title text* in the Scheme colors section.
f. Click the Change Color button.
g. At the Title Text Color dialog box, click a dark blue color of your choosing and then click OK.
h. Click the Apply button to apply the color changes and close the Edit Color Scheme dialog box.
6. Print the presentation as handouts with four slides per page.
7. Customize the background of the slide color scheme by completing the following steps:
   a. Click Format and then Background.
   b. At the Background dialog box, click the down-pointing triangle at the right side of the Background fill option box, and then click More Colors at the drop-down list.
   c. At the Colors dialog box with the Standard tab selected, click a light green color of your choosing, and then click the OK button.
   d. Click the Apply to All button at the Background dialog box.
8. Print the presentation as handouts with four slides per page.
9. Save the presentation again with the same name (Customized Networking Pres).
10. Run the presentation.
11. Close Customized Networking Pres.

Changing the Design Template

When preparing presentations for this and previous chapters, you have chosen a design template first and then created each slide. A different design template can be applied to an existing presentation. To do this, click the Slide Design button on the Formatting toolbar and then click the desired template in the Slide Design Task Pane.

exercise 4

CHANGING THE DESIGN TEMPLATE

1. Open Planning Presentation.
2. Choose a different design template for the presentation by completing the following steps:
   a. Click the Slide Design button on the Formatting toolbar.
   b. Click the *Layers* slide design in the Apply a design template list box in the Slide Design Task Pane. (You will need to scroll down the list to display this template.)
3. Run the presentation to see how it appears with the new design template applied.
4. Print all six slides on one page.
5. Close Planning Presentation without saving the changes.
6. Open Networking Presentation.
7. Apply a different design template of your choosing to this presentation.

POWERPOINT

Creating a Blank Presentation and then Applying a Design Template

Many of the presentations you have created in this and previous chapters have been based on a design template. You can also create a blank presentation and then apply your own formatting or apply a design template. To create a blank presentation, click the New button on the Standard toolbar. This displays an unformatted slide in the Slide pane. You can also create a blank presentation by displaying the New Presentation Task Pane and then clicking the *Blank Presentation* hyperlink.

New

Formatting with Format Painter

If you create a blank presentation and decide to apply your own formatting, consider using the Format Painter. Use Format Painter to apply the same formatting in more than one location in a slide or slides. To use the Format Painter, apply the desired formatting to text, position the insertion point anywhere in the formatted text, and then double-click the Format Painter button on the Standard toolbar. Using the mouse, select the additional text to which you want the formatting applied. After applying the formatting in the desired locations, click the Format Painter button to deactivate it. If you need to apply formatting in only one other location, click the Format Painter button once. The first time you select text, the formatting is applied and the Format Painter is deactivated.

Format
Painter

exercise 5

CREATING AND FORMATTING A BLANK PRESENTATION

1. At the blank PowerPoint window, click the New button on the Standard toolbar. (This displays an unformatted slide in the Slide pane and also displays the Slide Layout Task Pane.)
2. In the unformatted slide that displays in the Slide pane, key the title and subtitle for Slide 1 as shown in figure 3.8.
3. Create the remaining slides shown in figure 3.8 using the Title and Text slide layout for Slides 2 through 5. When keying the bulleted text, press the Tab key to move (promote) the insertion point to the previous tab stop or press Shift + Tab to move (demote) the insertion point to the next tab stop.
4. Save the presentation and name it Color Presentation.
5. Print the presentation as handouts with six slides per page. (The presentation contains only five slides.)
6. Suppose you are going to print transparencies for the slides in this presentation. To do this, apply a design template with a light background by completing the following steps:
   a. Click the Slide Design button on the Formatting toolbar.
   b. Click *Blends* in the Apply a design template list box. (You will need to scroll down the list to display this template.)

Step
6b

7. Change the font style and color of the terms using Format Painter by completing the following steps:
   a. Display Slide 4 in the Slide pane.
   b. Select the term *Balance:* (be sure to select the colon).
   c. Display the Font dialog box, change the font style to *Bold*, change the color to the red that follows the color scheme, and then click OK to close the dialog box.
   d. Deselect *Balance:* and then click anywhere in *Balance:*.
   e. Double-click the Format Painter button on the Standard toolbar.
   f. Using the mouse, select *Color Wheel:*. (The pointer displays as an I-beam with a paintbrush attached.)
   g. Using the mouse, select each of the other terms in Slide 4 (*Contrast:*, *Gradient:*, *Hue:*).
   h. Display Slide 5 and then use the mouse to select each of the terms (including the colon) in the slide.
   i. Click the Format Painter button to deactivate it.
   j. Deselect the text.
8. Print only Slide 4 by completing the following steps:
   a. Display Slide 4 in the Slide pane.
   b. Click File and then Print.
   c. At the Print dialog box, click the Current slide option in the Print range section.
   d. Click OK.
9. Save the presentation again with the same name (Color Presentation).
10. Run the presentation.
11. Close Color Presentation.

FIGURE

3.8 *Exercise 5*

Slide 1	Title	=	COMPANY PUBLICATIONS
	Subtitle	=	Using Color in Publications
Slide 2	Title	=	Communicating with Color
	Bullets	=	• Color in a publication can:
			- Elicit feelings
			- Emphasize important text
			- Attract attention
			• Choose one or two colors
			• Use "spot color" by using color only in specific areas

Slide 3	Title	=	Printing the Publication
	Bullets	=	• Print all copies on a color printer
			• Print on a color printer and duplicate with a color photocopier
			• Print on colored paper
			• Print on specialty paper

Slide 4	Title	=	Color Terminology
	Bullets	=	• Balance: Amount of light and dark in a picture
			• Color Wheel: Device used to illustrate color relationships
			• Contrast: Amount of gray in a color
			• Gradient: Gradual varying of color
			• Hue: Variation of a color such as green-blue

Slide 5	Title	=	Color Terminology
	Bullets	=	• Pixel: Each dot in a picture or graphic
			• Resolution: The number of dots that make up an image on a screen or printer
			• Reverse: White foreground on black background or white type against a colored background.
			• Saturation: Purity of a color

Formatting with Bullets and Numbers

Each design template contains a Title and Text slide layout containing bullets. The appearance and formatting of the bullets in this slide layout varies with each template. You can choose to use the bullet provided by the design template or you can insert different bullets and also change to numbering.

HINT

Use bullets for items that are not sequential or ranked in order of importance.

Changing Bullets

Customize bullets with options at the Bullets and Numbering dialog box with the Bulleted tab selected as shown in figure 3.9. Display this dialog box by clicking in a bulleted list object box, clicking Format, and then clicking Bullets and Numbering. At the Bullets and Numbering dialog box, choose one of the predesigned bullets from the list box, change the size of the bullets by percentage in relation to the text size, change the bullet color, and display bullet pictures and characters.

3.9   *Bullets and Numbering Dialog Box with Bulleted Tab Selected*

HINT

If you increase the size of bullets, you may need to increase paragraph indention or spacing between paragraphs.

Numbering

Click the <u>P</u>icture button located toward the bottom of the dialog box and the Picture Bullet displays. Click the desired bullet in the list box and then click OK. Click the C<u>u</u>stomize button located toward the bottom of the Bullets and Numbering dialog box and the Symbol dialog box displays. Choose a symbol bullet option at the Symbol dialog box and then click OK.

Inserting Numbering

A bulleted list can be easily changed to numbers. To do this, select the bulleted list and then click the Numbering button on the Formatting toolbar. You can also change to numbering by selecting the list and then displaying the Bullets and Numbering dialog box with the Numbered tab selected. At this dialog box, choose the desired numbering style, and then click OK.

exercise 6

CHANGING BULLETS AND APPLYING NUMBERING

1. Open Color Presentation.
2. Change the first-level bullets in Slides 2 through 5 by completing the following steps:
   a. Display Slide 2 in the Slide pane.
   b. Hold down the Shift key and then click the Slide Master View button on the View toolbar.
   c. Click in the text *Click to edit Master text styles*.
   d. Click F<u>o</u>rmat and then <u>B</u>ullets and Numbering.
   e. At the Bullets and Numbering dialog box with the Bulleted tab selected, click the up-pointing triangle at the right side of the <u>S</u>ize option until *85* displays in the text box.
   f. Click the <u>P</u>icture button located toward the bottom of the dialog box.

g. At the Picture Bullet dialog box, click the first bullet option from the left in the third row (gold, square bullet).

h. Click OK to close the Picture Bullet dialog box and the Bullets and Numbering dialog box.

i. Click the Normal View button. (This removes the slide master.)

3. Print only Slide 2.

4. Change the second-level bullets in Slide 2 by completing the following steps:

a. Make sure Slide 2 is displayed in Slide view.

b. Hold down the Shift key and then click the Slide Master View button on the View toolbar.

c. Click in the text *Second level*.

d. Click Format and then Bullets and Numbering.

e. At the Bullets and Numbering dialog box with the Bulleted tab selected, click the up-pointing triangle at the right side of the Size option until *70* displays in the text box.

f. Click the Customize button located toward the bottom of the dialog box.

g. At the Symbol dialog box, click the pen image (first image [in the second square] from the left in the top row).

h. Click OK to close the Symbol dialog box.

i. Click OK to close the Bullets and Numbering dialog box.

j. Click the Normal View button. (This removes the slide master.)

5. Print only Slide 2.

6. Save the presentation with the same name (Color Presentation).

7. Change the first-level bullets to numbers in Slides 2 through 5 by completing the following steps:

a. Make sure Slide 2 displays in the Slide pane.

b. Hold down the Shift key and then click the Slide Master View button on the View toolbar.

c. Click in the text *Click to edit Master text styles*.

d. Click the Numbering button on the Formatting toolbar.

e. Change the color of the numbers by completing the following steps:

1) Click Format and then Bullets and Numbering.

2) At the Bullets and Numbering dialog box, make sure the Numbered tab is selected.

3) Click the down-pointing triangle at the right side of the Color option and then click the green color that follows the color scheme.

4) Click OK to close the dialog box.

f. Click the Normal View button. (This removes the slide master.)

8. Save the presentation again with the same name (Color Presentation).

9. Display Slide 1 and then run the presentation.

10. Print all five slides on one page.

11. Close the presentation.

Step 2g

Step 4g

Step 7d

Step 7c

Step 7e3

Inserting Headers and Footers in a Presentation

Insert information that you want to appear at the top or bottom of each slide or on note and handout pages with options at the Header and Footer dialog box. Click <u>V</u>iew and then <u>H</u>eader and Footer to display the Header and Footer dialog box shown in figure 3.10.

FIGURE

3.10 *Header and Footer Dialog Box with Slide Tab Selected*

Include the date and time as fixed or automatic. To include a fixed date and time, click in the Fi<u>x</u>ed text box and then key the desired text. If you want the date and/or time inserted and then automatically updated when the presentation is opened, click the <u>U</u>pdate automatically option. Specify the format for the date and/or time by clicking the down-pointing triangle at the right side of the <u>U</u>pdate automatically text box and then click the desired format at the drop-down list. If you want the slide number inserted in a presentation, click the Slide <u>n</u>umber check box. Key any footer text desired in the <u>F</u>ooter text box. Click the Apply button to apply the element(s) to the current slide. If you want the element(s) inserted in all slides, click the Appl<u>y</u> to All button. Elements added to a slide or slides are previewed in the Preview section of the dialog box.

INSERTING THE DATE, TIME, SLIDE NUMBER, AND A FOOTER IN A PRESENTATION

1. Open Planning Presentation.
2. Save the presentation with Save As into the *PowerPoint Chapter 03* folder on your disk and name the presentation Planning Pres with Footer.
3. Insert the date, time, slide number, and footer text into the presentation by completing the following steps:
   a. Click View and then Header and Footer.
   b. At the Header and Footer dialog box with the Slide tab selected, make sure a check mark displays in the Date and time check box.
   c. Click the Update automatically option.
   d. Click the down-pointing triangle at the right side of the Update automatically text box and then click the option that displays the date in numbers followed by the time (i.e., 09/15/2002 12:35 PM).

   e. Click the Slide number option to insert a check mark in the check box.
   f. Click in the Footer text box and then key **Electronic Design**.
   g. Click the Apply to All button.
4. Save the document again with the same name (Planning Pres with Footer).
5. Run the presentation to see how the footer text displays in the slides.
6. Print all six slides on one page.
7. Close Planning Pres with Footer.

Inserting Information in the Footer Area of a Slide Master

You can include footer information in slides by keying the information in the slide master. To insert information in the Footer area of a slide master, display the Slide Master view, click in the desired section of the slide master, and then key or insert the desired information. Apply the desired formatting to the footer text at the Slide Master view.

INSERTING INFORMATION IN THE FOOTER AREA OF A SLIDE MASTER

1. Open Color Presentation.
2. Save the presentation with Save As into the *PowerPoint Chapter 03* folder on your disk and name the presentation Color Pres with Footer.
3. Insert and format a footer in the Slide Master by completing the following steps:
   a. Hold down the Shift key and then click the Slide Master View button on the View toolbar.

b. Click the Blends Slide Master miniature (the top miniature) located at the left side of the window.

c. Click the *<footer>* text in the Footer Area of the slide master.

d. Key **Using Colors in Publications**.

e. Select *Using Colors in Publications* and then change the font size to *12* and turn on bold.

f. Click the Normal View button on the View toolbar.

4. Print the presentation as handouts with six slides per page. (The footer text does print on Slide 1.)

5. Display Slide 1 and then run the presentation.

6. Save the presentation again with the same name (Color Pres with Footer).

7. Close Color Pres with Footer.

Inserting a Header and/or Footer in Notes and Handouts

Elements selected at the Header and Footer dialog box with the Slide tab selected are inserted in slides in a presentation. If you want elements inserted in notes or handouts, choose options at the Header and Footer dialog box with the Notes and Handouts tab selected as shown in figure 3.11. At this dialog box, choose to insert the date and/or time fixed or automatically, include a header and/or footer, and include page numbering. Choices made at this dialog box print when the presentation is printed as notes pages, handouts, or an outline.

FIGURE

3.11 *Header and Footer Dialog Box with Notes and Handouts Tab Selected*

Adding Speaker Notes

If you are going to give your presentation in front of an audience, consider creating speaker notes for some or all of the slides. Create speaker notes containing additional information about the slide that will help you during the presentation. Speaker notes do not display on a slide when the presentation is running. Speaker notes print when the *Notes Pages* option is selected at the Print dialog box.

To insert speaker notes, display slides in the Normal view, click in the Notes pane, and then key the information. Another method for inserting speaker notes is to display the presentation in Notes Page view. To do this, click View and then Notes Page. This displays the active slide with a text box below. Click inside the text box and then key the speaker note information. Format speaker notes in the normal manner. For example, you can change the font, change the text alignment, and insert bullets or numbering.

You can create and/or display speaker notes while a presentation is running. To do this, run the presentation, and then display the desired slide. Move the mouse to display the *Slide Show* menu icon. Click the *Slide Show* menu icon and then click Speaker Notes at the pop-up menu. This displays the Speaker Notes dialog box. View, key, or edit text at this dialog box and then click the Close button.

INSERTING A HEADER, FOOTER, AND THE DATE IN NOTES AND HANDOUTS

1. Open Planning Pres with Footer.
2. Insert a header and footer, the date, and page numbering in notes and handouts by completing the following steps:
   a. Click View and then Header and Footer.
   b. At the Header and Footer dialog box, click the Notes and Handouts tab.
   c. At the Header and Footer dialog box with the Notes and Handouts tab selected, click the Update automatically option. (Check to make sure the current date displays in the Update automatically text box. If not, click the down-pointing triangle at the right side of the text box, and then click the desired date style at the drop-down list.)
   d. Click in the Header text box and then key **Company Publications**.
   e. Click in the Footer text box and then key **Planning the Publication**.
   f. Make sure there is a check mark in the Page number check box.
   g. Click the Apply to All button.

3. Add and format speaker notes by completing the following steps:
   a. Display Slide 2 in the Slide pane.
   b. Click in the Notes pane. (This pane displays below the slide and contains the text *Click to add notes*.)

c. Click the Bold button on the Formatting toolbar and then click the Center button.
d. Key **Distribute publication examples.**, press Enter, and then key **Compare examples 1 and 2**.
e. Display Slide 4 in the Slide pane.
f. Click in the Notes pane.
g. Click the Bold button on the Formatting toolbar and then click the Center button.
h. Key **Elicit comments from participants regarding current corporate publications.**, press Enter, and then key **Ask what changes individuals would like to make.**

4. Print Slides 2 and 4 as notes pages by completing the following steps:
a. Display the Print dialog box.
b. Click the down-pointing triangle to the right of the Print what option and then click *Notes Pages* at the drop-down list.
c. Click the Slides option box and then key **2,4**.
d. Click OK. (This prints each slide [Slides 2 and 4] toward the top of the page on a separate piece of paper with the header, footer, date, page number, and speaker notes included.)

5. Save the presentation with the same name (Planning Pres with Footer).
6. Close Planning Pres with Footer.

CHAPTER summary

➤ Formatting such as changing fonts, changing font color, and changing paragraph alignment can be applied to text in slides.

➤ The Formatting toolbar contains several buttons you can use to apply formatting to text in slides.

➤ Change the font of selected text with options at the Font dialog box or with the Font and Font Size buttons on the Formatting toolbar.

➤ Increase or decrease line spacing or the spacing before or after paragraphs with options at the Line Spacing dialog box.

➤ Generally, a template contains a slide master as well as a title master. Changes made to a title master affect all slides with the Title Slide layout applied. Changes made to the slide master affect all other slides in a presentation.

➤ Change to the Slide Master view by holding down the Shift key and clicking the Slide Master View button on the View toolbar. (The Normal View button changes to the Slide Master View button when you hold down the Shift key.)

➤ In Slide Master view, a slide master displays in the Slide pane along with a slide-title master pair that display as slide miniatures at the left side of the window. Click the desired slide master miniature and then apply specific formatting to the slide master in the Slide pane.

➤ You can apply more than one design template to slides in a presentation. If more than one design template is applied to slides, multiple slide-title master pairs will display in the Slide Master view.

➤ A design template includes a default color scheme. Click the _Color Schemes_ hyperlink located toward the bottom of the Slide Design Task Pane and a number of additional color schemes display in the task pane.

➤ Click the _Edit Color Schemes_ hyperlink in the task pane to display the Edit Color Scheme dialog box. Use options at this dialog box to change color for specific items.

➤ Change the background color of a design template with options at the Background dialog box.

➤ You can apply a different design template to an existing presentation.

➤ Create a presentation with little formatting using the Blank Presentation template. To create a blank presentation, click the New button on the Standard toolbar or click the _Blank Presentation_ hyperlink in the New Presentation Task Pane.

➤ Use Format Painter to apply the same formatting to more than one location in a slide or slides.

➤ Customize bullets with options at the Bullets and Numbering dialog box with the Bulleted tab selected.

➤ Click the Picture button located toward the bottom of the Bullets and Numbering dialog box to display the Picture dialog box that contains bullet images. Click the Customize button at the dialog box to display the Symbol dialog box containing symbol options for bullets.

➤ Apply numbering to selected text by clicking the Numbering button on the Formatting toolbar or with options at the Bullets and Numbering dialog box with the Numbered tab selected.

➤ Insert elements in a slide or slides such as the date and time, slide number, and a footer with options at the Header and Footer dialog box with the Slide tab selected.

➤ You can create a footer for slides in the Footer Area of a slide master.

➤ Insert elements in notes and handouts such as the date and time, page number, and a header and footer with options from the Header and Footer dialog box with the Notes and Handouts tab selected.

➤ Insert speaker notes in the Notes pane that displays below the Slide pane in Normal view.

COMMANDS review

Command	Mouse/Keyboard
Display Font dialog box	Format, Font
Display Line Spacing dialog box	Format, Line Spacing
Display Slide Master view	Hold down Shift key, click Normal View button
Display additional color scheme options	Click _Color Schemes_ hyperlink in Slide Design Task Pane
Display Edit Color Scheme dialog box	Click _Edit Color Schemes_ hyperlink in Slide Design Task Pane with color scheme options displayed
Display Background dialog box	Format, Background
Display Bullets and Numbering dialog box	Format, Bullets and Numbering
Display Header and Footer dialog box	View, Header and Footer

CONCEPTS check

Completion: On a blank sheet of paper, indicate the correct term, symbol, or command.

1. Display the Font dialog box by clicking this option on the Menu bar and then clicking <u>F</u>ont at the drop-down menu.
2. Increase spacing before and after paragraphs with options at this dialog box.
3. Display the Slide Master view by holding down this key while clicking the Normal View button on the View toolbar.
4. Display additional color schemes for a design template by clicking this hyperlink in the Slide Design Task Pane.
5. Customize a color scheme with options at this dialog box.
6. Use this button on the Formatting toolbar to apply formatting to more than one location in a slide or slides.
7. Click this button at the Bullets and Numbering dialog box to display the Symbol dialog box.
8. Change a selected bulleted list to numbers by clicking this button on the Formatting toolbar.
9. Insert information you want to appear at the top or bottom of each slide or on note and handout pages with options at this dialog box.
10. Click in this pane in the Normal view to add speaker notes to a slide.

SKILLS check

Assessment 1

1. Create a presentation with the text shown in figure 3.12 using the Capsules design template. Choose the appropriate layout for each slide.
2. When all of the slides are created, complete a spelling check on the presentation.
3. Add a transition and sound of your choosing to each slide.
4. Save the presentation into the *PowerPoint Chapter 03* folder on your disk and name the presentation Benefits Presentation.
5. Run the presentation.
6. After running the presentation, print all of the slides on one page.
7. Close Benefits Presentation.

3.12 *Assessment 1*

Slide 1   Title   =   BENEFITS PROGRAM
            Subtitle =   Changes to Plans

Slide 2   Title   =   INTRODUCTION
            Bullets =
- Changes made for 2003
- Description of eligibility
- Instructions for enrolling new members
- Overview of medical and dental coverage

Slide 3   Title   =   INTRODUCTION
            Bullets =
- Expanded enrollment forms
- Glossary defining terms
- Telephone directory
- Pamphlet with commonly asked questions

Slide 4   Title   =   WHAT'S NEW
            Bullets =
- New medical plan
- Changes in monthly contributions
- Paying with pretax dollars
- Contributions toward spouse's coverage

Slide 5   Title   =   COST SHARING
            Bullets =
- Increased deductible
- New coinsurance amount
- Higher coinsurance amount for retail prescription drugs
- Co-payment for mail-order drugs
- New stop loss limit

Assessment 2

1. Open Benefits Presentation.
2. Save the presentation with Save As into the *PowerPoint Chapter 03* folder on your disk and name the presentation Formatted Benefits Pres.
3. Make the following changes to the presentation:
   a. Change to the Slide Master view.
   b. Make sure the Capsules Title Master slide miniature (the bottom miniature) is selected.
   c. Click in the text *Click to edit Master title style* and then click the Italic button on the Formatting toolbar.
   c. Click the Capsules Slide Master slide miniature (the top miniature).
   d. Click anywhere in the text *Click to edit Master title style* and then click the Italic button on the Formatting toolbar.
   e. Increase line spacing for the bulleted text by completing the following steps:
      1) Click anywhere in the text *Click to edit Master text styles*.
      2) Display the Line Spacing dialog box.
      3) Change the Line spacing number to *1.3*.

4) Close the Line Spacing dialog box.
      f. Click the Normal View button.
   4. Save the presentation again with the same name (Formatted Benefits Pres)
   5. Run the presentation.
   6. After running the presentation, print all of the slides on one page.
   7. Close Formatted Benefits Pres.

Assessment 3

   1. Open Formatted Benefits Pres.
   2. Save the presentation with Save As into the *PowerPoint Chapter 03* folder on your disk and name the presentation Modified Benefits Pres.
   3. Make the following changes to the presentation:
      a. Apply a different design template of your choosing.
      b. Insert the current date and slide number on all slides in the presentation. (Make sure there is no check mark in the Don't show on title slide option at the Header and Footer dialog box.)
      c. Change the bullets in Slide 2 to numbers.
   4. Save the presentation again with the same name (Modified Benefits Pres).
   5. Run the presentation.
   6. After running the presentation, print all of the slides on one page.
   7. Close Modified Benefits Pres.

Assessment 4

   1. Open Job Search Presentation. (This presentation is located in the *PowerPoint Chapter 03* folder on your disk.)
   2. Save the presentation with Save As and name it Revised Job Search Pres.
   3. Make the following change to the presentation:
      a. Create the header *Professional Employment Services*, the footer *Job Search Strategies*, and insert the date and page number for notes and handouts. (Make sure there is no check mark in the Don't show on title slide option at the Header and Footer dialog box with the Slide tab selected.)
      c. Display Slide 2 in Normal view and then add the speaker note *Refer participants to visual aids.*
      d. Display Slide 4 in Normal view and then add the speaker note *Provide participants with an example of a contact list.*
      e. Change the background color for all slides. (Make sure you choose a complementary color.)
   4. Add a transition and sound of your choosing to all slides in the presentation.
   5. Save the presentation again with the same name (Revised Job Search Pres).
   6. Run the presentation.
   7. Print Slides 2 and 3 as notes pages.
   8. Close Revised Job Search Pres.

Assessment 5

   1. Slides in a presentation generally display and print in landscape orientation. This orientation can be changed to portrait. Use PowerPoint's Help feature to learn about slide orientations and how to change the orientation.
   2. Open Job Search Presentation.
   3. Change the orientation of all slides in the presentation from landscape to portrait.
   4. Print all slides on one page.
   5. Close the Job Search Presentation without saving the changes.

ADDING VISUAL APPEAL AND ANIMATION TO PRESENTATIONS

PERFORMANCE OBJECTIVES

Upon successful completion of chapter 4, you will be able to:
- **Draw objects and autoshapes with buttons on the Drawing toolbar**
- **Select, delete, move, copy, size, and format objects**
- **Create a text box and wrap text within an autoshape**
- **Insert clip art images in a presentation**
- **Size, move, and format clip art images**
- **Insert a bitmap graphic in a slide**
- **Add an animation scheme to slides**
- **Add a build to slides**

PowerPoint Chapter 04

Add visual appeal to slides in a presentation by including shapes, objects, and autoshapes and by inserting clip art images or bitmap images. With buttons on the Drawing toolbar, you can format and customize object boxes in slides, draw objects, and create autoshapes. Insert clip art images in a slide with options at the Insert Clip Art Task Pane or at the Select Picture dialog box. Insert a bitmap graphic in a slide at the Insert Picture dialog box. Add an animation scheme to a presentation to add visual interest to your presentation as well as create focus on specific items. In this chapter you will learn a number of features for adding visual appeal and animation to presentations.

Formatting with Buttons on the Drawing Toolbar

Slides in a presentation contain placeholders where specific text or objects are inserted. A placeholder consists of an object box containing specific formatting. The formatting applied to placeholders in a design template will vary depending on the template selected. These placeholders (object boxes) can be customized by changing such items as the background color or adding a border or shadow. These types of changes can be made with buttons on the Drawing toolbar. The Drawing toolbar displays toward the bottom of the PowerPoint window (above the Status bar). Figure 4.1 describes the buttons on the Drawing toolbar.

4.1 *PowerPoint Drawing Toolbar Buttons*

Click this button	Named	To do this
Draw ▾	Draw	Display a pop-up menu with options for grouping and positioning drawings.
▸	Select Objects	Select text or objects.
AutoShapes ▾	AutoShapes	Display a palette of shapes that can be drawn in a document. (To draw a shape circumscribed within a perfect square, hold down the Shift key while drawing the shape.)
◹	Line	Draw a line in a document.
◥	Arrow	Insert a line with an arrowhead. (To draw at 15-degree angles, hold down the Shift key.)
▭	Rectangle	Draw a rectangle in a document. (To draw a perfect square, hold down the Shift key while drawing the shape.)
◯	Oval	Draw an oval in a document. (To draw a perfect circle, hold down the Shift key while drawing the shape.)
▤	Text Box	Create text in a text box. (To add text that does not wrap, click the button, click in the document, and then key the text. To add text that does wrap, click the button, drag to create a box, and then key the text.)
◢	Insert WordArt	Insert a Microsoft Office drawing object.
◫	Insert Diagram or Organization Chart	Insert and customize a predesigned diagram or organizational chart.
◫	Insert Clip Art	Display the Insert Clip Art Task Pane.
◫	Insert Picture	Display the Insert Picture dialog box containing pictures you can insert in the document.
◫	Fill Color	Fill selected object with a color, pattern, texture, or shaded fill.
◫	Line Color	Change color of selected line.
A	Font Color	Format selected text with a color.
≡	Line Style	Change thickness of selected line or change it to a compound line.
⋮	Dash Style	Change style of selected line, arc, or border to dashed.
⇄	Arrow Style	Add arrowheads to a selected line, arc, or open free-form.
◪	Shadow Style	Add or remove an object shadow.
◫	3-D Style	Add or remove a 3-D effect.

Drawing an Object

With buttons on the Drawing toolbar, you can draw a variety of shapes such as circles, squares, rectangles, ovals, and draw straight lines, free-form lines, and lines with arrowheads. If you draw a shape with the Line button or the Arrow button, the shape is considered a *line drawing*. If you draw a shape with the Rectangle or Oval button, the shape is considered an *enclosed object*. If you want to draw the same shape more than once, double-click the shape button on the Drawing toolbar. After drawing the shapes, click the button again to deactivate it.

Use the Rectangle button on the Drawing toolbar to draw a square or rectangle in a document. If you want to draw a square, hold down the Shift key while drawing the shape. The Shift key keeps all sides of the drawn object equal. Use the Oval button to draw a circle or an oval object. To draw a circle, hold down the Shift key while drawing the object.

Line

Arrow

Rectangle

Oval

Creating AutoShapes

With options from the AutoShapes button, you can choose from a variety of predesigned shapes. Click the AutoShapes button and a pop-up menu displays. Point to the desired menu option and a side menu displays. This side menu will offer autoshape choices for the selected option. For example, if you point to the Basic Shapes option, a number of shapes such as a circle, square, triangle, box, stop sign, and so on display at the right side of the pop-up menu. Click the desired shape and the mouse pointer turns into crosshairs. Position the crosshairs in the slide, hold down the left mouse button, drag to create the shape, and then release the button. You can also position the crosshairs in the desired location in the slide and then click the left mouse button. This inserts the autoshape in the slide.

AutoShapes ▾

AutoShapes

HINT

Many autoshapes have an adjustment handle you can use to change the most prominent feature of the autoshape.

Selecting an Object

After an object has been created, you may decide to make changes to the object or delete the object. To do this, the object must be selected. To select an enclosed object, position the mouse pointer anywhere inside the object (the mouse pointer displays with a four-headed arrow attached) and then click the left mouse button. To select a line, position the mouse pointer on the line until the pointer turns into an arrow with a four-headed arrow attached, and then click the left mouse button. When an object is selected, it displays surrounded by white sizing handles. Once an object is selected, it can be edited, such as changing the fill and the line, it can be moved, or it can be deleted.

If a slide contains more than one object, you can select several objects at once using the Select Objects button on the Drawing toolbar. To do this, click the Select Objects button, position the crosshairs in the upper left corner of the area containing the objects, hold down the left mouse button, drag the outline to the lower right corner of the area containing the objects, and then release the mouse button. You can also select more than one object by holding down the Shift key as you click each object.

Each object in the selected area displays surrounded by white sizing handles. Objects in the selected area are connected. For example, if you move one of the objects in the selected area, the other objects move relatively.

Select Objects

Deleting, Moving, and Copying an Object

Delete an object you have drawn by selecting the object and then clicking the Delete key. Move an object by selecting it, positioning the mouse pointer inside the object (mouse pointer displays with a four-headed arrow attached), holding down the left mouse button, and then dragging the outline of the object to the new location. If you select more than one object, moving one of the objects will move the other objects. Moving an object removes the object from its original position and inserts it into a new location. If you want the object to stay in its original location and an exact copy to be inserted in a new location, use the Ctrl key while dragging the object.

Sizing an Object

To change the size of an object, select it, and then position the mouse pointer on a sizing handle until it turns into a double-headed arrow. Hold down the left mouse button, drag the outline of the shape toward or away from the center of the object until it is the desired size, and then release the mouse button.

Formatting Objects

Fill Color

Line Color

With buttons on the Drawing toolbar you can add fill color and/or shading to an object, change the line style, and change the line color. Click the down-pointing triangle at the right side of the Fill Color or Line Color button and a palette of color choices displays. Choose a color at this palette or click an option to display more fill or line colors and fill or line patterns.

(Note: Before completing computer exercises, delete the PowerPoint Chapter 03 *folder on your disk. Next, copy to your disk the* PowerPoint Chapter 04 *subfolder from the* PowerPoint 2002 *folder on the CD that accompanies this textbook and then make* PowerPoint Chapter 04 *the active folder.)*

exercise 1

CREATING A PRESENTATION AND FORMATTING OBJECTS USING A MASTER SLIDE

1. Prepare the presentation on enhanced services for McCormack Financial Services shown in figure 4.2 by completing the following steps:
   a. At a blank PowerPoint screen, click the New button on the Standard toolbar.
   b. Click the Slide Design button on the Formatting toolbar.
   c. Click *Shimmer* in the Apply a design template list box in the Slide Design Task Pane.
   d. Create a title master slide for the presentation by completing the following steps:
      1) Position the arrow pointer on the Normal View button on the View toolbar, hold down the Shift key, and then click the left mouse button.

Step 1c

2) With the Shimmer Title Master slide displayed, click anywhere in the text *Click to edit Master title style*. (This selects the text in the object box.)

3) Change the horizontal alignment of text in the object box by clicking the Center button on the Formatting toolbar.

4) With the text in the object box still selected, add fill color by completing the following steps:

   a) Click the down-pointing triangle at the right side of the Fill Color button on the Drawing toolbar.

   b) At the pop-up menu that displays, click the second color from the right (light yellow).

5) With the text in the object box still selected, click the down-pointing triangle at the right side of the Font Color button on the Drawing toolbar and then click the dark blue color (third color from the left) at the pop-up menu that displays.

6) Click in the text *Click to edit Master subtitle style* and then click the Center button on the Formatting toolbar.

7) Draw and then copy diamond shapes in the upper left and lower right corners of the slide by completing the following steps:

   a) Click the AutoShapes button on the Drawing toolbar, point to Basic Shapes, and then click the diamond shape (last shape in the top row).

   b) Hold down the Shift key (this draws the diamond circumscribed in a square) and then position the arrow pointer (displays as a crosshair) in the upper left corner of the slide.

   c) With the Shift key still down, hold down the left mouse button, drag the mouse down and to the right until the diamond is about 0.5 inch tall, release the mouse button, and then release the Shift key. (If you do not like the size or position of the diamond, delete it. To do this, make sure the diamond is selected, and then press the Delete key.)

   d) Click the Fill Color button on the Drawing toolbar to change the diamond fill color to light yellow.

   e) If you need to move the diamond, make sure it is selected, position the arrow pointer inside the selected area, hold down the left mouse button, drag to the desired position, and then release the mouse button.

8) When the diamond is positioned in the desired location, copy it three times (you should end up with four diamond shapes—two in the upper left corner of the slide and two in the lower right corner of the slide) by completing the following steps:

   a) With the diamond selected, position the arrow pointer inside the selected box.

   b) Hold down the Ctrl key and the left mouse button.

to have on all Slides "Repeat Format" Go to Master Slide! (handwritten margin note)

c) Drag the outline to the desired position, release the mouse button, and then release the Ctrl key. Repeat these steps to create the third and fourth diamond shapes. (See slide at the right.)

e. Click the Normal View button on the View toolbar. (This removes the master slide and displays a slide with the formatted elements.)

f. Key the text shown in figure 4.2 by completing the following steps:
1) Click anywhere in the text *Click to add title*.
2) Key **McCormack Annuity Funds**.
3) Click anywhere in the text *Click to add subtitle*.
4) Key **Enhanced Services**.

g. Click the New Slide button on the Formatting toolbar.

h. Click the Title Slide layout in the Apply slide layout section of the Slide Layout Task Pane.

i. At the new slide, key the text shown in the second slide in figure 4.2.

j. Continue creating the remaining four slides shown in figure 4.2.

2. Add a transition and sound of your choosing to all slides.
3. Save the presentation and name it Enhanced Services Presentation.
4. Run the presentation.
5. Print all six slides as handouts on one page.
6. Close Enhanced Services Presentation.

FIGURE

4.2 *Exercise 1*

Slide 1	Title	=	McCormack Annuity Funds
	Subtitle	=	Enhanced Services
Slide 2	Title	=	Enhanced Services
	Subtitle	=	Set up future accumulations transfers
Slide 3	Title	=	Enhanced Services
	Subtitle	=	Receive automatic statement confirmation
Slide 4	Title	=	Enhanced Services
	Subtitle	=	Faster cash withdrawals
Slide 5	Title	=	Enhanced Services
	Subtitle	=	Personal service from 8 a.m. to 11 p.m. weekdays
Slide 6	Title	=	Enhanced Services
	Subtitle	=	Multiple transfers made with one telephone call

Creating a Text Box

With the Text Box button on the Drawing toolbar, you can create a box and then insert text inside the box. Text inside a box can be formatted in the normal manner. For example, you can change the font, alignment, or indent of the text.

HINT

Use a text box to place text anywhere in a slide.

Wrapping Text in an Autoshape

A text box can be drawn inside an autoshape. You can also click the Text Box button on the Drawing toolbar and then click in the autoshape. This positions the insertion point inside the shape where you can key text. If you want text to wrap within the autoshape, click Format and then AutoShape. At the Format AutoShape dialog box, click the Text Box tab. This displays the dialog box as shown in figure 4.3. At this dialog box, choose the Word wrap shape in AutoShape option. Choose the Resize AutoShape to fit text option if you want the size of the autoshape to conform to the text. Rotate text in a text box by choosing the Rotate text within AutoShape by 90° option.

Text Box

FIGURE

| 4.3 | **Format AutoShape Dialog Box with Text Box Tab Selected** |

1. Open Enhanced Services Presentation.
2. Save the presentation with Save As and name it Formatted Enhanced Presentation.
3. Create the slide shown in figure 4.4 by completing the following steps:

   a. Display Slide 6. (This is the last slide in the presentation.)
   b. Click the New Slide button on the Formatting toolbar.
   c. Click the Title Only layout in the Apply slide layout section of the Slide Layout Task Pane.
   d. Click the text *Click to add title* and then key **Enhanced Services Features**.
   e. Click the Center button on the Formatting toolbar.
   f. Draw the diamond at the left by completing the following steps:
      1) Click the AutoShapes button on the Drawing toolbar, point to Basic Shapes, and then click Diamond.
      2) Hold down the Shift key and then draw the diamond the size and position shown in figure 4.4.

      3) Insert the text and wrap the text in the autoshape by completing the following steps:
         a) Click the Text Box button on the Drawing toolbar.
         b) Click inside the diamond shape.
         c) Click Format and then AutoShape.
         d) At the Format AutoShape dialog box, click the Text Box tab.
         e) At the Format AutoShape dialog box with the Text Box tab selected, click the Word wrap text in AutoShape option. (This inserts a check mark.)
         f) Click OK to close the dialog box.
         g) Change the font size to 20, turn on bold, and change the font color to black.
         h) Key the text **Personal Service**. (Make sure the word *Personal* is not split between two lines. If it is, increase the size of the diamond.)
   g. Copy the diamond to the right two times.
   h. Select the text in the middle diamond and then key **Easy to Use**.
   i. Select the text in the diamond at the right and then key **Fast and Accurate**.
   j. Draw a text box and then key the text located toward the bottom of the slide in figure 4.4 by completing the following steps:
      1) Click the Text Box button on the Drawing toolbar.
      2) Position the crosshairs in the slide and then draw a text box in the slide that will hold the text *Quality Services for Our Customers*.
      3) Click the Center button on the Formatting toolbar.

4) Change the font size to 20, turn on bold, and turn on italics.
5) Key **Quality Services for Our Customers**.
6) Click outside the text box to deselect it.
4. Save the presentation again with the same name (Formatted Enhanced Presentation).
5. Print Slide 7 in grayscale.
6. Display Slide 1 and then run the presentation.
7. Close the presentation.

FIGURE

4.4 *Slide 7, Exercise 2*

Inserting Images in a Presentation

Microsoft Office includes a gallery of media images you can insert in a presentation, such as clip art, photographs, and movie images, as well as sound clips. To insert an image in a presentation, click the Insert Clip Art button on the Drawing toolbar or click <u>I</u>nsert, point to <u>P</u>icture, and then click <u>C</u>lip Art. This displays the Insert Clip Art Task Pane as shown in figure 4.5.

To view all picture, sound, and motion files, make sure no text displays in the Search text text box at the Insert Clip Art Task Pane and then click the Search button. Expand the viewing area of the task pane by clicking the button containing the left-pointing arrow that displays immediately below *Results*. Insert the image in the slide by clicking the desired image.

Insert
Clip Art

HINT
If you want the same image on every slide, insert it on the slide master.

4.5 *Insert Clip Art Task Pane*

Search for specific images by keying the desired category in this text box and then clicking the Search button.

Another method for inserting an image in a slide is to choose a slide layout containing a Contents placeholder. A Contents placeholder displays with four images including a table, a man's head, a chart, and a diagram. These images represent buttons. For example, the image of a man's head represents the Insert Clip Art button. At the slide, click the Insert Clip Art button in the Contents placeholder and the Select Picture dialog box displays as shown in figure 4.6. Like the Insert Clip Art Task Pane, the Select Picture dialog box contains a Search text text box.

4.6 *Select Picture Dialog Box*

Key search text in this text box and then click the Search button.

Narrowing a Search

By default (unless it has been customized), the Insert Clip Art Task Pane looks for all media images and sound clips found in all locations. You can narrow the search to specific locations and to specific images. The Search in option at the Insert Clip Art Task Pane has a default setting of *All collections*. You can change this to *My Collections*, *Office Collections*, and *Web Collections*. The Results should be option has a default setting of *All media file types*. Click the down-pointing triangle at the right side of this option to display media types. To search for a specific media type, remove the check mark before all options at the drop-down list but the desired type. For example, if you are searching only for clip art images, remove the check mark before Photographs, Movies, and Sound.

HINT

For additional clip art images, consider buying a commercial package of images.

If you are searching for specific images, click in the Search text text box, key the desired word, and then click the Search button. For example, if you want to find images related to computers, click in the Search text text box, key **computer**, and then click the Search button. To search for other images, click the Modify button. This redisplays the Search text text box. Click inside the text box and then key the desired word.

Sizing an Image

Size an image in a slide using the sizing handles that display around a selected image. To change the size of an image, click in the image to select it, and then position the mouse pointer on a sizing handle until the pointer turns into a double-headed arrow. Hold down the left mouse button, drag the sizing handle in or out to decrease or increase the size of the image, and then release the mouse button.

Use the middle sizing handles at the left or right side of the image to make the image wider or thinner. Use the middle sizing handles at the top or bottom of the image to make the image taller or shorter. Use the sizing handles at the corners of the image to change both the width and height at the same time. To deselect an image, click anywhere in the slide outside the image.

Moving and Deleting an Image

To move an image, select the image, and then position the mouse pointer inside the image until the pointer turns into a four-headed arrow. Hold down the left mouse button, drag the image to the desired position, and then release the mouse button. Rotate an image by positioning the mouse pointer on the green, round rotation handle until the pointer displays as a circular arrow. Hold down the left mouse button, drag in the desired direction, and then release the mouse button. Delete a clip art image by selecting the image and then pressing the Delete key.

Changing the Slide Layout

When preparing a presentation, you choose a slide layout containing placeholders (object boxes) that most closely matches the type of information you want to insert on the slide. If you decide you want to add information or rearrange information on an existing slide, you can choose a different slide layout. For example, in exercise 3, you will choose the Title and Text slide layout to create a slide and then change to the Title, Text, and Content slide layout to insert a clip art image. To change a slide layout, display the specific slide in the Slide pane, display the Slide Layout Task Pane, and then click the desired layout in the list box.

1. Open Networking Presentation.
2. Save the presentation with Save As into the *PowerPoint Chapter 04* folder on your disk and name the presentation Networking Pres with Images.
3. Insert a clip art image in Slide 4 as shown in figure 4.7 by completing the following steps:
    a. Make sure Normal view is selected and then display Slide 4 in the Slide pane.
    b. Click the Insert Clip Art button on the Drawing toolbar.
    c. At the Insert Clip Art Task Pane, click in the Search text text box.
    d. Key **computer** and then click the Search button.
    e. Click the image shown in figure 4.7 (and at the right). (If this clip art image is not available, click another image that interests you.)
    f. With the image selected (white sizing handles display around the image), position the mouse pointer on the bottom right sizing handle until it turns into a diagonally pointing two-headed arrow.
    g. Hold down the left mouse button, drag away from the image to increase the size until the image is approximately the size shown in figure 4.7, and then release the mouse button.
    h. Move the image so it is positioned as shown in figure 4.7. To do this, position the mouse pointer on the selected image, hold down the left mouse button, drag to the desired position, and then release the mouse button.
    i. Click outside the image to deselect it.
4. Create a new Slide 5 as shown in figure 4.8 by completing the following steps:
    a. With Slide 4 displayed in the Slide pane, click the New Slide button on the Formatting toolbar. (This displays a new slide with the Title and Text layout selected.)
    b. Click in the text *Click to add title* and then key **Using Modems**.
    c. Click in the text *Click to add text* and then key the bulleted text shown in figure 4.8.
    d. Change the slide layout by clicking the *Title, Text, and Content* slide layout in the Slide Layout Task Pane. (You will need to scroll down the list to display this layout.)
    e. Insert the image shown in figure 4.8 by completing the following steps:
        1) Click the Insert Clip Art button that displays in the Contents box in the slide.
        2) At the Select Picture dialog box, key **telephone** in the Search text text box and then click the Search button.

3) Click the image shown in figure 4.8 (and at the right) and then click OK.
4) Increase the size of the image and then move the image so it displays as shown in figure 4.8.
5) Deselect the image.
5. Save the presentation again with the same name (Networking Pres with Images).
6. Display Slide 1 in the Slide pane and then run the presentation.
7. Print all five slides as handouts on one page.
8. Close Networking Pres with Images.

FIGURE

4.7 **Slide 4, Exercise 3**

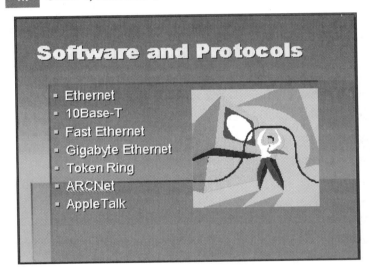

FIGURE

4.8 **Slide 5, Exercise 3**

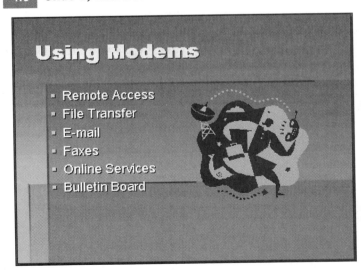

Formatting Images with Buttons on the Picture Toolbar

You can format images in a variety of ways. Formatting might include adding fill color and border lines, increasing or decreasing the brightness or contrast, choosing a wrapping style, and cropping the image. Format an image with buttons on the Picture toolbar or options at the Format Picture dialog box. Display the Picture toolbar by clicking an image or by right-clicking an image and then clicking Show Picture Toolbar at the shortcut menu. Figure 4.9 identifies the buttons on the Picture toolbar.

FIGURE

4.9 *Picture Toolbar Buttons*

Click this button	Named	To do this
	Insert Picture	Display the Insert Picture dialog box with a list of subfolders containing additional images.
	Color	Display a drop-down list with options for controlling how the image displays. Options include Automatic, Grayscale, Black & White, and Washout.
	More Contrast	Increase contrast of the image.
	Less Contrast	Decrease contrast of the image.
	More Brightness	Increase brightness of the image.
	Less Brightness	Decrease brightness of the image.
	Crop	Crop image so only a specific portion of the image is visible.
	Rotate Left	Rotate the image 90 degrees to the left.
	Line Style	Insert a border around the image and specify the border-line style.
	Compress Pictures	Reduce resolution or discard extra information to save room on the hard drive or to reduce download time.
	Recolor Picture	Display Recolor Picture dialog box with options for changing the colors of the selected image.
	Format Picture	Display Format Picture dialog box with options for formatting the image. Tabs in the dialog box include Colors and Lines, Size, Position, Picture Text Box, and Web.
	Set Transparent Color	This button is not active. (If an image contains a transparent area, the background color or texture of the page shows through the image. Set transparent color in Microsoft Photo Editor.)
	Reset Picture	Reset image to its original size, position, and color.

POWERPOINT

1. Open Networking Pres with Images.
2. Format the clip art image in Slide 4 by completing the following steps:
   a. Display Slide 4 in the Slide pane.
   b. Change the size of the image by completing the following steps:
      1) Click the clip art image to select.
      2) Click the Format Picture button on the Picture toolbar. (If the Picture toolbar is not visible, click View, point to Toolbars, and then click Picture.)
      3) At the Format Picture dialog box, click the Size tab.
      4) Select the current measurement in the Height text box (in the Size and rotate section) and then key **4**.
      5) Click OK to close the dialog box.
   c. Click three times on the Less Contrast button on the Picture toolbar.
   d. Click outside the image to deselect it.
3. Format the clip art image in Slide 5 by completing the following steps:
   a. Display Slide 5 in the Slide pane.
   b. Click the clip art image to select it. (Make sure the Picture toolbar displays.)
   c. Click the Recolor Picture button on the Picture toolbar.
   d. At the Recolor Picture dialog box, click the down-pointing triangle at the right side of the first button below the New section (contains the color black).
   e. At the color palette that displays, click the first green color from the left.
   f. Click the down-pointing triangle at the right side of the second button below the New section (contains the color blue).
   g. At the color palette, click the light yellow color.
   h. Click OK to close the Recolor Picture dialog box.
   i. Click outside the image to deselect it.
4. Save the presentation with the same name (Networking Pres with Images).
5. Display Slide 1 in the Slide pane and then run the presentation.
6. Print all six slides as handouts on one page.
7. Close Networking Pres with Images.

Downloading Images from the Microsoft Design Gallery Live Web Site

The Microsoft Design Gallery Live Web site offers a gallery with hundreds of images you can download. To display the Microsoft Design Gallery Live Web site, you must have access to the Internet. To download an image, display the Insert Clip Art Task Pane, and then click the *Clips Online* hyperlink located toward the bottom of the task pane. At the Microsoft Design Gallery Live Web site, click in the Search text box, key the desired category, and then click the Go button. Download the desired image by clicking the download button that displays below the image.

Adding Bitmapped Graphics to a Slide

PowerPoint recognizes a variety of picture formats dependent on the graphic filters installed with your program. Basically, pictures fall into one of two file categories—bitmaps and metafiles. Most clip art images are saved in a metafile format (named with a *.wmf* extension). Metafiles can be edited in PowerPoint, while bitmap files cannot. However, bitmaps can be edited in Microsoft Paint, Microsoft Photo Editor, or the program in which they were created. Pictures created in bitmap format are made from a series of small dots that form shapes and lines. Many scanned pictures are bitmapped. Bitmaps cannot be converted to drawing objects, but they can be scaled, sized, and moved.

Insert a bitmap image in a PowerPoint presentation by clicking Insert, pointing to Picture, and then clicking From File. At the Insert Picture dialog box, change to the folder containing the bitmap image, and then double-click the desired image in the list box.

exercise 5

INSERTING A BITMAP GRAPHIC IN A SLIDE

1. Open Waterfront Presentation. (This presentation is located in the *PowerPoint Chapter 04* folder on your disk.)
2. Save the presentation with Save As into the *PowerPoint Chapter 04* folder on your disk and name the presentation Waterfront Pres with Image.
3. Insert a bitmap graphic into Slide 1 by completing the following steps:
   a. Display Slide 1 in the Slide pane.
   b. Click Insert, point to Picture, and then click From File.
   c. At the Insert Picture dialog box, change the Look in option to the *PowerPoint Chapter 04* folder on your disk.
   d. Double-click the *Waterfrnt* bitmap image in the list box.
   e. With the bitmap image inserted in the slide, increase the size of the image and move it so it is positioned on the slide as shown in figure 4.10.

4. Save the presentation again with the same name (Waterfront Pres with Image).
5. Run the presentation.
6. Print the slides on one page.
7. Close Waterfront Pres with Image.

FIGURE

4.10 *Slide 1, Exercise 5*

Adding Animation Effects to a Presentation

You can animate objects in a slide to add visual interest to your presentation as well as create focus on specific items. PowerPoint includes preset animation schemes you can apply to objects in a presentation. Display these preset animation schemes by clicking Slide Show on the Menu bar and then clicking Animation Schemes at the drop-down list. This displays animation schemes in the Slide Design Task Pane as shown in figure 4.11. You can also display the animation schemes by clicking the *Animation Schemes* hyperlink located toward the top of the Slide Design Task Pane.

FIGURE

4.11 *Animation Schemes in Slide Design Task Pane*

Choose an animation scheme in this list box.

Click the desired animation scheme in the Apply to selected slides list box. Animation schemes are grouped into three categories—Subtle, Moderate, and Exciting. When you click an animation effect, the effect displays in the slide in the Slide pane. You can preview the animation again by clicking the Play button located toward the bottom of the Slide Design Task Pane. If you want the animation scheme to affect all slides in the presentation click the Apply to All Slides button located toward the bottom of the task pane. Apply an animation scheme to individual slides by selecting the slides first and then choosing an animation scheme.

When an animation scheme is applied to a slide, objects will appear on the slide in a specific order. When running the presentation, the slide will display on the screen followed by the slide title. To display any subtitles or bulleted text, click the mouse button. The animation scheme controls how much text displays when the mouse is clicked. If your slide contains bulleted text, clicking the left mouse button when running the presentation will cause the first bulleted item to display. Click the left mouse button again to display the next bulleted item, and so on.

exercise 6 Redo

ADDING AN ANIMATION SCHEME TO A PRESENTATION

1. Open Enhanced Services Presentation.
2. Save the presentation with Save As into the *PowerPoint Chapter 04* folder on your disk and name the presentation Enhanced Pres with Animation.
3. Add an animation scheme to each slide by completing the following steps:
   a. Make sure Normal view is selected and Slide 1 displays in the Slide pane.
   b. Click Slide Show on the Menu bar and then click Animation Schemes at the drop-down list. (This displays animation effects in the Slide Design Task Pane.)
   c. Scroll to the end of the Apply to selected slides list box and then click *Pinwheel*.
   d. Click the Apply to All Slides button located toward the bottom of the Slide Design Task Pane.
4. Run the presentation, clicking the left mouse button to display objects in the slide.
5. Save the presentation again with the same name (Enhanced Pres with Animation).
6. Close Enhanced Pres with Animation.

Step 3c

Step 3d

Customizing a Build

The preset animation schemes automatically create a *build* with objects on the slide. A build displays important points on a slide one point at a time, and is useful for keeping the audience's attention focused on the point being presented rather than reading ahead.

You can further customize the build in the animation scheme by causing a previous point to dim when the next point is displayed on the slide. To customize

P O W E R P O I N T

an animation scheme, click Sli<u>d</u>e Show on the Menu bar and then click Custo<u>m</u> Animation at the drop-down list. This displays the Custom Animation Task Pane as shown in figure 4.12.

F I G U R E

4.12 *Custom Animation Task Pane*

To add a dim effect to bulleted items, you would click the object box containing the bulleted text and then click the Add Effect button located toward the top of the Custom Animation Task Pane. At the drop-down list that displays, point to <u>E</u>ntrance, and then click the desired effect in the side menu. This causes a box to display in the Custom Animation Task Pane list box containing a number, an image of a mouse, and a down-pointing triangle. Click the down-pointing triangle and then click <u>E</u>ffect Options at the drop-down list. At the dialog box that displays, click the down-pointing triangle at the right of the <u>A</u>fter animation option box and then click the desired color.

exercise 7

CUSTOMIZING A BUILD FOR A PRESENTATION

1. Open Networking Presentation.
2. Save the presentation with Save As into the *PowerPoint Chapter* 04 folder on your disk and name the presentation Networking Pres with Builds.
3. Display the Custom Animation Task Pane by clicking Sli<u>d</u>e Show on the Menu bar and then clicking Custo<u>m</u> Animation at the drop-down list.
4. Add an animation scheme to the title of Slide 1 by completing the following steps:
   a. Make sure Normal view is selected and Slide 1 displays in the Slide pane.

b. Click in the text *NETWORKING* to select the object box.

c. Click the Add Effect button located toward the top of the Custom Animation Task Pane, point to <u>E</u>ntrance, and then click <u>2</u>. Box at the drop-down list.

d. Click the down-pointing triangle that displays at the right side of the Start option in the Modify: Box section and then click *With Previous* at the drop-down list.

5. Apply the same animation to the titles in Slides 2 through 4 using the Glass Layers Slide Master by completing the following steps:

a. Display Slide 2 in the Slide pane.

b. Hold down the Shift key and then click the Slide Master View button.

c. Click in the text *Click to edit Master title style* in the slide master.

d. Click the Add Effect button located toward the top of the Custom Animation Task Pane, point to <u>E</u>ntrance, and then click <u>2</u>. Box at the drop-down list.

e. Click the down-pointing triangle that displays at the right side of the Start option in the Modify: Box section and then click *With Previous* at the drop-down list.

f. Click the Normal View button.

6. Add a build to the bulleted items in Slide 2 by completing the following steps:

a. With Slide 2 displayed in the Slide pane, click anywhere in the bulleted text.

b. Click the Add Effect button located toward the top of the Custom Animation Task Pane, point to <u>E</u>ntrance, and then click <u>3</u>. Checkerboard at the side menu.

c. Click the down-pointing triangle at the right of the box in the Custom Animation Task Pane list box and then click <u>E</u>ffect Options at the drop-down list.

d. At the Checkerboard dialog box with the Effect tab selected, click the down-pointing triangle at the right of the <u>A</u>fter animation option box and then click the light yellow color.

e. Click OK to close the dialog box.

7. Display Slide 3 in the Slide pane and then complete steps similar to those in step 6 to add a build to the bulleted text.

8. Display Slide 4 in the Slide pane and then complete steps similar to those in step 6 to add a build to the bulleted text.

9. Save the presentation again with the same name (Networking Pres with Builds).

10. Run the presentation.

11. Close Networking Pres with Builds.

CHAPTER summary

- Use buttons on the Drawing toolbar to draw a variety of shapes and lines and to apply formatting to a drawn object.
- A shape drawn with the Line or Arrow buttons is considered a line drawing. A shape drawn with the Rectangle or Oval buttons is considered an enclosed object.
- A variety of predesigned shapes is available from the AutoShapes button on the Drawing toolbar.
- To select an enclosed object, position the mouse pointer inside the object and then click the left mouse button. To select a line, position the mouse pointer on the line until the pointer turns into an arrow with a four-headed arrow attached, and then click the left mouse button.
- To select several objects at once, click the Select Objects button and then draw a border around the objects. You can also select more than one object by holding down the Shift key and then clicking each object.
- To delete an object, select it, and then press the Delete key. To move an object, select it, and then drag it to the desired location. To copy an object, select it, and then hold down the Ctrl key while dragging the object.
- Use the sizing handles that display around a selected object to increase or decrease the size of the object.
- Apply formatting to an object such as fill color, shading, line color, and shadows with buttons on the Drawing toolbar.
- Create a text box in a slide by clicking the Text Box button on the Drawing toolbar and then drawing the box in the slide.
- A text box can be drawn inside an autoshape. Choose a text wrapping style for text inside an autoshape with options at the Format AutoShape dialog box with the Text Tab selected.
- Insert an image in a slide with options at the Insert Clip Art Task Pane or the Select Picture dialog box.
- With options at the Insert Clip Art Task Pane, you can narrow the search for images to specific locations and to specific images.
- Size an image using the sizing handles that display around a selected image and move a selected image to the desired location by dragging the image using the mouse. Delete a selected image by pressing the Delete key.
- Format a clip art image with buttons on the Picture toolbar.
- If you are connected to the Internet, you can download images from the Microsoft Design Gallery Live Web site.
- Pictures fall into one of two basic file categories—bitmaps and metafiles. Most clip art images are saved in a metafile format. Insert a bitmap image in a slide by displaying the Insert Picture dialog box, and then double-clicking the desired image.
- Animate objects in slides to add visual interest and create focus on specific items in a presentation.
- PowerPoint includes preset animation schemes. Display animation schemes in the Slide Design Task Pane by clicking Slide Show on the Menu bar and then clicking Animation

Schemes or by clicking the *Animation Schemes* hyperlink located toward the top of the Slide Design Task Pane.

➤ Customize animation with options at the Custom Animation Task Pane. Display this task pane by clicking Sli<u>d</u>e Show on the Menu bar and then clicking Cust<u>o</u>m Animation.

COMMANDS review

Commmand	Mouse/Keyboard
Display Format AutoShape dialog box	With autoshape selected, click F<u>o</u>rmat, Aut<u>o</u>Shape.
Display Insert Clip Art Task Pane	Click Insert Clip Art button on Drawing toolbar; or click <u>I</u>nsert, <u>P</u>icture, <u>C</u>lip Art
Display Select Picture dialog box	Click Insert Clip Art button in Contents placeholder on slide
Display Format Picture dialog box	Click Format Picture button on Picture toolbar
Display Recolor Picture dialog box	Click Recolor Picture button on Picture toolbar
Display Insert Picture dialog box	Click <u>I</u>nsert, <u>P</u>icture, <u>F</u>rom File
Display animation schemes	Click Slide Show, Animation S<u>c</u>hemes; or click *Animation Schemes* hyperlink in Slide Design Task Pane
Display Custom Animation Task Pane	Click Sli<u>d</u>e Show, Cust<u>o</u>m Animation

CONCEPTS check

Completion: On a blank sheet of paper, indicate the correct term, symbol, or command.

1. A variety of predesigned shapes is available with options from this button on the Drawing toolbar.
2. Change the size of a selected object using these items that display around a selected object.
3. Choose a text wrapping style for text inside an autoshape with options at the Format AutoShape dialog box with this tab selected.
4. Insert an image in a slide with options at this task pane.
5. Select a clip art image in a slide and this toolbar displays containing buttons for formatting the image.
6. Change the colors of a selected clip art image with options at this dialog box.
7. Pictures generally fall into one of two file categories—metafiles and this.
8. Click Sli<u>d</u>e Show and then Animation S<u>c</u>hemes and preset animation schemes display in this task pane.
9. Animation schemes are grouped into three categories—Subtle, Moderate, and this.
10. Customize an animation scheme with options at this task pane.

POWERPOINT

SKILLS check

1. Open Enhanced Services Presentation. (You created this presentation in exercise 1.)
2. Save the presentation with Save As into the *PowerPoint Chapter 04* folder on your disk and name the presentation Edited Enhanced Services Pres.
3. Change to the Slide Master view and then make the following changes:
   a. With the Shimmer Title Master slide miniature selected at the left side of the screen, click anywhere in the text *Click to edit Master title style*, and then change the fill color to the light blue that follows the scheme of the design template.
   b. Select and then delete each of the four diamond shapes.
   c. Using the 5-Point Star autoshape (click AutoShapes, point to Stars and Banners, click the 5-Point Star autoshape), draw a small star in the upper left corner of the slide master. (When you release the mouse button, the star should fill with the same light blue color you chose in step 3a.)
   d. Copy the star to the right two times. (You should have a total of three stars in the upper left corner of the slide all containing light blue fill.)
   e. Click the Normal View button to remove the slide master.
4. Create a new Slide 7 that displays as shown in figure 4.13 with the following specifications:
   a. Create the new slide with the Title Only slide layout.
   b. Change to center alignment for the title *Enhanced Services Launch Date*.
   c. Use the Text Box button on the Drawing toolbar to draw a text box for the text *May 1, 2003*. Set the text in 28-point size, turn on bold, and change the alignment to center.
   d. Use the Right Arrow autoshape (AutoShapes, Block Arrows, Right Arrow) to draw the arrow at the left side. Use the Left Arrow autoshape (AutoShapes, Block Arrows, Left Arrow) to draw the arrow at the right.
5. Save the presentation again with the same name (Edited Enhanced Services Pres).
6. Run the presentation.
7. Print all of the slides as handouts on one page.
8. Print only Slide 7.
9. Close Edited Enhanced Services Pres.

4.13 *Slide 7, Assessment 1*

Assessment 2

1. Open Waterfront Presentation.
2. Save the presentation with Save As into the *PowerPoint Chapter 04* folder on your disk and name the presentation Edited Waterfront Pres.
3. Make the following changes to the presentation:
   a. Delete Slide 1.
   b. Apply the *Ripple* design template to the presentation.
   c. Check each slide and make any needed adjustments (such as repositioning elements).
   d. In Slide 3, insert a clip art image related to food. You determine the size and position of the image. Recolor the image so it follows the color scheme of the design template.
   e. In Slide 4, insert another clip art image related to food (use a different image from the one you chose for Slide 3). You determine the size and position of the image. Recolor the image so it follows the color scheme of the design template.
   f. Apply an animation scheme of your choosing to all slides in the presentation.
4. Save the presentation again with the same name (Edited Waterfront Pres).
5. Run the presentation.
6. Print all four slides as handouts on one page.
7. Close Edited Waterfront Pres.

Assessment 3

1. Open Job Search Presentation.
2. Save the presentation with Save As into the *PowerPoint Chapter 04* folder on your disk and name the presentation Edited Job Search Pres.
3. Make the following changes to the presentation:
   a. Apply the *Radial* design template to the presentation.
   b. Display color schemes for the Radial design template and then choose a color scheme other than the default.

POWERPOINT

    c. Add an animation scheme of your choosing to the title of Slide 1. *(Hint: Refer to exercise 7, step 4.)*

    d. Apply the same animation scheme to the titles in Slides 2 through 9 in Slide Master view using the Radial Slide Master. *(Hint: Refer to exercise 7, step 5.)*

    e. Add a build to the bulleted items in Slide 2. You determine the <u>E</u>ntrance animation and also the <u>A</u>fter animation color. *(Hint: Refer to exercise 7, step 6.)*

    f. Apply the same build to the bulleted items in Slides 3 through 9.

4. Save the presentation again with the same name (Edited Job Search Pres).
5. Print all nine slides as handouts on one page.
6. Run the presentation. (Make sure the animation and builds function properly.)
7. Close Edited Job Search Pres.

Assessment 4

1. Use PowerPoint's Help feature to learn about adding music or sound effects to a slide. Learn specifically how to insert a sound from the Clip Organizer.

2. Open Networking Presentation.
3. Save the presentation with Save As into the *PowerPoint Chapter 04* folder on your disk and name the presentation Networking Pres with Sound.
4. Insert a sound clip of your choosing from the Clip Organizer into Slide 1.
5. Run the presentation and make sure you hear the sound you inserted in Slide 1.
6. Save and then close Networking Pres with Sound.

WORK IN Progress

ASSESSING proficiency

In this unit, you have learned to create, print, save, close, open, view, run, edit, and format a PowerPoint presentation. You also learned how to add transition and sound to presentations, rearrange slides, customize presentations by changing the design template and color scheme, make global formatting changes with slide and title masters, add visual appeal to slides by inserting drawn objects and clip art images, and how to add animation and build to items in slides.

(Note: Before completing the unit assessments, delete the PowerPoint Chapter 04 *folder on your disk. Next, copy to your disk the* PowerPoint Unit 01 *subfolder from the* PowerPoint 2002 *folder on the CD that accompanies this textbook and then make* PowerPoint Unit 01 *the active folder.)*

Assessment 1

1. Create a presentation with the text shown in figure U1.1 using the *Pixel* design template. Use the appropriate slide layout for each slide. After creating the slides, complete a spelling check on the text in slides.
2. Add a transition and sound of your choosing to all slides.
3. Save the presentation into the *PowerPoint Unit 01* folder on your disk and name the presentation Cornerstone Presentation.
4. Run the presentation.
5. Print all six slides as handouts on one page.
6. Close Cornerstone Presentation.

Slide 1	Title	=	CORNERSTONE SYSTEMS
	Subtitle	=	Yearly Report
Slide 2	Title	=	Financial Review
	Bullets	=	• Net Revenues
			• Operating Income
			• Net Income
			• Return on Average Equity
			• Return on Average Asset
Slide 3	Title	=	Corporate Vision
	Bullets	=	• Expansion
			• Increased Productivity

```
                              •   Consumer Satisfaction
                              •   Employee Satisfaction
                              •   Market Visibility

Slide 4      Title    =   Consumer Market
             Bullets  =   •   Travel
                          •   Shopping
                          •   Entertainment
                          •   Personal Finance
                          •   E-mail

Slide 5      Title    =   Industrial Market
             Bullets  =   •   Finance
                          •   Education
                          •   Government
                          •   Manufacturing
                          •   Utilities

Slide 6      Title    =   Future Goals
             Bullets  =   •   International Market
                          •   Acquisitions
                          •   Benefits Packages
                          •   Product Expansion
```

Figure U1.1 • Assessment 1

Assessment 2

1. Open Cornerstone Presentation.
2. Save the presentation with Save As into the *PowerPoint Unit 01* folder on your disk and name the presentation Edited Cornerstone Pres.
3. Make the following changes to Slide 2:
   a. Key **Net Income per Common Share** over *Net Income*.
   b. Delete *Return on Average Equity*.
4. Make the following changes to Slide 4:
   a. Delete *Shopping*.
   b. Key **Business Finance** between *Personal Finance* and *E-mail*.
5. Rearrange the slides in the presentation so they are in the following order (only the slide titles are shown below):

   Slide 1   =   CORNERSTONE SYSTEMS
   Slide 2   =   Corporate Vision
   Slide 3   =   Future Goals
   Slide 4   =   Industrial Market
   Slide 5   =   Consumer Market
   Slide 6   =   Financial Review

6. Increase spacing between bulleted items by completing the following steps:
   a. Display the Pixel Slide Master in Slide Master view.
   b. Click the text *Click to edit Master text styles*.

    c. Display the Line Spacing dialog box, change the <u>L</u>ine spacing to *1.4*, and then close the dialog box.

    d. Return to the Normal view.

7. Apply a different color scheme to the presentation.

8. Save the presentation again with the same name (Edited Cornerstone Pres).

9. Run the presentation.

10. Print all six slides as handouts on one page.

    11. Close Edited Cornerstone Pres.

Assessment 3

1. Open Artworks Presentation. (This presentation is located in the *PowerPoint Unit 01* folder on your disk.)

2. Save the presentation with Save As into the *PowerPoint Unit 01* folder on your disk and name the presentation Formatted Artworks Pres.

3. Insert in Slide 1 the autoshape and text shown in figure U1.2 with the following specifications:

    a. Use the Horizontal Scroll autoshape (A<u>u</u>toShapes, <u>S</u>tars and Banners, Horizontal Scroll) to create the banner autoshape. Make sure the banner fill color is the green color shown in figure U1.2 that follows the design color scheme. (This should be the default fill color.)

    b. Insert a text box in the autoshape and then key the text **Rainbow Artworks** as shown in figure U1.2 with the following specifications:

       1) Change the alignment to center.

       2) Change the font to 88-point Comic Sans MS bold. (If this font is not available, choose a similar font.)

       3) Change the font color to the medium blue that follows the design color scheme.

WORD WRAP PG 90 #3C

4. Change the font for slide titles on Slides 2 through 4 by completing the following steps:

    a. Display the Blends Title Master in Slide Master view.

    b. Click the text *Click to edit Master title style*.

    c. Change the alignment to center.

    d. Change the font to 44-point Comic Sans MS bold (or the font you chose in 3b2) and the font color to red (that follows the design color scheme).

    e. Click the text *Click to edit Master subtitle style*.

    f. Change the font to 28-point Comic Sans MS bold (or the font you chose in 3b2) and the font color to medium blue (that follows the design color scheme).

    g. Return to the Normal view.

5. Add a transition and sound of your choosing to all slides.

6. Save the presentation again with the same name (Formatted Artworks Pres).

7. Run the presentation.

8. Print all four slides as handouts on the same page.

9. Print only Slide 1.

10. Close Formatted Artworks Pres.

Figure U1.2 • Assessment 3

Assessment 4

1. Open Job Search Presentation. (This presentation is located in the *PowerPoint Unit 01* folder on your disk.)
2. Save the presentation into the *PowerPoint Unit 01* folder on your disk and name the presentation Enhanced Job Search Pres.
3. Make the following changes to the presentation:
   a. Change the design template. (Choose something appropriate for the subject matter.)
   b. In Slide 5, insert a clip art image related to *telephone, people, Internet,* and so on. Search for a clip art image that is related to at least one of the bulleted items. You determine the size and position of the image. Recolor the image so it follows the color scheme of the design template.
   c. In Slide 6, insert a clip art image related to *clock* or *time.* You determine the size and position of the element. Recolor the image so it follows the color scheme of the design template.
   d. Insert the current date and slide number on all slides in the presentation. (Make sure there is no check mark in the Don't show on title slide option at the Header and Footer dialog box.)
   e. Create the header *Job Search Seminar,* the footer *Employment Strategies,* and insert the date and page number for notes and handouts.
   f. Add the speaker note *Handout list of Internet employment sites.* to Slide 5.
4. Save the presentation again with the same name (Enhanced Job Search Pres).
5. Run the presentation.
6. Print all nine slides as handouts on one page.
7. Print Slide 5 as notes pages.
8. Close Enhanced Job Search Pres.

Assessment 5

1. Open Medical Plans Presentation. (This presentation is located in the *PowerPoint Unit 01* folder on your disk.)
2. Save the presentation with Save As in the *PowerPoint Unit 01* folder on your disk and name the presentation Formatted Plans Pres.
3. Make the following changes to the presentation:
   a. In Slide 3, insert a clip art image related to *medicine*. You determine the size and position of the image. Recolor the image so it follows the color scheme of the design template.
   b. In Slide 4, insert a clip art image related to *buildings*. You determine the size and position of the image. Recolor the image so it follows the color scheme of the design template.
   c. Display the Custom Animation Task Pane and then use the Add Effect button in the task pane to apply an animation of your choosing to the title of Slide 1. (Refer to chapter 4, exercise 7, step 4.)
   d. Apply the same animation to the titles in Slides 2 through 4 in Slide Master view using the Capsules Slide Master. (Refer to chapter 4, exercise 7, step 5.)
   e. Add a build to the bulleted items in Slide 2. You determine the Entrance animation and also the After animation color. (Refer to chapter 4, exercise 7, step 6.)
   f. Apply the same build to the bulleted items in Slides 3 and 4.
4. Save the presentation again with the same name (Formatted Plans Pres).
5. Print all four slides as handouts on one page.
6. Run the presentation. (Make sure the animation and builds function properly.)
7. Close Formatted Plans Pres.

WRITING activities

The following activities give you the opportunity to practice your writing skills along with demonstrating an understanding of some of the important PowerPoint features you have mastered in this unit. Use correct grammar, appropriate word choices, and clear sentence structure.

Activity 1

Using PowerPoint's Help feature, learn more about animating slides and then prepare a PowerPoint presentation with the information by completing the following steps:

1. Display the Microsoft PowerPoint Help window with the Answer Wizard tab selected.
2. Key **custom animation** in the What would you like to do? text box and then press Enter.

3. With *Animate text and objects* selected in the Select topic to display list box, click the *Show All* hyperlink in the upper right corner of the Help window and then print the information that displays.
4. Select the text *custom animation* in the **W**hat would you like to do? text box, key **animation order**, and then press Enter.
5. With *About timing animations* selected in the Select topic to display list box, print the information that displays.
6. Read the information you printed on custom animation and animation order and then prepare a PowerPoint presentation with the following information:
   Slide 1 = Title of presentation and your name
   Slide 2 = Steps on how to apply a preset animation scheme
   Slide 3 = Steps on how to display the Custom Animation Task Pane
   Slide 4 = Explanation of the three options (*Entrance, Emphasis*, and *Exit*) available with the Add Effect button
   Slide 5 = Steps on changing the order of an animation
7. Save the completed presentation and name it Animation Presentation.
8. Run the presentation.
9. Print all five slides as handouts on one page.
10. Close Animation Presentation.

The Formatted Plans Pres you customized in Assessment 5 contains clip art images on Slides 3 and 4. When you ran the presentation, the clip art image automatically displayed in the slide and then the title displayed. Using the information you learned about animation order, open the Formatted Plans Pres, change the animation order of objects on Slides 3 and 4 so the title displays first, followed by the clip art image, and then the bulleted items. Run the presentation to make sure the items animate in the proper order. Save the presentation with the same name.

Activity 2

1. Open Word and then open, print, and close Key Life Health Plan. Looking at the printing of this document, create a presentation in PowerPoint that presents the main points of the plan. (Use bullets in the presentation.) Add a transition and build to the slides.
2. Save the presentation and name it Key Life Presentation.
3. Run Key Life Presentation.
4. Print the slides as handouts with six slides per page.
5. Close Key Life Presentation.

INTERNET project

Analyzing a Magazine Website

Make sure you are connected to the Internet and then explore the Time Magazine Web site at www.time.com. Discover the following information for the site:

- Magazine sections (i.e., *Nation, World, Business,* and so forth.)
- The type of information presented in each section
- Services available
- Information on how to subscribe

Use the information you discovered about the Time Magazine Web site and create a PowerPoint presentation that presents the information in a clear, concise, and logical manner. Add formatting and enhancements to the presentation to make it more interesting. When the presentation is completed, save it and name it Time Mag Presentation. Run, print, and then close the presentation.

JOB study

Presenting Career Options

As a Counselor in the university's Career Development office, you have been asked to give a presentation to a group of seniors. Research career paths (feel free to use the Internet) related to their field of study and create a PowerPoint presentation that explains your selections. You must "sell" your examples to the students and make them see why these are good choices. (Hint: You may want to click on File, New and use a Wizard.)

Your PowerPoint presentation should contain at least 10 slides. You determine the design template. Edit the slide master layout for both the title and slide master layouts to feature a clip art image of someone performing a job similar to one you have chosen. Include this image in the upper left corner on all of your slides. Apply any formatting options you think are appropriate. Print the slides as handouts with six slides per page. Print an outline of your presentation.

POWERPOINT

UNIT 2: CUSTOMIZING AND ENHANCING POWERPOINT PRESENTATIONS

Adding Visual Elements to a Presentation

Sharing and Connecting Data

Linking and Embedding Objects and Files

Sharing Presentations

MICROSOFT® POWERPOINT 2002

BENCHMARK MOUS SKILLS-UNIT 2

Reference No.	Skill	Pages
PP2002-2	**Inserting and Modifying Text**	
PP2002-2-1	Import text from Word	150-152
PP2002-3	**Inserting and Modifying Visual Elements**	
PP2002-3-1	Add tables, charts, clip art, and bitmap images to slides	
	Create, edit, and modify a chart	127-132
	Create, edit, and modify a table	132-135
	Insert a scanned image and animated GIF	137
PP2002-3-3	Add OfficeArt elements to slides	
	Create, size, move, and customize WordArt	119-123
	Create and customize organizational charts and diagrams	124-126
PP2002-3-4	Apply custom formats to tables	133-135
PP2002-4	**Modifying Presentation Formats**	
PP2002-4-5	Customize slide templates	140-141
PP2002-4-7	Rehearse timing	161-164
PP2002-4-10	Add links to a presentation	
	Add action buttons	156-160
	Create hyperlinks	160-161
	Link to other programs	176-177
PP2002-5	**Printing Presentations**	
PP2002-5-1	Preview and print slides, outlines, handouts, and speaker notes	
	Printing comments	194-195
PP2002-6	**Working with Data from Other Sources**	
PP2002-6-1	Import Excel charts to slides	
	Link Excel chart to a slide	174-175
	Edit a linked Excel chart	175
PP2002-6-2	Add sound and video to slides	138-139
PP2002-6-3	Insert Word tables on slides	
	Embed a Word table on a slide	164-172
	Edit an embedded Word table	172-173
PP2002-6-4	Export a presentation as an outline	
	Export an outline to Word	154-155
	Save a presentation as an Outline/RTF	155-156
PP2002-7	**Managing and Delivering Presentations**	
PP2002-7-1	Set up slide shows	195-206
PP2002-7-2	Deliver presentations	
	Set automatic times for slides	161-164
PP2002-7-3	Manage files and folders for presentations	
	Create a folder	178-179
	Select, copy, delete, rename files and folders	179-182
PP2002-7-4	Work with embedded fonts	197-198
PP2002-7-5	Publish presentations to the Web	
	Save a presentation as a Web page	198-202
	Preview a Web page	202-203
	Format Web pages	203-204
PP2002-7-6	Use Pack and Go	195-196
PP2002-8	**Workgroup Collaboration**	
PP2002-8-1	Set up a review cycle	188-193
PP2002-8-2	Review presentation comments	193-195
PP2002-8-3	Schedule and deliver presentation broadcasts	204-206
PP2002-8-4	Publish presentations to the Web	198-206

6.9

4.5

ADDING VISUAL ELEMENTS TO A PRESENTATION

PERFORMANCE OBJECTIVES

Upon successful completion of chapter 5, you will be able to:
- Create, size, move, modify, and format WordArt text
- Create and format an organizational chart
- Create and format a diagram
- Create, edit, and modify a chart
- Create and format a table
- Add a scanned image to a slide
- Add animated GIFs to slides
- Add sound and video effects to a presentation
- Create and apply a custom template

PowerPoint Chapter 05

A presentation consisting only of text slides may have important information in it that will be overlooked by the audience because a slide contains too much text. Adding visual elements, where appropriate, can help to deliver the message by adding interest and impact to the information. In this chapter, you will learn how to create visual elements on slides such as WordArt, organizational charts, diagrams, miscellaneous charts, and tables. You will also learn how to add scanned images, sound, video, and animated GIFs, which are multimedia effects that will make the delivery of your presentation a dynamic experience for your audience. This chapter also includes information on how to customize a design template and then save it as a template for future use.

Creating WordArt

With the WordArt application, you can distort or modify text to conform to a variety of shapes. This is useful for creating company logos and headings. With WordArt, you can change the font, style, and alignment of text. You can also use different fill patterns and colors, customize border lines, and add shadow and three-dimensional effects. To insert WordArt in a slide, click the Insert WordArt button on the Drawing toolbar. You can also click Insert, point to Picture, and then click WordArt. This displays the WordArt Gallery shown in figure 5.1.

Insert
WordArt

5.1 *WordArt Gallery*

HINT
Use WordArt to create interesting text effects in slides.

Double-click the desired style.

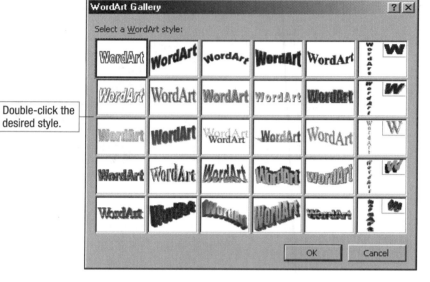

Entering Text

Double-click a WordArt choice at the WordArt Gallery, and the Edit WordArt Text dialog box displays as shown in figure 5.2. At the Edit WordArt Text dialog box, key the WordArt text and then click the OK button. At the Edit WordArt Text dialog box, you can change the font and/or size of text and also apply bold or italic formatting.

5.2 *Edit WordArt Text Dialog Box*

Key the WordArt text and then click OK.

POWERPOINT

Sizing and Moving WordArt

WordArt text is inserted in the workbook with the formatting selected at the WordArt Gallery. The WordArt text is surrounded by white sizing handles and the WordArt toolbar displays near the text. Use the white sizing handles to change the height and width of the WordArt text. Use the yellow diamond located at the bottom of the WordArt text to change the slant of the WordArt text. To do this, position the arrow pointer on the yellow diamond, hold down the left mouse button, drag to the left or right, and then release the mouse button.

To move WordArt text, position the arrow pointer on any letter of the WordArt text until the arrow pointer displays with a four-headed arrow attached. Hold down the left mouse button, drag the outline of the WordArt text box to the desired position, and then release the mouse button.

HINT

Edit WordArt by double-clicking the WordArt text.

HINT

Delete WordArt by clicking it and then pressing the Delete key.

exercise 1

INSERTING WORDART IN A SLIDE

1. Open Waterfront Presentation.
2. Save the presentation with Save As in the *PowerPoint Chapter 05* folder on your disk and name the presentation Waterfront Pres with WordArt.
3. Change the accent color of the design scheme by completing the following steps:
   a. Click the Slide Design button on the Formatting toolbar.
   b. Click the *Color Schemes* hyperlink located toward the top of the Slide Design Task Pane.
   c. Click the *Edit Color Schemes* hyperlink located toward the bottom of the Slide Design Task Pane.
   d. At the Edit Color Scheme dialog box, click the Accent option in the Scheme colors section, and then click the Change Color button.
   e. At the Accent Color dialog box, click the Standard tab.
   f. Click the medium blue color shown below and at the right and then click OK.
   g. At the Edit Color Scheme dialog box, click the Apply button.
4. Insert the WordArt shown in figure 5.3 by completing the following steps:
   a. Click the Insert WordArt button on the Drawing toolbar. (If the Drawing toolbar is not displayed, click View, point to Toolbars, and then click Drawing.)
   b. At the WordArt Gallery, double-click the fifth option from the left in the third row.
   c. At the Edit WordArt Text dialog box, key **Waterfront cafe** and then click OK.
   d. Using the sizing handles that display around the selected WordArt text, increase the size of the WordArt so it is approximately the size shown in figure 5.3.
   e. Move the WordArt text so it is positioned approximately as shown in figure 5.3.

Step 3d

Step 3e

Step 3f

Step 4b

5. Add a transition and sound of your choosing to all slides in the presentation.
6. Run the presentation.
7. Print only Slide 1.
8. Save and then close Waterfront Pres with WordArt.

5.3 *Slide 1, Exercise 1*

WordArt Gallery

Edit Text

Format WordArt

WordArt Shape

Customizing WordArt

The WordArt toolbar, shown in figure 5.4, contains buttons for customizing the WordArt text. Click the Insert WordArt button or the WordArt Gallery button to display the WordArt Gallery shown in figure 5.1, and click the Edit Text button to display the Edit WordArt Text dialog box shown in figure 5.2. Click the Format WordArt button, and the Format WordArt dialog box displays containing a number of options for formatting and customizing WordArt text. Display a palette of shape choices by clicking the WordArt Shape button. Use the last four buttons on the WordArt toolbar to specify letter heights, change horizontal and vertical alignment of WordArt text, as well as the character spacing.

FIGURE

5.4 *WordArt Toolbar*

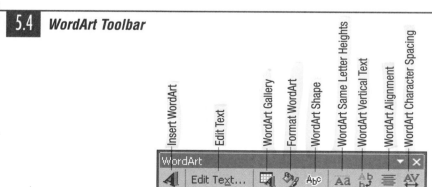

POWERPOINT

1. Open Artworks Presentation.
2. Save the presentation with Save As in the *PowerPoint Chapter 05* folder on your disk and then name it Artworks Pres with WordArt.
3. Insert WordArt in Slide 1 as shown in figure 5.5 by completing the following steps:
   a. With Slide 1 displayed in the Slide pane, click the Insert WordArt button on the Drawing toolbar.
   b. At the WordArt Gallery, double-click the fourth option from the left in the third row.
   c. At the Edit WordArt Text dialog box, key **Rainbow Artworks** and then click OK.
   d. Click the WordArt Shape button on the WordArt toolbar and then click the first option from the left in the second row from the top (Arch Up [Curve]).
   e. Click the Format WordArt button on the WordArt toolbar.
   f. At the Format WordArt dialog box, click the Size tab.
   g. At the Format WordArt dialog box with the Size tab selected, select the current measurement in the Height text box and then key **7**.
   h. Select the current measurement in the Width text box and then key **6.5**.
   i. Click OK to close the dialog box.
   j. Drag the WordArt text so it is positioned on the slide as shown in figure 5.5.
4. Add an animation scheme of your choosing to all slides in the presentation.
5. Run the presentation.
6. Print only Slide 1.
7. Save and then close Artworks Pres with WordArt.

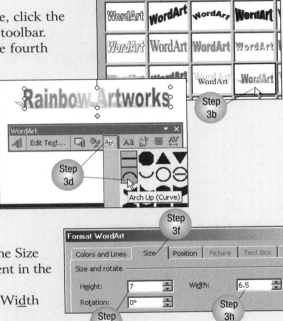

FIGURE

5.5 **Slide 1, Exercise 2**

Creating Organizational Charts and Diagrams

Insert Diagram or Organization Chart

Use the Diagram Gallery to create organizational charts or other types of diagrams. Display the Diagram Gallery dialog box, shown in figure 5.6, by clicking the Insert Diagram or Organization Chart button on the Drawing toolbar or by clicking Insert and then Diagram. You can also display the Diagram Gallery dialog box by choosing a slide layout containing a content placeholder and then clicking the Insert Diagram or Organization Chart button in the content placeholder.

F I G U R E

5.6 *Diagram Gallery Dialog Box*

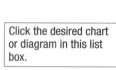

Click the desired chart or diagram in this list box.

HINT

Use an organizational chart to visually illustrate hierarchical data.

At the Diagram Gallery dialog box, click the desired option in the Select a diagram type list box and then click OK. If you click an organizational chart option, chart boxes appear in the slide and the Organization Chart toolbar displays. Use buttons on this toolbar to create additional boxes in the chart, specify the layout of the chart, expand or scale the chart, select specific elements in the chart, apply an autoformat to the chart, or specify a text wrapping option.

HINT

Use a diagram to illustrate a concept and enhance the visual appeal of a document.

If you click a diagram option at the Diagram Gallery dialog box, the diagram is inserted in the slide and the Diagram toolbar displays. Use buttons on this toolbar to insert additional shapes; move shapes backward or forward or reverse the diagram; expand, scale, or fit the contents of the diagram; apply an autoformat to the diagram; or change the type of diagram (choices include Cycle, Radial, Pyramid, Venn, and Target).

exercise 3

CREATING AND CUSTOMIZING AN ORGANIZATIONAL CHART AND A DIAGRAM

1. Open Waterfront Pres with WordArt.
2. Add a new Slide 6 containing an organizational chart as shown in figure 5.7 by completing the following steps:
   a. Display Slide 5 in the Slide pane.
   b. Click the New Slide button on the Formatting toolbar.

c. At the Slide Layout Task Pane, click the Title and Content slide layout.

d. Click in the text *Click to add title* and then key **Executive Officers**.

e. Click the Insert Diagram or Organization Chart button located in the middle of the slide in the content placeholder.

f. At the Diagram Gallery dialog box, make sure the first option from the left in the top row is selected, and then click OK.

g. Create the organizational chart shown in figure 5.7 by completing the following steps:
   1) Click the Autoformat button on the Organization Chart toolbar.
   2) At the Organization Chart Style Gallery, double-click *Double Outline* in the Select a Diagram Style list box.
   3) Click in the top box, key **Tanya Mitchell**, press Enter, and then key **Owner**.
   4) Click in each of the remaining boxes and then key the text as shown in figure 5.7.

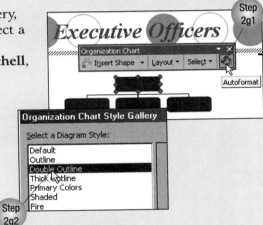

3. Add a new Slide 7 containing a diagram as shown in figure 5.8 by completing the following steps:
   a. Click the New Slide button on the Formatting toolbar.
   b. At the Slide Layout Task Pane, click the Title and Content slide layout.
   c. Click in the text *Click to add title* and then key **Company Divisions**.
   d. Click the Insert Diagram or Organization Chart button located in the middle of the slide in the content placeholder.
   e. At the Diagram Gallery dialog box, click the middle diagram in the top row, and then click OK.
   f. Create the diagram shown in figure 5.8 by completing the following steps:
      1) Click the AutoFormat button on the Diagram Chart toolbar.
      2) At the Diagram Style Gallery, double-click *Double Outline* in the Select a Diagram Style list box.
      3) Click the text *Click to add text* located at the right side of the diagram and then key **Dining Room**.

4) Click the text *Click to add text* located at the left side of the diagram and then key **Catering**.
5) Click the text *Click to add text* located at the bottom side of the diagram and then key **Wine Cellar**.
6) Select the text *Catering* and then click the Bold button on the Formatting toolbar.
7) Select and then bold *Dining Room*.
8) Select and then bold *Wine Cellar*.
4. Run the presentation.
5. Print only Slides 6 and 7.
6. Save and then close Waterfront Pres with WordArt.

FIGURE

5.7 *Slide 6, Exercise 3*

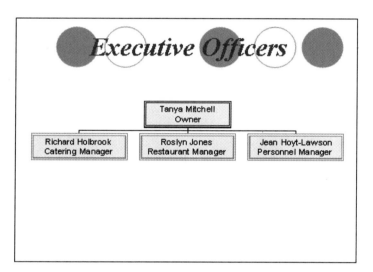

FIGURE

5.8 *Slide 7, Exercise 3*

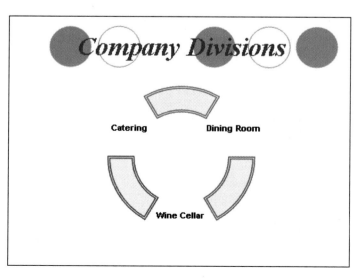

POWERPOINT

Creating a Chart

A chart is an effective way of visually presenting relationships between numerical data. The audience will be able to quickly grasp the largest expenditure, or the sales trend line, because the information is displayed in a graph format. Microsoft Office includes a feature called Microsoft Graph Chart you can use to create charts.

To add a chart to your presentation, insert a new slide with a slide layout that contains a content placeholder. Click the Insert Chart button in the content placeholder and a chart displays in the slide along with a datasheet as shown in figure 5.9. You can also insert a chart by clicking the Insert Chart button on the Standard toolbar or by clicking Insert and then Chart.

Insert
Chart

FIGURE

5.9 *Chart and Datasheet*

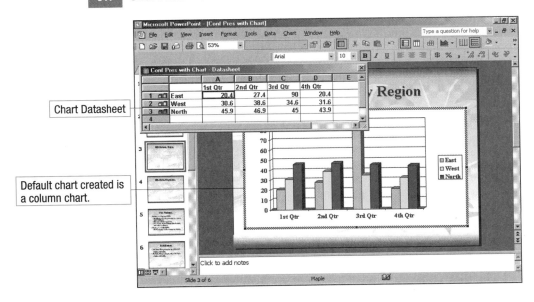

Chart Datasheet

Default chart created is
a column chart.

Editing the Datasheet

The datasheet is set up similar to an Excel worksheet with columns and rows. Data is entered into a cell, which is the intersection of a column with a row. Each row in the datasheet represents a series in the chart as noted by the colored bars to the right of the row numbers. Key your data by clicking the required cell in the datasheet and then typing the correct label or value. Press Tab or use the arrow keys on the keyboard to move from cell to cell in the datasheet. As you make changes to the contents of the datasheet, the chart will update automatically. You can also clear the entire datasheet first and then key the data for the chart into an empty datasheet. To do this, select all of the cells in the datasheet, press the Delete key or click Edit, point to Clear, and then click All.

Changing the Chart Type

Once the correct data has been entered, you can modify the chart settings to suit your needs. You can choose from several standard chart types. Each chart category includes several subtypes. In addition to the standard chart types, PowerPoint includes some custom charts that are preformatted combinations of charts with various colors, patterns, gridlines, and other options. Select a custom chart at the Chart Type dialog box. Display this dialog box by clicking Chart on the Chart Menu bar and then clicking Chart Type at the drop-down menu. The standard chart types and a brief description of each are listed in figure 5.10.

FIGURE

5.10 *Standard Chart Types*

Type	Description
Column	Can be used to compare related items and show changes over a period of time.
Bar	Similar to a column chart except the x-axis is displayed vertically, and the y-axis is displayed horizontally.
Line	Use a line chart to illustrate changes in values or to show trends over time.
Pie	Individual items are displayed as they relate to the sum of all of the items in a pie chart.
XY (Scatter)	Values are plotted as individual points in the chart. Each point is the interception of the x and y values. XY charts are commonly used for scientific data.
Area	This chart is similar to a line chart with a solid color filling in the area of the chart below the line.
Doughnut	The doughnut chart illustrates each item as it relates to the sum of all of the items. It is used instead of a pie chart when more than one data series is to be graphed.
Radar	In this chart, the axis radiates from the center of the chart. Data is plotted along the axes radiating from the center and then lines are shown joining axis to axis.
Surface	Two sets of data can be illustrated topographically with peaks and valleys in a surface chart. Areas with the same color and pattern indicate similar values.
Bubble	Three values are required to create a bubble chart. Two of the values cause the bubble to be positioned on the chart similar to an XY chart. The third value affects the size of the bubble.
Stock	Stock prices are graphed according to their *high-low-close* prices. Graphing a particular stock is useful to see the beginning value, how much the value fluctuated, and the ending value.
Cylinder	This is the column or bar chart shown with a cylinder series instead of a rectangular bar.
Cone	This is the column or bar chart shown with a cone series instead of a rectangular bar.
Pyramid	This is the column or bar chart shown with a pyramid series instead of a rectangular bar.

1. Open Conference Presentation from the *PowerPoint Chapter 05* folder on your disk.
2. Save the presentation with Save As into the *PowerPoint Chapter 05* folder on your disk and name the presentation Conf Pres with Chart.
3. Add a chart to the presentation, edit the datasheet, and change the chart type by completing the following steps:
   a. Display Slide 3 in the Slide pane.
   b. Click the Insert Chart button in the middle of the slide in the content placeholder.
   c. Delete the existing data in the datasheet by completing the following steps:
      1) Click the Select All button at the top left corner of the datasheet. This button is located at the top of the row indicators and to the left of the column indicators.
      2) Press the Delete key on the keyboard.
   d. Key the data displayed at the right into the datasheet. Press the Tab key to move from one cell to the next. As you enter new data, the chart will update automatically to reflect the changes.
   e. Change to a 3-D clustered bar chart by completing the following steps:
      1) Click Chart and then Chart Type.
      2) Click Bar in the Chart type list box.
      3) Click the first sub-type in the second row in the Chart sub-type section.
      4) Click OK.
4. Click in an area on the slide outside the chart to deselect it.
5. Make Slide 1 active and then run the presentation.
6. Print only Slide 3.
7. Save and then close Conf Pres with Chart.

Modifying a Chart

The chart created in exercise 4 needs more information added to it to make it more readily understood by the conference participants. You can tell by looking at the chart that the East region had the largest sales volume, but what do the values represent? Are the sales figures represented in thousands, millions, or billions? The legend in the chart created in exercise 4 is not necessary since the slide title provides the same information.

Additional elements such as titles can be added to the chart, or, existing elements can be deleted or formatted by modifying the chart. Double-click a chart to edit it. The chart displays with a thick shaded border surrounding it, the datasheet window opens, and the chart options appear on the Menu bar and toolbar.

View Datasheet

Click the Close button (contains an *X*) on the datasheet Title bar or click the View Datasheet button on the Chart Standard toolbar to remove the datasheet from the screen. The View Datasheet button on the toolbar is a toggle. Clicking it once will remove the datasheet; clicking it again will redisplay it.

Once a chart has been created on a slide, clicking the chart once will display eight white sizing handles around the chart. Drag the sizing handles to change the size of the chart. Press the Delete key to delete the chart from the slide. To move the chart, position the mouse pointer inside the chart until the four-headed move icon displays, and then drag the chart to the new location on the slide. Click in an area on the slide outside the chart to deselect it.

HINT

Click a chart once to select it and then move or size it. Double-click a chart to edit the chart contents or elements.

Adding Chart Titles

Three titles can be added to a chart: the Chart title; the Category title, and the Value title. To add a title to the chart, click Chart and then Chart Options, or right-click the chart and then click Chart Options at the shortcut menu. This opens the Chart Options dialog box with the Titles tab selected as displayed in figure 5.11. Key the titles in the appropriate text boxes then click OK.

FIGURE

5.11 **Chart Options Dialog Box**

Click a tab to display formatting options for that particular chart element.

Formatting Chart Elements

HINT

Right-click any of the chart elements to display a format dialog box for the selected element.

A chart is comprised of several elements as shown in figure 5.12. Double-clicking a chart element will open a dialog box with formatting options that are available for the selected element. You can also right-click the object and then click the desired option at the shortcut menu, or click to select the object and then use options from the Format or Chart menus on the Menu bar.

5.12 Chart Elements

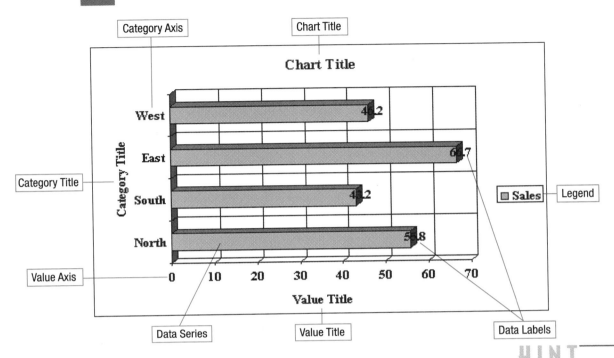

In exercise 5 you will add a title to the axis displaying the dollar amounts, delete the legend, format the value axis to display the numbers in currency format, change the shape of the bars, and add value labels to the bars.

exercise 5

ENHANCING THE CHART

1. Open Conf Pres with Chart.
2. Display Slide 3 in the Slide pane.
3. Double-click the chart to edit it.
4. Click the Close button (contains an *X*) on the datasheet title bar to remove it from the slide.
5. Add a value title by completing the following steps:
   a. Click **C**hart and then Chart Op**t**ions.
   b. Click in the **V**alue (Z) axis text box and then key **Sales in Millions**.
   c. Click OK.
6. Click the legend to select it. Make sure black sizing handles appear around the legend and then press the Delete key. (Sales)
7. Change the format of the numbers in the value axis to Currency by completing the following steps:

a. Point the tip of the mouse pointer at one of the values along the bottom of the chart until a yellow pop-up box appears which reads *Value Axis*.

b. Click the right mouse button and then click F<u>o</u>rmat Axis at the shortcut menu.

c. At the Format Axis dialog box, click the Number tab.

d. Click *Currency* in the <u>C</u>ategory list box.

e. Change the number in the <u>D</u>ecimal places text box to zero (0).

f. Click OK.

8. Change the shape of the bars in the chart by completing the following steps:

a. Point to any of the bars in the chart, click the right mouse button, and then click F<u>o</u>rmat Data Series at the shortcut menu.

b. At the Format Data Series dialog box, click the <u>S</u>hape tab.

c. Click the first shape in the second row (shape 4 in the Bar <u>s</u>hape section).

d. Click OK.

9. Add data labels to the chart and reposition the labels by completing the following steps:

a. Click <u>C</u>hart and then Chart Opti<u>o</u>ns.

b. At the Chart Options dialog box, click the Data Labels tab.

c. Click in the <u>V</u>alue check box to insert a check mark.

d. Click OK.

e. The values are placed at the end of the cylinders, but are partly obstructed from view by the cylinders. Move the values by completing the following steps:

1) Point to the first value label and click the left mouse button. (This selects all of the value labels.)

2) Click the left mouse button again and sizing handles appear around the first value label only.

3) Point the mouse pointer at the border around the sizing handles and then drag the value label to the right of the cylinder until the entire value is visible.

4) Repeat steps 9e2 and 9e3 to move the remaining value labels.

10. Click in an area on the slide outside the chart to deselect it.

11. Make Slide 1 active and then run the presentation.

12. Print only Slide 3.

13. Save and then close Conf Pres with Chart.

Creating a Table

Insert Table

Tables are useful for numbers and lists where you want to present the data in column format. Each entry in a table is called a cell and can be formatted independently. If you want to arrange the content of a slide in columns and rows, insert a new slide with the slide layout that includes a content placeholder. Click the Insert Table button in the content placeholder and the Insert Table dialog box displays. At the Insert Table dialog box, key the number of columns, press the Tab key, key the number of rows, and then press Enter.

POWERPOINT

You can also insert a table using the Insert Table button on the Standard toolbar. Click the Insert Table button, drag the mouse down and to the right to select the desired number of columns and rows, and then click the left mouse button.

HINT

Use PowerPoint to create a table with simple formatting. For more complex formatting, consider creating the table in Word or Excel and then embedding it in a slide.

Entering Text in Cells in a Table

To enter text in the table, click in the desired cell and then key the text. Press the Tab key to move the insertion point to the next cell to the right. Press Shift + Tab to move the insertion point to the previous cell. If you want to insert a tab within a cell, press Ctrl + Tab. If you press the Tab key when the insertion point is positioned in the last cell in the table, a new row is automatically added to the bottom of the table.

exercise 6

CREATING A TABLE IN A SLIDE

1. Open Conf Pres with Chart.
2. Display Slide 4 in the Slide pane.
3. Add a table to the slide and enter text into the cells by completing the following steps:
   a. Click the Insert Table button located in the middle of the slide in the content placeholder.
   b. At the Insert Tab dialog box, press the Tab key. (This accepts the default of *2* in the Number of columns text box.)
   c. Key 5 in the Number of rows text box.
   d. Click OK or press Enter.
   e. Key the text as displayed in the table at the right. Press the Tab key to move from cell to cell. Do not press Tab after keying the last cell entry.
   f. Click outside the table to deselect it.
4. Make Slide 1 active and then run the presentation.
5. Print only Slide 4.
6. Save and then close Conf Pres with Chart.

Step 3e

Region	In millions of dollars
North	68.3
South	55.2
East	77.8
West	59.9

Modifying a Table

Once a table has been created it can be resized and moved to another position on the slide. Click the table to select it and then use the sizing handles that display around the table to increase or decrease the size. To move the table, point to the border of the table until the mouse pointer displays with a four-headed arrow attached, and then drag the table to the desired position.

HINT

Text in a table does not display in the Outline/Slides pane with the Outline tab selected.

Use buttons on the Tables and Borders toolbar shown in figure 5.13 to format a table. For example, you can insert and/or delete rows and columns from the table. To delete a column or row, select the cells in the column or row to be deleted, click the Table button on the Tables and Borders toolbar, and then click Delete Columns or Delete Rows. Insert a column or row by following a similar procedure. You can also use buttons on the toolbar to change the border style, width, and color and add fill color or effects to the table.

The Tables and Borders toolbar should appear automatically when you click inside a cell. If the toolbar has been closed, redisplay it by clicking View, pointing to Toolbars, and then clicking Tables and Borders.

5.13 Tables and Borders Toolbar

Adjust column widths by positioning the pointer on the column gridline until the pointer changes to a double vertical line with a left- and right-pointing arrow attached to it. Drag the column gridline to the left or right to decrease or increase the width. Other options available from the Table button on the Tables and Borders toolbar allow you to merge and split cells and apply borders and fill.

exercise 7

MODIFYING A TABLE

1. Open Conf Pres with Chart.
2. Display Slide 4 in the Slide pane.
3. Modify the table by completing the following steps:
   a. Click the table to select it.
   b. Position the mouse pointer on the bottom right sizing handle until the pointer turns into a diagonally pointing double-headed arrow and then drag up and to the left approximately 0.5 inch.
   c. Position the mouse pointer on the gridline at the left edge of the table until the pointer turns into a double vertical bar with a left- and right-pointing arrow attached and then drag to the right approximately 1 inch.

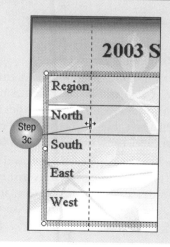

Step 3c

d. Delete the words **of dollars** from the second cell in the first row.

e. Decrease the width of the second column by positioning the mouse pointer on the gridline at the right edge of the table until the pointer turns into a double vertical bar with a left- and right-pointing arrow attached, and then dragging to the left approximately 1 inch.

f. Position the arrow pointer along the border of the table until the pointer displays with a four-headed arrow attached, and then drag the table until it displays centered in the middle of the slide.

g. Select the cells in the second column and then click the Center button on the Formatting toolbar.

h. Select all of the cells in the table.

i. Click the down-pointing arrow on the Border Width button on the Tables and Borders toolbar and then click *4½ pt* at the drop-down list.

j. Click the Border Color button on the Tables and Borders toolbar and then click the fifth color (blue) from the left (see figure at right).

k. Click the down-pointing arrow at the right of the Outside Borders button on the Tables and Borders toolbar and then click the All Borders button (second button from the left in the top row).

l. Click the down-pointing arrow to the right of the Fill Color button on the Tables and Borders toolbar and then click the first color from the left (white).

m. Click outside the table to deselect it.

4. Make Slide 1 active and then run the presentation.

5. Print only Slide 4.

6. Save and then close Conf Pres with Chart.

Inserting a Scanned Image

Many computer systems are sold today with color scanners as part of the multimedia package. Scanners can be used to capture pictures, logos, or other artwork that you want to insert into a presentation. Scanned images are stored as files and can easily be placed on a slide. Once the image has been inserted, you can use the sizing handles to resize or move it around on the slide.

   To insert a scanned image, click the Insert Picture button on the Drawing toolbar (or click Insert, point to Picture, and then click From File). At the Insert Picture dialog box, navigate to the folder where the picture is stored, and then double-click the file name. This picture will be inserted in the current slide and white sizing handles will display around it. Move and resize the picture as required.

HINT

PowerPoint contains a variety of filters that allow you to insert many popular graphic file formats into a presentation.

Insert
Picture

1. Open Semester Presentation.
2. Save the presentation with Save As into the *PowerPoint Chapter 05* folder on your disk and name the presentation Semester Pres with Images.
3. Add a scanned logo into Slide 1 (shown in figure 5.14) by completing the following steps:
    a. Display Slide 1 in the Slide pane.
    b. Click the Insert Picture button on the Drawing toolbar.
    c. At the Insert Picture dialog box, navigate to the *Logos* folder on the CD that accompanies this textbook, and then double-click the file named *Redwood*.
    d. Resize the logo and reposition it in the slide as shown in figure 5.14.
4. Insert a scanned picture as shown in figure 5.14 by completing the following steps:
    a. Click the Insert Picture button on the Drawing toolbar.
    b. At the Insert Picture dialog box, navigate to the *Pictures* folder on the CD that accompanies this textbook, and then double-click the file named *Building1*.
    c. Resize the picture and reposition it in the slide as shown in figure 5.14.
5. Print only Slide 1.
6. Run the presentation.
7. Save and then close Semester Pres with Images.

FIGURE

5.14 *Slide 1, Exercise 8*

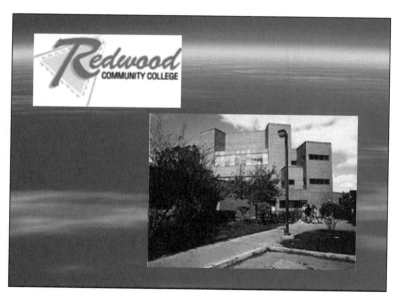

HINT

You can move and size an animated GIF, but you have to edit and format it in an animated GIF editing program.

Adding Animated GIFs

GIF files are graphic files saved in *Graphics Interchange Format*, which is a type of file format commonly used for graphics on Web pages. Animated GIFs are GIF files that have been programmed to display a series of images one on top of another that give the illusion of motion. If you surf the Internet you will see most Web sites have incorporated one or more animated GIFs on their pages to add interest and variety to their site.

Animated GIFs do not display the motion until you display the slide in a slide show. To insert an animated GIF that you have stored as a file on disk, click the Insert Picture button on the Drawing toolbar (or click Insert, point to Picture, and then click From File). Navigate to the folder containing the GIF file and then double-click the file name. Once the GIF image has been placed in the slide it can be resized and moved using the sizing handles.

exercise 9

ADDING ANIMATED GIFS

1. Open Design Presentation.
2. Save the presentation with Save As into the *PowerPoint Chapter 05* folder on your disk and name the presentation Design Pres with GIF.
3. Add an animated GIF from a file to Slide 1 as shown in figure 5.15 by completing the following steps:
   a. Click the Insert Picture button on the Drawing toolbar.
   b. At the Insert Picture dialog box, navigate to the *Pictures* folder on the CD that accompanies this textbook, and then double-click the file named *Banner*.
   c. Slightly increase the size of the image and then position it inside the circle at the upper left side of the slide as shown in figure 5.15.
4. Run the presentation and notice the animation (the red circles move around the text) in the image you inserted.
5. Print only Slide 1.
6. Save and then close Design Pres with GIF.

FIGURE

5.15 *Slide 1, Exercise 9*

Adding Sound and Video

Adding sound and/or video effects to a presentation will turn a slide show into a true multimedia experience for your audience. Including a variety of elements in a presentation will stimulate interest in your presentation and keep the audience motivated.

To add a sound to your presentation, choose Insert, point to Movies and Sounds, and then click Sound from Clip Organizer or click Sound from File. Clicking Sound from Clip Organizer will display sound files in the Insert Clip Art Task Pane. Click the desired sound to insert it in the active slide. If the sound you want to incorporate into your presentation is not part of the gallery but stored in a file on disk, click Sound from File. This displays the Insert Sound dialog box where you can navigate to the file's location and then double-click the sound to insert it in the active slide.

When a sound is inserted, you will be prompted with a message asking if you want the sound to start playing automatically when the slide is displayed in a slide show. If you click No at this message, clicking the sound icon on the slide during the presentation will cause the sound clip to start playing.

Adding a video clip is a similar process to adding sound. Click Insert, point to Movies and Sounds, and then click either Movie from Clip Organizer or Movie from File.

exercise 10

ADDING SOUND AND VIDEO TO A PRESENTATION

1. Open Potential Presentation.
2. Save the presentation with Save As into the *PowerPoint Chapter 05* folder on your disk and name the presentation Potential Pres with Video and Sound.
3. Add a movie clip and sound to the Slide 6 as shown in figure 5.16 by completing the following steps:
   a. Display Slide 6 in the Slide pane.
   b. Click Insert, point to Movies and Sounds, and then click Movie from File.
   c. At the Insert Movie dialog box, navigate to the *Sound and Video* folder on the CD that accompanies this textbook, and then double-click the file named *sts-95-launch*.
   d. At the message asking if you want your movie to play automatically, click No.
   e. Resize and position the movie on the slide as shown in figure 5.16.
   f. Add a sound clip to Slide 6 that will automatically play by completing the following steps:
      1) Click Insert, point to Movies and Sounds, and then click Sound from File.
      2) At the Insert Sound dialog box, navigate to the *Sound and Video* folder on the CD that accompanies this textbook, and then double-click the file named *greatfire*.
      3) At the message asking if you want your sound to play automatically, click Yes.
      4) Resize and position the sound icon as shown in figure 5.16.
4. Display Slide 1 in the Slide pane and then run the presentation. When the last slide (Slide 6) displays, as soon as you hear the music, click the video image to begin the video. After viewing the video and listening to the music for about 30 seconds, end the slide show.
5. Sounds and videos can be set to loop continuously. The sound and/or video will continue playing over and over again until the slide show is ended. In this exercise, when the

speaker has finished the presentation, he or she might choose to have the sound and video play for a few minutes until the audience has left the room. Change the video and sound in Slide 6 to loop continuously by completing the following steps:

   a. Display Slide 6 in the Slide pane.

   b. Right-click the video and then click Edit Movie Object at the shortcut menu.

   c. At the Movie Options dialog box, click Loop until stopped to insert a check mark, and then click OK.

   d. Right-click the sound icon and then click Edit Sound Object at the shortcut menu.

   e. At the Sound Options dialog box, click Loop until stopped, and then click OK.

   f. Deselect the sound icon.

6. Display Slide 1 and then run the presentation. When you reach Slide 6, click the video image when you hear the music. Watch the video and listen to the sound repeat a few times and then end the slide show.

7. Print only Slide 6.

8. Print the slides as handouts with all six slides on one page.

9. Save and then close Potential Pres with Video and Sound.

FIGURE

5.16 *Slide 6, Exercise 10*

Creating and Applying a Custom Template

Each PowerPoint presentation is based on a template. The Slide Design Task Pane offers a number of design templates that apply specific formatting to slides in a presentation. If you customize a design template and then decide you want to use the customized template in the future, save it as a template.

To save a customized design as a design template, click File and then Save As. At the Save As dialog box, key a name for the template, click the down-pointing triangle at the right side of the Save as type option box, and then click *Design Template* at the drop-down list. Specify the location where you want the design template saved and then click the Save button.

exercise 11

CREATING AND APPLYING A CUSTOM DESIGN

1. At a blank PowerPoint screen, click the New button on the Standard toolbar. (This displays a blank, unformatted slide.)
2. Click the Slide Design button on the Formatting toolbar.
3. Click the *Crayons* design template in the Apply a design template list box at the Slide Design Task Pane.
4. Customize the design template by completing the following steps:
   a. Click the *Color Schemes* hyperlink located toward the top of the Slide Design Task Pane.
   b. Click the first color scheme option in the second row.
   c. Click the *Edit Color Schemes* hyperlink located toward the bottom of the Slide Design Task Pane.
   d. At the Edit Color Scheme dialog box, click the Accent color option, and then click the Change Color button.
   e. At the Accent Color dialog box with the Standard tab selected, click a bright yellow color of your choosing, and then click OK.
   f. At the Edit Color Scheme dialog box, click the Accent and followed hyperlink color option, and then click the Change Color button.
   g. At the Accent and Followed Hyperlink Color dialog box with the Standard tab selected, click a bright red color of your choosing, and then click OK.
   h. Click the Apply button at the Edit Color Scheme dialog box.
5. Save the customized design as a design template by completing the following steps:
   a. Click File and then Save As.
   b. At the Save As dialog box, key **Artworks Template** in the File name text box.
   c. Click the down-pointing triangle at the right side of the Save as type option box and then click *Design Template* at the drop-down list.

POWERPOINT

d. Change the Save in option to the *PowerPoint Chapter 05* folder on your disk.
e. Click the Save button.
6. Close Artworks Template.
7. Apply the Artworks Template to the Artworks Pres with WordArt presentation by completing the following steps:
   a. Open Artworks Pres with WordArt. (You saved this presentation in exercise 2. If you did not complete exercise 2, open Artworks Presentation.)
   b. Apply the Artworks Template by completing the following steps:
     1) Click the Slide Design button on the Formatting toolbar.
     2) Click the *Design Templates* hyperlink located toward the top of the Slide Design Task Pane.
     3) Click the *Browse* hyperlink located toward the bottom of the Slide Design Task Pane.
     4) At the Apply Design Template dialog box, change the Look in option to the *PowerPoint Chapter 05* folder on your disk.
     5) Double-click *Artworks Template* in the list box. (This applies the customized template to the slides in the presentation.)
8. Make the following changes to the slides:
   a. With Slide 1 displayed in the Slide pane, click the *Rainbow Artworks* WordArt text to select it and then drag the WordArt so it is balanced in the slide.
   b. Display Slide 2 in the Slide pane, click to select the subtitle placeholder (contains the Goal 1 text), and then drag the placeholder up slightly so the text does not touch the wavy red line that is part of the design template.
   c. Display Slide 3 and then drag the subtitle placeholder up slightly so the text does not touch the wavy red line.
   d. Display Slide 4 and then drag the subtitle placeholder up slightly so the text does not touch the wavy red line.
9. Display Slide 1 in the Slide pane and then run the presentation.
10. Print the presentation as handouts with all four slides on one page.
11. Save and then close Artworks Pres with WordArt.

CHAPTER summary

➤ Use WordArt to create, distort, modify, and/or conform text to a variety of shapes.

➤ The WordArt Gallery contains a variety of predesigned WordArt styles.

➤ Size WordArt using the sizing handles that display around selected WordArt text and move selected WordArt by dragging it to the desired location using the mouse.

➤ Customize WordArt text with buttons on the WordArt toolbar and/or with options at the Format WordArt dialog box.

➤ Create organizational charts and diagrams with options at the Diagram Gallery. Use buttons on the Organization Chart toolbar to customize an organizational chart. Use buttons on the Diagram toolbar to customize a diagram.

➤ Add a chart to a slide to visually present relationships between numerical data. Use the Microsoft Graph Chart feature to create a variety of charts.

➤ Data for a chart is entered in the datasheet. When a new chart is created, a sample datasheet and chart display. Edit the datasheet to insert the values you want to plot on the graph.

➤ Double-click a chart to edit it. A chart is comprised of several chart elements that can be added, deleted, or formatted.

➤ Create a table on a slide when you want to present information in columns and/or rows. Each entry in a table is entered into a cell that can be formatted independently of the other cells.

➤ In a table, press the Tab key to move the insertion point to the next cell or press Shift + Tab to move the insertion point to the previous cell.

➤ Click a table to select it. You can resize, move, or delete a selected table.

➤ Use buttons on the Tables and Borders toolbar to customize and format cells in a table.

➤ Insert a scanned image or animated GIF by double-clicking the desired image at the Insert Picture dialog box. You can resize and/or move a scanned image or GIF on a slide.

➤ An animated GIF is a graphic file that displays motion when running a presentation.

➤ Sound and/or video effects that will play as the presentation runs can be added. You can configure a sound or video object to play continuously until the slide show is ended.

➤ Save a customized template you want to use in the future as a design template. To do this, display the Save As dialog box, key a name for the customized template, change the Save as type option to *Design Template*, identify the Save in location, and then click Save.

COMMANDS review

Command	Mouse
Display WordArt Gallery	Click Insert WordArt button on Drawing toolbar or in content placeholder; or click Insert, Picture, WordArt
Display Diagram Gallery	Click Insert Diagram or Organization Chart button on Drawing toolbar or in content placeholder; or click Insert, Diagram
Insert a chart	Click Insert Chart button on Standard toolbar or in content placeholder; or click Insert, Chart
Insert a table	Click Insert Table button in content placeholder and then key the desired number of columns and rows at the Insert Table dialog box; or click Insert Table button on Standard toolbar and then drag to specify the desired number of rows and columns
Insert a scanned image/animated GIF	Click Insert Picture button on Drawing toolbar and then double-click desired image at Insert Picture dialog box
Insert a video file from a disk	Click Insert, Movies and Sounds, Movie from File, double-click desired file
Insert a sound file from a disk	Click Insert, Movies and Sounds, Sound from File, double-click desired file

CONCEPTS check

Completion: On a blank sheet of paper, indicate the correct term, symbol, or command.

1. Click the Insert WordArt button on the Drawing toolbar and this displays.
2. Display a palette of shape choices by clicking this button on the WordArt toolbar.
3. Click this button on the Drawing toolbar to display the Diagram Gallery.
4. If you click an organizational chart option at the Diagram Gallery, this toolbar displays.
5. Use this Microsoft Office feature to create charts.
6. Click this button on the Chart Standard toolbar to remove the datasheet from the screen.
7. Three titles can be added to a chart: the Category title, the Value title, and this title.
8. Press this key in a table to move the insertion point to the next cell.
9. Use buttons on this toolbar to customize and format a table.
10. Insert a scanned image by double-clicking the desired image at this dialog box.
11. The initials *GIF* stand for this.
12. To save a customized design as a design template, change the Save as type option at the Save As dialog box to this.

SKILLS check

Assessment 1

1. Open Corporate Presentation.
2. Save the presentation with Save As in the *PowerPoint Chapter 05* folder on your disk and name the presentation Enhanced Corporate Pres.
3. Create the WordArt on Slide 1 as shown in figure 5.17 with the following specifications:
   a. At the WordArt Gallery, double-click the second option from the left in the second row.
   b. Change the shape of the WordArt to the Deflate shape (second shape from the left in the fourth row from the top).
   c. Display the Format WordArt dialog box with the Colors and Lines tab selected, change the Color option in the Fill section to black, and then close the dialog box.
   d. Size and move the WordArt so it displays on the slide as shown in figure 5.17.
4. Create the organizational chart on Slide 3 as shown in figure 5.18 with the following specifications:
   a. Display the Diagram Gallery and then choose the first option from the left in the top row.
   b. Display the Organization Chart Style Gallery dialog box and then double-click the *Outline* style.
   c. Key the text in bold in the organizational chart boxes as shown in figure 5.18.

5. Create the diagram on Slide 4 as shown in figure 5.19 with the following specifications:
   a. Display the Diagram Gallery and then choose the second option from the left in the top row.
   b. Key the text in bold in the diagram as shown in figure 5.19.
6. Add an animation scheme of your choosing to the presentation.
7. Run the presentation beginning with Slide 1.
8. Print the presentation as handouts with all four slides on one page.
9. Save and then close Enhanced Corporate Pres.

FIGURE

5.17 *Slide 1, Assessment 1*

FIGURE

5.18 *Slide 3, Assessment 1*

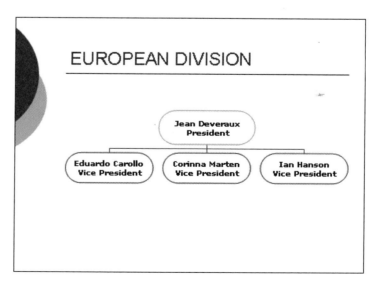

POWERPOINT

5.19 *Slide 4, Assessment 1*

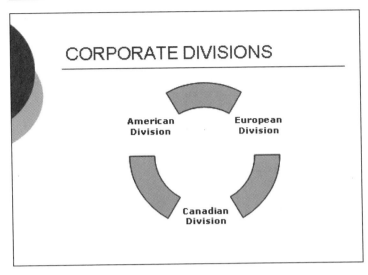

Assessment 2

1. Open Greenspace Presentation.
2. Save the presentation with Save As in the *PowerPoint Chapter 05* folder on your disk and name it Enhanced Greenspace Pres.
3. Insert the Greenspace Architects logo in Slide 1 as shown in figure 5.20 by completing the following steps:
   a. Click Insert, point to Picture, and then click From File.
   b. At the Insert Picture dialog box, navigate to the *Pictures* folder on the CD that accompanies this textbook, and then double-click the file named *Grnspc Logo*.
   c. Size and move the logo so it is positioned on the slide as shown in figure 5.20.
4. Add a chart to Slide 5 with the following specifications:
   a. Click the Insert Chart button in the content placeholder in the slide.
   b. Delete the data in the datasheet and then key the following:

	Court Bldg.	Rose Mall	East Hills	RW Const.
Contract	34.1	58.2	23.7	19.5

   c. Change the chart type to a pie.
   d. Remove the border from the perimeter of the pie. *(Hint: To do this, position mouse pointer anywhere on the line around the pie until* Plot Area *displays in a yellow bow. Click the right mouse button and then click Format Plot Area at the shortcut menu. At the Format Plot Area dialog box, click None in the Border section, and then click OK.)*
   e. Insert data labels around the pie chart that will display the values.
   f. Resize the chart as large as possible to fill the slide.
5. Add a table to Slide 6 with the following specifications:
   a. Create a table with two columns and five rows.
   b. Key the following data in the cells:

Course Title	Participating Division
Telecommunications	Mechanical Engineering
Air Particle Analysis	Environmental Group
Wireless Networks	Technical Support
Security Online	Security Engineers

   c. Bold the text in the first row.

   d. Change all of the border lines to *3 pt* and change the border color to match one of the design colors.

6. Create a new Slide 7 with the Blank slide layout and include the following objects:

   a. Create the words *Thank you* as WordArt. Size and position the WordArt text so it fills most of the slide.

   b. Insert the sound file named Greenspace located in the *Sound and Video* folder on the CD that accompanies this textbook and specify that the sound begin automatically when the slide displays. Position the sound icon in the lower right corner of the slide.

7. Apply an animation scheme of your choosing to all slides in the presentation.

8. Run the presentation beginning with Slide 1.

9. Print the presentation as handouts with all seven slides on one page.

10. Save and then close Enhanced Greenspace Pres.

FIGURE

5.20 **Slide 1, Assessment 2**

Assessment 3

1. Open Enhanced Greenspace Pres.
2. Display Slide 5 and then double-click the pie chart.
3. Use the Microsoft Graph Help feature to learn how to pull out a slice of the pie chart.
4. Pull the pie slice representing the Court Bldg. contract away from the pie approximately 0.5 inch.
5. Print only Slide 5.
6. Save and then close Enhanced Greenspace Pres.

6

SHARING AND CONNECTING DATA

P E R F O R M A N C E   O B J E C T I V E S

Upon successful completion of chapter 6, you will be able to:
- **Copy an Excel chart to a slide and then modify the chart**
- **Copy text from Word to a slide**
- **Import text from Word**
- **Copy and paste text using the Clipboard Task Pane**
- **Export an outline to Word**
- **Save a presentation as an Outline/RTF**
- **Add action buttons connecting slides within a presentation**
- **Add action buttons connecting to a Web site and another presentation**
- **Insert hyperlinks in slides connecting to a Web site**
- **Rehearse and set timings for each slide in a presentation**
- **Create a summary slide**

PowerPoint Chapter 06

A variety of methods are available for sharing data between PowerPoint and other Office programs. You can copy data in one program and then paste it in another. You can also copy and then embed or copy and then link data. In this chapter you will learn how to use the Copy and Paste buttons on the Standard toolbar and you will also learn commands for importing and exporting data. In the next chapter, you will learn how to copy and embed and copy and link objects between programs.

Use action buttons to facilitate the navigation of your PowerPoint presentation. These buttons can be used to connect to slides within the same presentation, connect to another presentation, connect to a Web site, or connect to a file in another program. You can also use the Insert Hyperlink dialog box to create a hyperlink in a slide to a Web site or file.

If you are preparing a self-running presentation, consider using the Rehearse Timings feature in PowerPoint. With this feature you can rehearse running the presentation and determine how much time each slide should remain on the screen.

Copy

Paste

Copying and Pasting Data

Use the Copy and Paste buttons on the Standard toolbar to copy data such as text or an object from one program and then paste it into another program within the Microsoft Office suite. For example, in exercise 1, you will copy an Excel chart and then paste it into a PowerPoint slide. A copied object, such as a chart, can be moved and sized like any other object. You can also edit a copied object by double-clicking the object.

COPYING AN EXCEL CHART TO A SLIDE AND THEN MODIFYING THE CHART

1. Open Travel Presentation.
2. Save the presentation with Save As into the *PowerPoint Chapter 06* folder on your disk and name the presentation Travel Pres with Chart.
3. Insert an Excel chart on Slide 2 as shown in figure 6.1 by completing the following steps:
   a. Display Slide 2 in the Slide pane.
   b. Open Microsoft Excel.
   c. Open the file named Top 5 Tours from the *PowerPoint Chapter 06* folder on your disk.
   d. Click the chart to select it. (Click near the outside of the chart. Make sure you select the entire chart and not an element inside the chart.)
   e. Click the Copy button on the Standard toolbar.
   f. Close Top 5 Tours. (If a message displays asking if you want to save the file, click No.)
   g. Exit Microsoft Excel.
   h. In PowerPoint, click the Paste button on the Standard toolbar. (This inserts the chart in Slide 2.)
   i. Resize and move the chart so it displays in the slide as shown in figure 6.1.
4. Modify the chart by removing the border and changing the title by completing the following steps:
   a. Double-click the chart.
   b. Position the tip of the mouse pointer on the single-line border until *Chart Area* displays in a yellow box.
   c. Click the *right* mouse button and then click Format Chart Area at the shortcut menu.
   d. At the Format Chart Area dialog box, click the Patterns tab.
   e. At the Format Chart Area dialog box with the Patterns tab selected, click None in the Border section, and then click OK.
   f. Click the chart title to select it.
   g. Click inside the chart title.

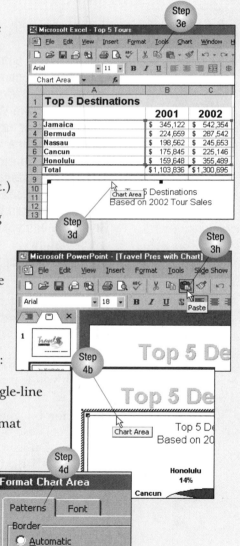

h. Delete the first line of the title, *Top 5 Destinations*.
   i. Deselect the chart by clicking in the slide but outside the chart.
5. Display Slide 1 in the Slide pane and then run the presentation.
6. Print only Slide 2.
7. Save and then close Travel Pres with Chart.

FIGURE

6.1 **Slide 2, Exercise 1**

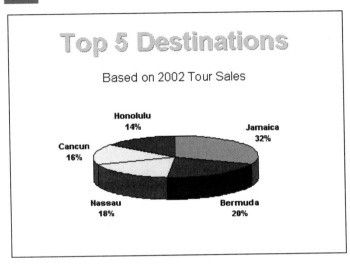

Copying and Pasting Word Text

You can copy text from a Word document and paste the text in a PowerPoint slide. To specify the area on the slide where you want the text inserted, draw a text box. To do this, click the Text Box button on the Drawing toolbar and then drag in the slide to create the box. With the insertion point positioned inside the text box, click the Paste button on the Standard toolbar to insert the copied text.

Text Box

INTEGRATED

COPYING TEXT FROM WORD TO A SLIDE

1. Open Travel Pres with Chart.
2. Copy text in a Word document and paste it in Slide 3 as shown in figure 6.2 by completing the following steps:
   a. Display Slide 3 in the Slide pane.
   b. Click the Text Box button on the Drawing toolbar.
   c. Drag in the slide to create a text box approximately the size shown at the right.
   d. Open Microsoft Word.
   e. Open the file named New Cruises from the *PowerPoint Chapter 06* folder on your disk.

New Cruise Packages

Step 2c

f. Select the text *Worldwide Cruises*, the paragraph below it, *Somerset Cruises*, and the paragraph below it.

g. Click the Copy button on the Standard toolbar.

h. Close the New Cruises file.

i. Exit Microsoft Word.

j. In PowerPoint, click the Paste button on the Standard toolbar.

k. Click at the beginning of the heading *Somerset Cruises* and then press the Enter key.

l. Select the text inside the placeholder and then change the font size to 20.

m. If necessary, move the text box so it is positioned as shown in figure 6.2.

3. Display Slide 1 in the Slide pane and then run the presentation.

4. Print only Slide 3.

5. Save and then close Travel Pres with Chart.

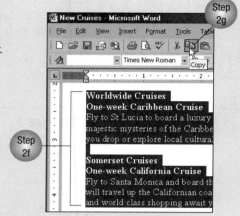

F I G U R E

6.2 **Slide 3, Exercise 2**

New Cruise Packages

Worldwide Cruises
One-week Caribbean Cruise
Fly to St. Lucia to board a luxury ship, then relax and enjoy as the next 7 days unveil the majestic mysteries of the Caribbean! This cruise will stop at 5 ports so you can shop till you drop or explore local cultural attractions. Call us today to check availability.

Somerset Cruises
One-week California Cruise
Fly to Santa Monica and board the newest luxury ship in the Somerset fleet. This cruise will travel up the Californian coast toward San Francisco. Mystic sunsets, ocean breezes, and world-class shopping await you. Don't delay—this package will sell fast.

Importing Data

A Word document containing heading styles can be imported into a PowerPoint presentation. To do this, open the document in Word, click File, point to Send To, and then click Microsoft PowerPoint. Paragraphs formatted with a Heading 1 style become the title of a new slide. Paragraphs formatted with a Heading 2 style become the first level of text, paragraphs formatted as a Heading 3 style become the second level, and so on. PowerPoint creates a presentation with the imported

text using the Blank Presentation template. After importing the text into
PowerPoint, apply the desired formatting, or apply a design template.

Changing the Slide Layout

Text imported from Word into PowerPoint is inserted in a slide with a specific
slide layout. In some cases, this slide layout is appropriate for the imported text.
In other cases, you may need to change the layout. To do this, click Format on
the Menu bar, and then click Slide Layout at the drop-down list. Click the desired
layout at the Slide Layout Task Pane.

INTEGRATED

3

IMPORTING TEXT FROM WORD

1. Make sure PowerPoint is open and then open Word.
2. With Word the active program, open Word Outline 01 (located in the *PowerPoint Chapter
   06* folder on your disk).
3. Import the document (formatted with Heading 1 and
   Heading 2 styles) into PowerPoint by clicking File,
   pointing to Send To, and then clicking Microsoft
   PowerPoint.
4. With Slide 1 of the presentation displayed in PowerPoint,
   change the slide layout for Slide 1 by completing the
   following steps:
   a. Click Format and then Slide Layout.
   b. Click the Title Slide layout in the Slide Layout
      Task Pane.
5. Click the Slide Design button on the Formatting
   toolbar and then click the *Satellite Dish* design template
   in the Apply a design template list box at the Slide
   Design Task Pane. (You will need to scroll down the list
   to display this template.)
6. Make the following changes to the presentation:
   a. Increase the font size and/or line spacing of the
      bulleted text in Slides 2 through 4 so the bulleted
      lists are better spaced on the slides.
   b. Consider inserting an appropriate clip art image in
      one or two of the slides. (If you cannot find an
      appropriate clip art image at the Insert Clip Art
      Task Pane, consider downloading a clip from the Microsoft Design Gallery Live Web
      site.)
   c. Add a transition and sound of your choosing to each slide.
7. Save the presentation and name it Internet Presentation.
8. Run the presentation.
9. Print the presentation as handouts with all four slides on the same page.
10. Close Internet Presentation.
11. Make Word the active program, close Word Outline 01, and then exit Word.

Using the Clipboard Task Pane

HINT

To delete one item from the Clipboard Task Pane, point to the item, click the down-pointing triangle, and then click Delete.

Use the Clipboard Task Pane to collect and paste multiple items. You can collect up to 24 different items and then paste them in various locations. Turn on the display of the Clipboard Task Pane by clicking Edit and then Office Clipboard or by clicking the Other Task Panes button (displays as a down-pointing triangle) located in the upper right corner of the current task pane, and then clicking Clipboard at the drop-down list. The Clipboard Task Pane displays at the right side of the screen in a manner similar to what you see in figure 6.3.

FIGURE

6.3 *Clipboard Task Pane*

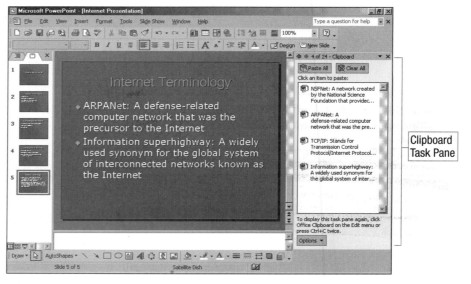

HINT

Click the Options button at the bottom of the Clipboard Task Pane to customize the display of the task pane.

Select data or an object you want to copy and then click the Copy button on the Standard toolbar. Continue selecting text or items and clicking the Copy button. To insert an item, position the insertion point in the desired location and then click the button in the Clipboard Task Pane representing the item. If the copied item is text, the first 50 characters display. When all desired items are inserted, click the Clear All button to remove any remaining items from the Clipboard Task Pane.

In exercise 2, you drew a text box in a slide and then pasted text inside the text box. In exercise 4, you will copy text in a Word document and then paste it in a slide containing a bulleted list placeholder. Since the slide contains a placeholder where you can insert the text, you do not need to draw a text box.

INTEGRATED *exercise* **4**

COLLECTING TEXT IN WORD AND PASTING IT IN A POWERPOINT SLIDE

1. In PowerPoint, open Internet Presentation.
2. Create a new Slide 5 by completing the following steps:
   a. Display Slide 4 and then click the New Slide button on the Formatting toolbar.
   b. Click the text *Click to add title* and then key **Internet Terminology**.

c. Click the text *Click to add text* and then copy terms from Word and paste them into slides by completing the following steps:
1) Open Word and then open Word Terms.
2) Display the Clipboard Task Pane by clicking Edit and then Office Clipboard.
3) Select the first term *(Information superhighway)* and its definition by triple-clicking with the mouse.
4) With the term and definition selected, click the Copy button on the Standard toolbar. (Notice that the copied item displays in the Clipboard Task Pane.)
5) Select the second term *(TCP/IP)* and its definition and then click the Copy button.
6) Select the third term *(ARPANet)* and its definition and then click the Copy button on the Clipboard toolbar.
7) Select the fourth term *(NSFNet)* and its definition and then click the Copy button on the Clipboard toolbar.
8) Click the button on the Taskbar representing Internet Presentation.
9) Click Edit and then Office Clipboard to display the Clipboard Task Pane.
10) Make sure the insertion point is positioned in the bulleted list placeholder and then click the item on the Clipboard Task Pane representing the term *ARPANet*.
11) Press the Enter key.
12) Click the item on the Clipboard Task Pane representing the term *Information superhighway*.

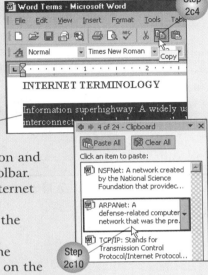

3. Create a new Slide 6 by completing the following steps:
   a. Click the New Slide button on the Standard toolbar.
   b. Click the text *Click to add title* and then key **Internet Terminology**.
   c. Click the text *Click to add text* and then paste terms in the slide by completing the following steps:
      1) Display the Clipboard Task Pane by clicking the Other Task Panes button (displays as a down-pointing triangle) located in the upper right corner of the task pane and then clicking *Clipboard* at the drop-down list.
      2) Make sure the insertion point is positioned in the bulleted list placeholder and then click the item on the Clipboard Task Pane representing the term *NFSNet*.
      3) Press the Enter key.
      4) Click the item on the Clipboard Task Pane representing the term *TCP/IP*.

4. Clear the Clipboard Task Pane by clicking the Clear All button located in the upper right corner of the task pane.
5. Close the Clipboard Task Pane by clicking the Close button (contains an *X*) located in the upper right corner of the task pane.

6. Make Slide 1 the active slide and then run the presentation.
7. Save the presentation again with the same name (Internet Presentation).
8. Print the six slides on one page.
9. Close Internet Presentation.
10. Make Word the active program, close Word Terms, and then exit Word.

Exporting an Outline to Word

A PowerPoint presentation can be exported to a Word document which can then be edited and formatted using Word's capabilities. You can print slides as handouts in PowerPoint; however, you may prefer to export the presentation to Word to have greater control over the formatting of the handouts. To export the presentation that is currently open, click File, point to Send To, and then click Microsoft Word. At the Send To Microsoft Word dialog box shown in figure 6.4, select the page layout you want to use in Word, and then click OK.

FIGURE

6.4 *Send To Microsoft Word Dialog Box*

The first four page layout options will export slides as they appear in PowerPoint with lines to the right or below the slides. The last option will export the text only as an outline. If you select the Paste link option, the Word document will be automatically updated whenever changes are made to the PowerPoint presentation.

EXPORTING A PRESENTATION AS AN OUTLINE TO WORD

1. Open Potential Presentation.
2. Create an outline in Word by completing the following steps:
   a. Click File, point to Send To, and then click Microsoft Word.
   b. At the Send To Microsoft Word dialog box, click the Outline only option.
   c. Click OK.
3. Save the Word document in the *PowerPoint Chapter 06* folder on your disk and name it Word Potential Outline.
4. Click the Print button on the Standard toolbar to print Word Potential Outline.
5. Close Word Potential Outline and then exit Word.
6. In PowerPoint, close Potential Presentation.

Saving a Presentation as an Outline/RTF

With the Save as type option at the Save As dialog box, you can save a presentation in a different format such as a Web page, a previous version of PowerPoint, a design template, and as an outline in rich text format (RTF). In exercise 6, you will use the *Outline/RTF* option save a PowerPoint presentation as an outline in Word in rich text format. In this format, the presentation loses graphical elements but retains the character formatting of the presentation.

SAVING A PRESENTATION IN OUTLINE/RTF FORMAT

1. Open Design Presentation.
2. Save the presentation as a Word outline in rich text format by completing the following steps:
   a. Click File and then Save As.
   b. At the Save As dialog box, key **Design Outline** in the File name text box.
   c. Click the down-pointing triangle at the right side of the Save as type option box and then click *Outline/RTF*

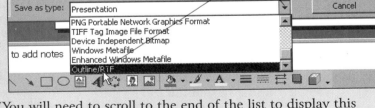

   at the drop-down list. (You will need to scroll to the end of the list to display this option.)
   d. Change the Save in option to the *PowerPoint Chapter 06* folder on your disk.
   e. Click the Save button.
3. Close Design Presentation.

4. Open and then close the Design Outline document in Word by completing the following steps:
   a. Open Word.
   b. Click the Open button on the Standard toolbar.
   c. At the Open dialog box, change the Look in option to the *PowerPoint Chapter 06* folder on your disk.
   d. Double-click *Design Outline* in the file list box.
   e. With the Design Outline document open, click the Print button on the Standard toolbar.
   f. Click File and then Close to close the Design Outline document.
   g. Exit Word.

Adding Action Buttons

HINT

Action buttons contain commonly understood symbols.

Action buttons are drawn objects on a slide that have a routine attached to them that is activated when the viewer or the speaker clicks the button. For example, you could include an action button that displays a specific Web page, a file in another program, or the next slide in the presentation. Creating an action button is a two-step process. The button is drawn using the AutoShapes button on the Drawing toolbar and then the action that will take place is defined in the Action Settings dialog box. Once an action button has been created it can be customized using the same techniques employed for customizing drawn objects. When the viewer or speaker moves the mouse over an action button during a presentation, the pointer changes to a hand with a finger pointing upward to indicate clicking will result in an action.

exercise 7

ADDING ACTION BUTTONS

1. Open Job Search Presentation.
2. Save the presentation with Save As in the *PowerPoint Chapter 06* folder on your disk and name the presentation Job Search Pres with Action.
3. Add an action button that will display the next slide on the title slide by completing the following steps:
   a. Make sure Slide 1 displays in the Slide pane.
   b. Draw an action button in the lower right corner of Slide 1 by completing the following steps:
      1) Click the AutoShapes button on the Drawing toolbar, point to Action Buttons, and then click Action Button: Forward or Next (second option from the left in the second row).
      2) Move the crosshair pointer to the lower right corner of Slide 1 and drag to create a button that is approximately 0.5 inch wide by 1 inch in height.

Step 3b1

3) At the Action Settings dialog box that displays, click OK. (The default setting is <u>H</u>yperlink to Next Slide.)
4) Deselect the action button.
4. Add an action button on the Slide Master that will display the next slide by completing the following steps:
   a. Change to the Slide Master view.
   b. Click the Ripple Slide Master miniature in the Outline/Slides pane.
   c. Click the A<u>u</u>toShapes button on the Drawing toolbar, point to Action Buttons, and then click Action Button: Forward or Next (second option from the left in the second row).
   d. Move the crosshair pointer to the lower right corner of the Slide Master and drag to create a button that is approximately 0.5 inch wide by 1 inch in height. (The button will overlap the Number Area on the Slide Master. Creating the action button on the slide master means the button will automatically appear on all slides except the title slide.)
   e. At the Action Settings dialog box, click OK. (The default setting is <u>H</u>yperlink to Next Slide.)
   f. Click the Normal View button on the View toolbar.
5. Click the Slide Show button on the View toolbar and then navigate through the slide show by clicking the action button. At the last slide, click in the slide (outside the action button).
6. Save and then close Job Search Pres with Action.

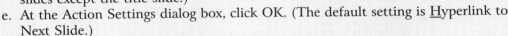

In exercise 7, creating the action button on the Slide Master saved the work of drawing a button on each slide. However, the next slide action button on the last slide does not make sense since there is no next slide. In the next exercise you will create action buttons using the copy and paste routine, which will still be efficient but allows you to control to which slide a button is pasted.

 exercise 8

COPYING AND PASTING ACTION BUTTONS

1. Open Potential Presentation.
2. Save the presentation with Save As in the *PowerPoint Chapter 06* folder on your disk and name the presentation Potential Pres with Action.
3. Add an action button that will display the next slide on the title slide by completing the following steps:
   a. Make sure Slide 1 displays in the Slide pane.
   b. Draw an action button in the lower right corner of Slide 1 that will display the next slide by completing steps similar to those in exercise 7, step 3b (except, do not deselect the action button).
   c. With the action button selected, click the down-pointing triangle at the right of the Fill Color button on the Drawing toolbar, and then click the green color.

d. With the action button still selected, click the Copy button on the Standard toolbar.

e. Display Slide 2 and then click the Paste button on the toolbar.

f. Paste the action button to Slides 3 through 5 by completing steps similar to those in 3e.

4. Create an action button on the last slide that returns to the beginning of the presentation by completing the following steps:

a. Display Slide 6 in the Slide pane.

b. Click AutoShapes, point to Action Buttons, and then click Action Button: Home (second from the left in the first row).

c. Drag to create a button in the lower right corner of Slide 6 that is approximately 0.5 inch wide by 1 inch in height.

d. At the Action Settings dialog box with the Hyperlink to First Slide option selected, click OK.

e. With the button selected, click the Fill Color button on the Drawing toolbar. (This changes the color of the button to green.)

f. Deselect the button.

5. Display Slide 1 in the Slide pane and then run the presentation. Navigate through the slide show by clicking the action button. When you click the action button on the last slide the first slide displays. End the slide show by pressing the Esc key.

6. Print the presentation as handouts with all six slides on one page.

7. Save and then close Potential Pres with Action.

HINT
Hyperlinks are active when running the presentation, not when creating it.

You can specify that an action button links to a Web site during a presentation. To do this, draw an Action button. At the Action Settings dialog box, click the Hyperlink to option, click the down-pointing triangle at the right side of the Hyperlink to option box, and then click URL at the drop-down list. At the Hyperlink To URL dialog box, key the Web address in the URL text box, and then click OK. Click OK to close the Action Settings dialog box.

Other actions you can link to using the Hyperlink to drop-down list include: Next Slide, Previous Slide, First Slide, Last Slide, Last Slide Viewed, End Show, Custom Show, Slide, Other PowerPoint Presentation, and Other File. The Action Settings dialog box can also be used to run another program when the action button is selected, to run a macro, or to activate an embedded object.

LINKING TO A WEB SITE AND ANOTHER PRESENTATION

1. Open Job Search Presentation.

2. Save the presentation with Save As in the *PowerPoint Chapter 06* folder on your disk and then name the presentation Job Search Pres with Action.

3. Add an action button that will link to another presentation by completing the following steps:

a. Display Slide 4 in the Slide pane.

b. Click AutoShapes, point to Action Buttons, and then click Action Button: Help (third from the left in the top row).

POWERPOINT

c. Draw the action button in the lower right corner of Slide 4. (You determine the size of the button.)

d. At the Action Settings dialog box, click the <u>H</u>yperlink to option.

e. Click the down-pointing triangle at the right side of the <u>H</u>yperlink to option box and then click *Other PowerPoint Presentation* at the drop-down list. (You will need to scroll down the list to display this option.)

f. At the Hyperlink to Other PowerPoint Presentation dialog box, navigate to the *PowerPoint Chapter 06* folder on your disk, and then double-click the presentation named *Contacts Presentation*.

g. At the Hyperlink to Slide dialog box, click OK.

h. Click OK to close the Action Settings dialog box.

i. With the button selected, click the down-pointing triangle at the right side of the Fill Color button on the Drawing toolbar, and then click a color of your choosing that follows the color scheme of the design template.

j. Deselect the action button.

4. Add an action button that will link to a Web site address by completing the following steps:

a. Display Slide 5 in the Slide pane.

b. Click A<u>u</u>toShapes, point to Act<u>i</u>on Buttons, and then click Action Button: Information (fourth from the left in the top row).

c. Draw the action button in the lower right corner of Slide 5.

d. At the Action Settings dialog box, click the <u>H</u>yperlink to option.

e. Click the down-pointing triangle at the right of the <u>H</u>yperlink to option box, and then click *URL* at the drop-down list.

f. At the Hyperlink To URL dialog box, key **www.jobresourceonline.com** and then press Enter.

g. Click OK to close the Action Settings dialog box.

h. With the button selected, click the Fill Color button on the Drawing toolbar.

i. Click outside the button to deselect it.

5. Run the presentation by completing the following steps:

a. Make sure you are connected to the Internet.

b. Display Slide 1 in the Slide pane.

c. Click the Slide Show button on the View toolbar.

d. Navigate through the slide show to Slide 4.

e. Click the action button on Slide 4. (This displays Slide 1 of the Contacts Presentation.)

f. Navigate through the three slides in the Contacts Presentation. Continue clicking the mouse button until you return to Slide 4 of the Job Search Pres with Action presentation.

g. Display Slide 5 and then click the action button. (If you are connected to the Internet, the Job Resources Online Web site displays.)

h. Click a few links at the Job Resources Online site.

i. When you are finished with the Job Resources Online site, close Internet Explorer (click File and then Close).

j. Continue viewing the remainder of the presentation.

6. Print the presentation as handouts with all nine slides on one page.

7. Save and then close Job Search Pres with Action.

Creating Hyperlinks

Insert Hyperlink

In exercise 9, you created hyperlinks using action buttons. You can also create hyperlinks with options at the Insert Hyperlink dialog box shown in figure 6.5. To display this dialog box, select a key word or phrase in a slide, and then click the Insert Hyperlink button on the Standard toolbar. At the Insert Hyperlink dialog box, key the Web address in the Address text box, and then click OK.

FIGURE

6.5 *Insert Hyperlink Dialog Box*

POWERPOINT

1. Open Job Search Presentation.
2. Save the presentation with Save As in the *PowerPoint Chapter 06* folder on your disk and name the presentation Job Search Pres with Hyperlinks.
3. Add a new Slide 6 by completing the following steps:
   a. Display Slide 5 in the Slide pane.
   b. Click the New Slide button on the Formatting toolbar.
   c. Click the Title Slide layout in the Slide Layout Task Pane.
   d. Click the text *Click to add title* and then key **Internet Job Resources**.
   e. Click the text *Click to add subtitle* and then key **Job Resources Online**, press Enter, and then key **America's Job Bank**.
4. Add a hyperlink to the Internet Job Resources site by completing the following steps:
   a. Select *Job Resources Online* in Slide 6.
   b. Click the Insert Hyperlink button on the Standard toolbar.
   c. At the Insert Hyperlink dialog box, key **www.jobresourceonline.com** in the Address text box. (PowerPoint automatically inserts *http://* at the beginning of the address.)
   d. Click OK.

Step 4c

5. Add a hyperlink to the America's Job Bank site by completing the following steps:
   a. Select *America's Job Bank* in Slide 6.
   b. Click the Insert Hyperlink button on the Standard toolbar.
   c. At the Insert Hyperlink dialog box, key **www.ajb.dni.us** in the Address text box.
   d. Click OK.
6. Run the presentation by completing the following steps:
   a. Make sure you are connected to the Internet.
   b. Display Slide 1 in the Slide pane.
   c. Click the Slide Show button on the View toolbar.
   d. Navigate through the slides. When you reach Slide 6, click the *Job Resources Online* hyperlink.
   e. Scroll through the Job Resources Online site and then close Internet Explorer.
   f. Click the *America's Job Bank* hyperlink.
   g. Scroll through the America's Job Bank site and then close Internet Explorer.
   h. Continue viewing the remainder of the presentation.
7. Print only Slide 6 of the presentation.
8. Save and then close Job Search Pres with Hyperlinks.

Setting Automatic Times for Slides

The time a slide remains on the screen during a slide show can be manually set using the Automatically after option at the Slide Transition Task Pane. Key the number of seconds in the seconds text box and the time is applied to the current slide. If you want the time to apply to all slides in the presentation, click the Apply to All Slides button.

Rehearse
Timings

Next

Pause

Repeat

Applying the same time to all slides is not very practical unless the same amount of text occurs on every slide. In most cases, some slides should be left on the screen longer than others. Use the Rehearse Timings feature to help set the times for slides as you practice delivering the slide show.

To set times for slides using Rehearse Timings, display the presentation in Slide Sorter view, and then click the Rehearse Timings button on the Slide Sorter toolbar. The first slide displays in Slide Show view and the Rehearsal toolbar displays on the slide. The buttons on the Rehearsal toolbar are identified in figure 6.6.

When the slide displays on the screen, the timer on the Rehearsal toolbar begins. Click the Next button on the Rehearsal toolbar when the slide has displayed for the appropriate amount of time. If you want to stop the timer, click the Pause button. Click the Pause button again to resume the timer. Use the Repeat button on the Rehearsal toolbar if you get off track and want to reset the time for the current slide. Continue through the presentation until the slide show is complete. After the last slide, a message displays showing the total time for the presentation and asks if you want to record the new slide timings. At this message, click Yes to set the times for each slide recorded during the rehearsal.

FIGURE

6.6 *Rehearsal Toolbar*

Use options at the Set Up Show dialog box shown in figure 6.7 to control the slide show. Display this dialog box by clicking Slide Show and then Set Up Show.
Use options in the Show type section to specify the type of slide show you want to display. If you want the presentation to be totally automatic and run continuously until you end the show, click the Loop continuously until 'Esc' check box to insert a check mark. In the Advance slides section, the Using timings, if present option should be selected by default. Select Manually if you want to advance the slides using the mouse during the slide show instead of the slides advancing using your preset times.

HINT

If your computer is equipped with a sound card, microphone, and speakers, you can record a voice narration for a presentation.

6.7 *Set Up Show Dialog Box*

USING REHEARSE TIMINGS TO SET TIMES FOR SLIDES

1. Open Job Search Presentation.
2. Save the presentation with Save As in the *PowerPoint Chapter 06* folder on your disk and name the presentation Job Search Pres with Timings.
3. Set times for the slides to display during a slide show by completing the following steps:
   a. Display the presentation in Slide Sorter view.
   b. Click the Rehearse Timings button on the Slide Sorter toolbar.
   c. The first slide displays in Slide Show view and the Rehearsal toolbar displays. Wait until the time displayed for the current slide reaches four seconds and then click Next. (If you miss the time, click the Repeat button to reset the clock back to zero for the current slide.)
   d. Set the times for remaining slides as follows:

Slide 2	=	8 seconds
Slide 3	=	6 seconds
Slide 4	=	8 seconds
Slide 5	=	4 seconds
Slide 6	=	6 seconds
Slide 7	=	8 seconds
Slide 8	=	8 seconds
Slide 9	=	6 seconds

   e. After the last slide has displayed, click Yes at the message asking if you want to record the new slide timings.

4. Set up the slide show to run continuously by completing the following steps:
   a. Click Sli_de Show and then select _Set Up Show.
   b. At the Set Up Show dialog box, click the _Loop continuously until 'Esc' check box.
   c. Click OK to close the Set Up Show dialog box.
5. Click Slide 1 and then click the Slide Show button on the View toolbar. The slide show will start and run continuously. Watch the presentation until it has started for the second time and then end the show by pressing the Esc key.
6. Save and then close Job Search Pres with Timings.

Step 4b

Creating a Summary Slide

Summary Slide

A summary slide is a slide created by PowerPoint that lists the titles of the other slides in your presentation. Create a summary slide if you want to include a slide at the beginning of the presentation that outlines what topics will follow. To create a summary slide, change to the Slide Sorter view, click the slides you want included in the summary slide, and then click the Summary Slide button on the Slide Sorter toolbar. The Summary Slide is inserted immediately before the first selected slide and includes the titles from the selected slides in a bulleted list.

exercise 12

CREATING A SUMMARY SLIDE

1. Open Job Search Presentation.
2. Save the presentation with Save As in the *PowerPoint Chapter 06* folder on your disk and name the presentation Job Search with Summary.
3. Create a summary slide between Slides 1 and 2 by completing the following steps:
   a. Display the presentation in Slide Sorter view.
   b. Click Slide 2 to select it, hold down the Shift key, and then click Slide 9. (This selects Slides 2 through 9.)
   c. Click the Summary Slide button on the Slide Sorter toolbar. (This creates a new Slide 2 containing the titles of Slides 2 through 9 in a bulleted list.)

Step 3c

4. Display Slide 1 in Normal view.
5. Run the presentation. (Notice the new summary slide [Slide 2].)
6. Print only Slide 2.
7. Save and then close Job Search with Summary.

CHAPTER summary

- Use the Copy and Paste buttons on the Standard toolbar to copy data from one program to another.
- Import a Word document into a PowerPoint presentation by opening the document in Word, clicking File, pointing to Send To, and then clicking Microsoft PowerPoint.
- Use the Clipboard Task Pane to collect up to 24 different items and paste them in various locations within or between programs.
- Clear all items from the Clipboard Task Pane by clicking the Clear All button located toward the top of the task pane.
- Export a PowerPoint presentation to a Word document by clicking File, pointing to Send To, and then clicking Microsoft Word. Choose the desired page layout for the Word document at the Send To Microsoft Word dialog box.
- Save a presentation in a different format, such as Outline/RTF format, with the Save as type option at the Save As dialog box.
- Action buttons are drawn objects on a slide that have a routine attached, such as displaying the next slide, the first slide, a Web site, or another PowerPoint presentation.
- Create an action button by clicking the AutoShapes button on the Drawing toolbar, pointing to Action Buttons, and then clicking the desired button. Drag in the slide to create the button.
- Create a hyperlink in a document by selecting text in the slide and then clicking the Insert Hyperlink button on the Standard toolbar. At the Insert Hyperlink dialog box, key the Web site address or file location, and then click OK.
- Set times for slides by displaying the presentation in Slide Sorter view and then clicking the Rehearse Timings button on the Slide Sorter toolbar. Use the timer and buttons on the Rehearsal toolbar to establish specific times for each slide.
- Use options at the Set Up Show dialog to control the slide show.
- A summary slide lists the titles of the other slides in a presentation. Create a summary slide by displaying the presentation in Slide Sorter view, clicking the slides to be included, and then clicking the Summary Slide button on the Slide Sorter toolbar.

COMMANDS review

Command	Mouse
Import Word document in PowerPoint presentation	Click File, Send To, Microsoft PowerPoint
Display Clipboard Task Pane	Click Edit, Office Clipboard; or click Other Task Panes button on task pane, then click Clipboard
Export presentation to Word document	Click File, Send To, Microsoft Word
Display action buttons	Click AutoShapes, point to Action Buttons

Display Insert Hyperlink dialog box	Click Insert Hyperlink button on Standard toolbar
Display Rehearsal toolbar	Click Rehearse Timings button on Slide Sorter toolbar
Display Set Up Show dialog box	Click Slide Show, Set Up Show
Create summary slide	Click slides to be included, then click Summary Slide button on Slide Sorter toolbar

CONCEPTS check

Completion: On a blank sheet of paper, indicate the correct term, symbol, or command.

1. Use the Copy and Paste buttons on this toolbar to copy data from one program to another.
2. To import a Word document into a PowerPoint presentation, click File on the Menu bar, point to this option, and then click Microsoft PowerPoint.
3. Using the Clipboard Task Pane, you can collect up to this number of items and then paste them in various locations.
4. Click Edit on the Menu bar and then click this option to display the Clipboard Task Pane.
5. Click this button in the Clipboard Task Pane to remove all items from the task pane.
6. With this option at the Save As dialog box, you can save a presentation in a different format.
7. Insert this action button in a slide to display the next slide in the presentation.
8. Insert this action button in a slide to display the first slide in the presentation.
9. Draw an action button in a slide and this dialog box displays.
10. To rehearse times for slides, display the presentation in Slide Sorter view, and then click this button on the Slide Sorter toolbar.
11. Click this button on the Rehearsal toolbar if you get off track and want to reset the time for the current slide.
12. This dialog box contains the Loop continuously until 'Esc' option.

SKILLS check

Assessment 1

1. Open Herbal Presentation.
2. Save the presentation with Save As in the *PowerPoint Chapter 06* folder on your disk and name the presentation Enhanced Herbal Pres.
3. Copy and paste an Excel chart to Slide 2 by completing the following steps:
   a. Display Slide 2 in the Slide pane.
   b. Open Excel and then open the workbook named Sales Projections (located in the *PowerPoint Chapter 06* folder).
   c. Copy the chart to Slide 2 in the presentation.
   d. Resize and move the chart so it fills most of the slide below the title.
   e. Display the Sales Projections workbook, close the workbook, and then exit Excel.

POWERPOINT

4. Copy and paste text from Word to Slide 4 and Slide 5 by completing the following steps:
   a. Display Slide 4 in the Slide pane.
   b. Draw a text box in the slide.
   c. Open Word and then open the document named Remedies.
   d. Copy the first three terms and paragraphs in the document to the text box in Slide 4.
   e. Add a blank line above *Chamomile* and above *Evening Primrose Oil*.
   f. Select the text in the placeholder and change the font size to 24 and turn on bold.
   g. Move and/or resize the placeholder so it fills most of the slide below the title.
5. Copy and paste the last two terms and paragraphs in the Remedies document to Slide 5 following steps similar to those in step 4.
6. Apply an animation scheme of your choosing to all slides in the presentation.
7. Run the presentation beginning with Slide 1.
8. Print the presentation as handouts with all six slides on one page.
9. Save and then close Enhanced Herbal Pres.

Assessment 2

1. Open Enhanced Herbal Pres.
2. Export the presentation to Word as an outline.
3. Save the Word document in the *PowerPoint Chapter 06* folder on your disk and name it Word Herbal Outline.
4. Click the Print button on the Standard toolbar to print Word Herbal Outline.
5. Close Word Herbal Outline and then exit Word.
6. In PowerPoint, close Enhanced Herbal Pres.

Assessment 3

1. Make sure PowerPoint is open and then open Word.
2. With Word the active program, open Word Outline 02 (located in the *PowerPoint Chapter 06* folder on your disk).
3. Import the document into PowerPoint.
4. Make the following changes to the presentation:
   a. With Slide 1 of the presentation displayed in PowerPoint, change the slide layout to Title Slide.
   b. Apply the Cascade slide design template to all slides in the presentation.
   c. Increase the font size and/or line spacing of the bulleted text in Slides 2 through 4 so the bulleted lists are better spaced in the slides.
   d. Consider inserting an appropriate clip art image in one or two of the slides. (If you cannot find an appropriate clip art image at the Insert Clip Art Task Pane, consider downloading a clip from the Microsoft Design Gallery Live Web site.)
   e. Apply an animation scheme of your choosing to all slides in the presentation.
5. Save the presentation and name it Telecom Presentation.
6. Run the presentation.
7. Print the presentation as handouts with all four slides on the same page.
8. Close Telecom Presentation.
9. Make Word the active program, close Word Outline 02, and then exit Word.

Assessment 4

1. Open Perennials Presentation.
2. Save the presentation with Save As in the *PowerPoint Chapter 06* folder on your disk and name the presentation Enhanced Perennials Pres.
3. Create the following action buttons:

a. Insert an action button in the lower right corner of Slides 1 through 7 that displays the next slide (change to a fill color that matches the design template color scheme).

b. Insert an action button in the lower right corner of Slide 8 that displays the first slide in the presentation.

c. Insert a second action button in the lower right corner of Slide 2 that will link to another PowerPoint presentation named Maintenance Presentation (located in the *PowerPoint Chapter 06* folder).

4. Display Slide 8 and then create a hyperlink with the text *Better Homes and Gardens* that connects to the Web site www.bhg.com.

5. Make sure you are connected to the Internet and then run the presentation beginning with Slide 1. Navigate through the slide show by clicking the next action button and display the connected presentation by clicking the information action button. At Slide 8, click the *Better Homes and Gardens* hyperlink (if you are connected to the Internet). Close the subscription page that displays and then navigate the magazine Web site. After viewing a few Web pages in the magazine, close your Web browser. When you click the action button on the last slide the first slide displays. End the slide show by pressing the Esc key.

6. Print the presentation as handouts with all eight slides on one page.

7. Save and then close Enhanced Perennials Pres.

Assessment 5

1. Open Perennials Presentation.

2. Save the presentation with Save As in the *PowerPoint Chapter 06* folder on your disk and name the presentation Rehearsed Perennials Pres.

3. Create a summary slide between Slides 1 and 2 that includes topics for Slides 2 through 8.

4. Use the Rehearse Timings feature to set the following times for the slides to display during a slide show:

Slide 1	=	3 seconds
Slide 2	=	7 seconds
Slide 3	=	4 seconds
Slide 4	=	6 seconds
Slide 5	=	5 seconds
Slide 6	=	6 seconds
Slide 7	=	6 seconds
Slide 8	=	7 seconds
Slide 9	=	4 seconds

5. Set up the slide show to run continuously.

6. Run the presentation beginning with Slide 1. Watch the slide show until the presentation has started for the second time and then end the show.

7. Print the presentation as handouts with all nine slides on one page.

8. Save and then close Rehearsed Perennials Pres.

Assessment 6

1. When running some presentations, you may decide that certain slides in your presentation are not relevant to a specific audience. In this situation you can hide slides in your presentation. Use PowerPoint's Help feature to learn how to hide slides in a presentation.

2. Open Perennials Presentation.

3. Hide Slides 6 and 7.

4. Run the presentation beginning with Slide 1 (Slides 6 and 7 will not display).

5. Close Perennials Presentation without saving the changes.

POWERPOINT

LINKING AND EMBEDDING OBJECTS AND FILES

PERFORMANCE OBJECTIVES

Upon successful completion of chapter 7, you will be able to:
- Embed a Word table in a PowerPoint presentation
- Embed and edit an Excel chart in a PowerPoint presentation
- Link a Word table in a PowerPoint presentation
- Link and edit an Excel chart in a PowerPoint presentation
- Break a link between a source and destination program
- Launch another program from a PowerPoint presentation
- Create a folder
- Select, copy, delete, and rename presentations

PowerPoint Chapter 07

Share objects between programs in the Microsoft Office suite by copying and pasting objects, copying and embedding objects, or copying and linking objects. In chapter 6, you learned how to copy and paste data and objects. In this chapter you will learn how to copy and embed and copy and link objects between programs. You will also learn some basic file maintenance activities such as creating a folder and selecting, copying, deleting, and renaming presentations.

Linking and Embedding Objects

One of the reasons the Microsoft Office suite is used extensively in business is because it allows data from an individual program to seamlessly integrate into another program. For example, a chart depicting the sales projections created in Excel can easily be added to a slide in a presentation to the company board of directors on the new budget forecast.

Integration is the process of completing a file by adding parts to it from other sources. Duplicating data that already exist in another program should be a rare instance. In chapter 6, you learned how to insert a chart from Excel and text from Word into slides in a PowerPoint presentation using the copy and paste method. The copy and paste method is fast and is used in situations where the content is not likely to change. If the content is dynamic, the copy and paste method becomes problematic and prone to error. To illustrate this point, assume one of the outcomes from the presentation to the board of directors is a revision to the sales projections. The chart that was originally created in Excel has to be updated to reflect the new projections. The existing chart in PowerPoint needs to be deleted and then the revised chart in Excel copied and pasted to the slide. Both Excel and PowerPoint need to be opened and edited to reflect this change in projection. In this case, copying and pasting the chart was not efficient.

In other situations, the source of the content may not be readily apparent, requiring the user to go searching for the program that was used for the original task. Individual programs may also be updated without the corresponding updates to other programs to which the data was copied, thus resulting in potential errors.

To eliminate the inefficiency of the copy and paste method, you can integrate data between programs using *object linking and embedding*. Object linking and embedding (OLE) is the sharing of data from one program to another. An object can be text in a document, data in a table, a chart, a picture, a slide, or any combination of data that you would like to share between programs. The program that was used to create the object is called the *source* and the program the object is linked or embedded to is called the *destination*.

Embedding versus Linking

Embedding and linking are two methods that can be used to integrate data in addition to the copy and paste routine discussed in chapter 6. When an object is embedded, the content in the object is stored in both the source and the destination programs. When you edit an embedded object in the destination program, the source program in which the program was created opens. If the content in the object is changed in the source program, the change is not reflected in the destination program and vice versa.

Linking inserts a code into the destination file connecting the destination to the name and location of the source object. The object itself is not stored within the destination file. If a change is made to the content in the source program, the destination program reflects the change automatically.

Your decision to integrate data by embedding or linking will depend on whether the data is dynamic or static. If the data is dynamic, then linking the object is the most efficient method of integration. Static data can be embedded or copied and pasted from the source to the destination program.

Embedding Objects

As previously discussed, an object that is embedded will be stored in both the source *and* the destination programs. The content of the object can be edited in *either* the source or the destination; however, a change made in one will not be reflected in the other. The difference between copying and pasting and embedding is that embedded objects can be edited with the source program's editing menus and toolbars. Figure 7.1 illustrates a table from Word embedded in a slide in PowerPoint that has been opened for editing. Notice the Word options on the menu and toolbars displayed in figure 7.1, as well as the horizontal and vertical ruler bars from Word that are visible within the editing window.

7.1 Editing a Word Table Embedded in PowerPoint

Word's menus and toolbars are active.

Double-click embedded Word object to edit it. Word's ruler bars become active.

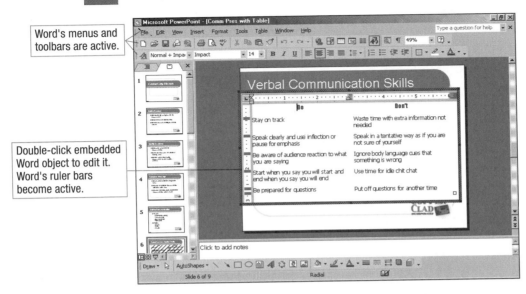

Since embedded objects are edited within the source program, the source program must reside on the computer when the presentation is opened for editing. If you are preparing a presentation that will be edited on another computer, you may want to check before embedding any objects to verify that the other computer has the same programs. You would complete the following basic steps to embed an object from one program to another:

1. Open both programs and open both files needed for the integration.
2. Activate the source program.
3. Select the desired object.
4. Copy the selected object using the Copy button on the Standard toolbar.
5. Activate the destination program.
6. Move to the location where you want the object inserted.
7. Click Edit and then Paste Special.
8. At the Paste Special dialog box, click the source of the object in the As list box, and then click OK.

INTEGRATED

EMBEDDING A WORD TABLE IN A POWERPOINT PRESENTATION

1. In PowerPoint, open Communication Presentation from the *PowerPoint Chapter 07* folder on your disk.
2. Save the presentation with Save As and name it Comm Pres with Table.
3. Copy and embed a Word table in Slide 5 by completing the following steps:
   a. Open Microsoft Word.
   b. Open the Verbal Skills document from the *PowerPoint Chapter 07* folder on your disk.
   c. Below the second paragraph is a two-column table set in a different font that begins with the title row *Do,* and *Don't.* Select the table by completing the following steps:
      1) Click in any text below *Do* or *Don't.*

2) Click Table on the Menu bar, point to Select, and then click Table.

d. Click the Copy button on the Standard toolbar.
e. Click the button on the Taskbar representing PowerPoint.
f. Display Slide 5 in the Slide pane.
g. Click the New Slide button on the Formatting toolbar.
h. Click the Title Only slide layout in the Slide Layout Task Pane.
i. Click Edit and then Paste Special.
j. At the Paste Special dialog box, click *Microsoft Word Document Object* in the As list box, and then click OK.
k. Resize the table as large as possible without overlapping the logo at the bottom right of the slide.
l. Deselect the table
m. Click the text *Click to add title* and then key **Verbal Communication Skills**.

4. Display Slide 1 in the Slide pane and then run the presentation.
5. Print only Slide 6 (this is the new slide you created).
6. Save and then close Comm Pres with Table.
7. Switch to Word, close Verbal Skills, and then exit Word.

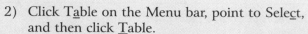

Editing an Embedded Object

Once an object has been embedded it can be edited by double-clicking the object. When you double-click an embedded object, the object displays in an editing window with the source program's menu options and toolbars displayed in the current program (see figure 7.1). Make any changes necessary using the normal editing features available in the source program and then click outside the object to exit the source program's editing tools.

Click to select an embedded object and then use the white sizing handles that appear around the object to move and/or size it. Embedded objects can also be animated or edited by the same techniques as used in editing drawn objects discussed in chapter 5.

INTEGRATED

EMBEDDING AND EDITING AN EXCEL CHART IN A SLIDE

1. In PowerPoint, open Comm Pres with Table.
2. Open Microsoft Excel.
3. Open the workbook named Nonverbal Cues from the *PowerPoint Chapter 07* folder on your disk.
4. Copy and embed the chart to a slide by completing the following steps:
   a. Click the chart to select it.
   b. Click the Copy button on the Standard toolbar.

c. Click the button on the Taskbar representing PowerPoint.

d. Display Slide 6 in the Slide pane.

e. Click the New Slide button on the Formatting toolbar.

f. Click the Title Only slide layout in the Slide Layout Task Pane.

g. Click Edit and then Paste Special.

h. In the Paste Special dialog box, make sure *Microsoft Excel Chart Object* is selected in the As list box, and then click OK.

5. Edit the chart in the slide by completing the following steps:

   a. Double-click the chart.

   b. Click Chart and then Chart Type.

   c. At the Chart Type dialog box, click Bar in the Chart type list box.

   d. Click the first sub-type in the second row in the Chart sub-type section.

   e. Click OK.

   f. Click Chart and then Chart Options.

   g. At the Chart Options dialog box, with the Titles tab selected, change the chart title to **Cues Causing a Response**.

   h. Click the Data Labels tab.

   i. At the Chart Options dialog box with the Data Labels tab selected, click the Category name option to remove the check mark and then click the Value option to remove the check mark.

   j. Click OK to close the Chart Options dialog box.

   k. Right-click one of the blue bars inside the chart and then click Format Data Series at the shortcut menu.

   l. At the Format Data Series dialog box with the Patterns tab selected, click a yellow color in the Area section that closely matches the yellow of the accent line in the slide.

   m. Click OK to close the Format Data Series dialog box.

   n. Click outside the chart to exit editing in Excel.

   o. Resize the chart so it fills the slide without overlapping the accent line or logo.

   p. Key **Nonverbal Cues** as the title for the slide.

6. Display Slide 1 in the Slide pane and then run the presentation.

7. Print only Slide 7 (this is the new slide containing the chart).

8. Save and then close Comm Pres with Table.

9. Switch to Excel, close Nonverbal Cues, and then exit Excel.

Linking Objects

If the content of the object that will be integrated between programs is likely to change, then the object should be linked from the source program to the destination program. Linking the object establishes a direct connection between the source and destination program. The object will be stored in the source program only. The destination program will have a code inserted into it that indicates the name and location of the source of the object. Whenever the document containing the link is opened, a message displays saying that the document contains links and the user is prompted to update the links. This process of updating links is referred to as *Dynamic Data Exchange* (DDE). You would complete these basic steps to link an object from one program to another:

1. Open both programs and open both files needed for the link.
2. Activate the source program.
3. Select the desired object.
4. Click the Copy button on the Standard toolbar.
5. Activate the destination program.
6. Move to the location where you want the object inserted.
7. Click Edit and then Paste Special.
8. At the Paste Special dialog box, click the source program for the object in the As list box.
9. Click the Paste link option located at the left side of the As list box.
10. Click OK to close the Paste Special dialog box.

INTEGRATED exercise 3

LINKING EXCEL CHARTS TO A POWERPOINT PRESENTATION

1. In PowerPoint, open Funds Presentation from the *PowerPoint Chapter 07* folder on your disk.
2. Save the presentation with Save As in the *PowerPoint Chapter 07* folder on your disk and name the presentation Funds Pres with Links.
3. Open Microsoft Excel.
4. Open Excel Workbook 01 from the *PowerPoint Chapter 07* folder on your disk.
5. Save the workbook by completing the following steps:
   a. Click File and then Save As.
   b. At the Save As dialog box, key **Funds Workbook 01**.
   c. Click the Save button.
6. Copy and link the chart to a slide in the presentation by completing the following steps:
   a. Click the chart to select it.
   b. Click the Copy button on the Standard toolbar.
   c. Click the button on the Taskbar representing PowerPoint.
   d. Display Slide 2 in the Slide pane.
   e. Click Edit and then Paste Special.
   f. In the Paste Special dialog box, make sure *Microsoft Excel Chart Object* is selected in the As list box.
   g. Click the Paste link option.
   h. Click OK.

i. Increase the size of the chart in the slide so it fills a good portion of the slide below the title. Move the chart so it appears balanced below the title.

7. Click the button on the Taskbar representing Excel and then close Funds Workbook 01.
8. Open Excel Workbook 02.
9. Save the workbook with Save As and name it Funds Workbook 02.
10. Link the chart in the workbook to Slide 3 by completing steps similar to those in step 6.
11. In PowerPoint, print the presentation as handouts with all slides on one page (the fourth slide is blank, except for the title).
12. Display Slide 1 in the Slide pane and then run the presentation.
13. Save and then close Funds Pres with Links.
14. Click the button on the Taskbar representing Excel, close Funds Workbook 02, and then exit Excel.

Editing Linked Objects

Linked objects are edited in the source program in which they were created. Open the document, workbook, or presentation in which the object was created, make the changes as required, and then save and close the file. If both the source and destination programs are open at the same time, the changed content is reflected immediately in both programs. In exercise 4, you will make changes to information in the Excel charts, and this will update the charts in the PowerPoint presentation.

INTEGRATED

CHANGING DATA IN LINKED CHARTS

1. Open Excel and then open Funds Workbook 01.
2. Make the following changes to the data in the cells in the workbook:
   a. Change B2 from *18%* to *10%*.
   b. Change B3 from *28%* to *20%*.
3. Save the workbook again with the same name (Funds Workbook 01).
4. Close Funds Workbook 01.
5. Open Funds Workbook 02.
6. Make the following changes to the data in the cells in the worksheet:
   a. Change B2 from *13%* to *17%*.
   b. Change B3 from *9%* to *4%*.
   c. Change B6 from *15%* to *19%*.
7. Save the workbook again with the same name (Funds Workbook 02).
8. Close Funds Workbook 02.
9. Exit Excel.
10. With PowerPoint the active program, open Funds Pres with Links.
11. At the message telling you that the presentation contains links, click the Update Links button.
12. Save the presentation with the same name (Funds Pres with Links).
13. Print the presentation as handouts with all slides on one page. (The fourth slide will be blank, except for the title.)
14. Close Funds Pres with Links.

Breaking a Link

HINT

Control how linked objects are updated with options at the Links dialog box.

If you linked an object from one program to another and then determined afterward that the data are not likely to change, you can break the link between the two files. Breaking the link does not remove the object from the destination program. It removes the direct connection between the source and the destination file. To do this, open the destination file, click Edit and then Links. At the Links dialog box as shown in figure 7.2, click the linked object in the Links list box, and then click the Break Link button. The object becomes an embedded object in the destination file and will no longer be updated if changes occur to the source.

FIGURE

7.2 Links Dialog Box

To break a link, click the desired object in this list box and then click the Break Link button.

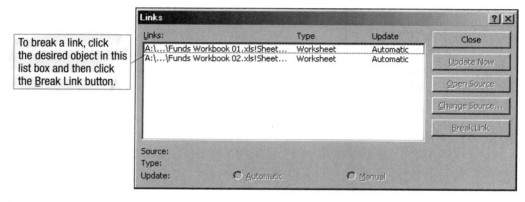

Linking to Other Programs

In chapter 6, you learned how to create action buttons on slides that could be used to jump to other slides within the presentation, to another PowerPoint presentation, or to a Web site on the Internet. You have also learned in this chapter how to embed and link objects from other programs. Sometimes you may want to create a link in a presentation that will launch another program altogether. For example, in the previous exercises, you linked an Excel chart to a slide in a PowerPoint presentation. What if you wanted to launch Excel instead and have the worksheet and chart display side by side? To do this, you can create an action button on the slide as discussed in chapter 6, or you can select a word in a slide, click Slide Show, and then click Action Settings. This displays the Action Settings dialog box where you can specify the file to which you want to create the hyperlink.

When a program is launched from a PowerPoint presentation, the other program is opened in its own window on top of the slide show. When the other program is exited, the presentation resumes from the slide where it was left.

LAUNCHING OTHER PROGRAMS FROM A POWERPOINT PRESENTATION

1. Open Communication Presentation.
2. Save the presentation with Save As in the *PowerPoint Chapter 07* folder on your disk and name the presentation Comm Pres with Action.
3. Create a link that will launch Excel from a slide in the presentation by completing the following steps:
   a. Display Slide 5 in the Slide pane.
   b. Select the word *Verbal* in the slide.
   c. Click Sli_d_e Show on the Menu bar and then click _A_ction Settings at the drop-down menu.
   d. At the Action Settings dialog box, click the _H_yperlink to option.
   e. Click the down-pointing triangle at the right of the _H_yperlink to option box, and then click *Other File* at the drop-down list.

   f. At the Hyperlink to Other File dialog box, navigate to the *PowerPoint Chapter 07* folder on your disk, and then double-click the Excel workbook named *Nonverbal Cues*.
   g. Click OK to close the Action Settings dialog box.
4. Select the word *Written* in the slide and then create a hyperlink to the Word document named Written Skills by completing steps similar to those in steps 3c through 3g.
5. Apply a transition and sound of your choosing to all slides in the presentation.
6. Run the presentation beginning with Slide 1. At Slide 5, click the _Verbal_ hyperlink. Look at the Excel workbook that displays and then click the Close button (contains an *X*) in the upper right corner of the screen. Click the _Written_ hyperlink, look at the Word document that displays, and then click the Close button.
7. Print the presentation as handouts with all six slides on the same page.
8. Save and then close Comm Pres with Action.

Maintaining Presentation Files

When you have been working with PowerPoint for a period of time, you will have accumulated a number of presentation files. These files should be organized into folders to facilitate fast retrieval of information. Occasionally you should perform file maintenance activities such as copying, moving, renaming, and deleting presentation files to ensure the presentations in your various folders are manageable.

Many file management tasks can be completed at the Open dialog box (and some at the Save As dialog box). These tasks can include creating a new folder; copying, moving, printing, and renaming presentation files; and opening and

Open

closing multiple presentations. Display the Open dialog box, shown in figure 7.3, by clicking the Open button on the Standard toolbar. Some file maintenance tasks such as creating a folder and deleting files are performed by using buttons on the Open dialog box toolbar. Figure 7.3 identifies the dialog box toolbar.

FIGURE

7.3 *Open Dialog Box*

Creating a Folder

In PowerPoint, presentations should be grouped logically and stored in folders. For example, all of the presentations related to one department within a company could be stored in one folder with the department name being the folder name. A folder can be created within a folder (called a *subfolder*). If you create presentations for a department by individual, each individual could have a subfolder name within the department folder. The main folder on a disk or drive is called the *root folder*. Additional folders are created as a branch of this root folder.

Create
New Folder

At the Open dialog box, presentation file names display in the list box preceded by a presentation file icon, and a folder name is preceded by a folder icon. The folder and presentation icons are identified in figure 7.3.

Create a new folder by clicking the Create New Folder button located on the Open dialog box toolbar. At the New Folder dialog box shown in figure 7.4, key a name for the folder in the Name text box, and then click OK or press Enter. The new folder becomes the active folder.

FIGURE

7.4 *New Folder Dialog Box*

Key a name for the new folder in this text box.

Up One Level

Back

If you want to make the previous folder the active folder, click the Up One Level button on the dialog box toolbar. Clicking this button changes to the folder that was up one level from the current folder. After clicking the Up One Level button, the Back button becomes active. Click this button and the previously active folder becomes active again. A folder name can contain a maximum of 255 characters.

exercise **6**

CREATING A FOLDER

1. Create a folder named *Career Department* on your disk by completing the following steps:
   a. Display the Open dialog box with the *PowerPoint Chapter 07* folder on your disk the active folder.
   b. Click the Create New Folder button (located on the dialog box toolbar).
   c. At the New Folder dialog box, key **Career Department**.
   d. Click OK or press Enter. (The *Career Department* folder is now the active folder.)
   e. Change back to the *PowerPoint Chapter 07* folder by clicking the Up One Level button on the dialog box toolbar.
2. Click the Cancel button to close the Open dialog box.

Step 1c

Selecting Files

File management tasks can be completed on one file or more than one selected file. For example, you can move one file to a different folder, or you can select several files and move them all in one operation. Selected files can be opened, deleted, copied, moved, or printed.

To select one file, display the Open dialog box, and then click the desired file in the file list. To select several adjacent files (files displayed next to each other), click the first file, hold down the Shift key, click the last file to be selected, and then release the Shift key.

You can also select files that are not adjacent in the Open dialog box. To do this, click the first file, hold down the Ctrl key, click each additional file to be selected, and then release the Ctrl key.

Copying Files

In this and previous chapters, you opened a file from the chapter folder on your data disk and saved it with a new name on the same disk. This process makes an exact copy of the file, leaving the original on the disk. You can also copy a file into another folder and use the file's original name, give it a different name, or select files at the Open dialog box and copy them to the same folder or into a different folder.

To copy a file into another folder, open the file, display the Save As dialog box, change to the desired folder, and then click the Save button. A file also can be copied to another folder without opening the file first. To do this, use the Copy and Paste options from a shortcut menu at the Open (or Save As) dialog box.

A file or selected files can be copied into the same folder. When you do this, PowerPoint names the duplicated file(s) "Copy of xxx" (where *xxx* is the current file name). You can copy one file or selected files into the same folder.

exercise 7

COPYING SELECTED FILES INTO A DIFFERENT FOLDER

1. Copy selected files to the *Career Department* folder by completing the following steps:
   a. Display the Open dialog box with *PowerPoint Chapter 07* the active folder.
   b. Click *Job Search Presentation*, hold down the Ctrl key, and then click *Potential Presentation* and *Contacts Presentation*. (This selects the three, nonadjacent presentations.)
   c. Position the arrow pointer on one of the selected files, click the right mouse button, and then click Copy at the shortcut menu.
   d. Double-click the *Career Department* folder.
   e. Position the arrow pointer in any white area in the list box, click the right mouse button, and then click Paste at the shortcut menu.
   f. Click the Up One Level button to change back to the *PowerPoint Chapter 07* folder.
2. Close the Open dialog box.

Deleting Files and Folders

Delete

Tools ▾

Tools

At some point, you may want to delete certain files from your data disk or any other disk or folder in which you may be working. If you use PowerPoint on a regular basis, you should establish a periodic system for deleting files that are no longer used. The system you choose depends on the work you are doing and the amount of folder or disk space available. To delete a file, display the Open or Save As dialog box, select the file, and then click the Delete button on the dialog box toolbar. At the dialog box asking you to confirm the deletion, click Yes.

You can also delete a file by displaying the Open dialog box, selecting the file to be deleted, clicking the Tools button on the dialog box toolbar, and then clicking Delete at the drop-down menu. Another method for deleting a file is to display the Open dialog box, right-click the file to be deleted, and then click Delete at the shortcut menu. Delete a folder and all of its contents in the same manner as deleting a file or selected files.

POWERPOINT

1. Display the Open dialog box with the *PowerPoint Chapter 07* folder active.
2. Double-click the *Career Department* folder.
3. Delete the Job Search Presentation by completing the following steps:
   a. Right-click *Job Search Presentation* in the list box.
   b. At the shortcut menu that displays, click <u>D</u>elete.
   c. At the message telling you that Job Search Presentation is a read-only file, click <u>Y</u>es.
4. Click the Up One Level button to return to the *PowerPoint Chapter 07* folder.
5. Close the Open dialog box.

1. Display the Open dialog box with the *PowerPoint Chapter 07* folder active.
2. Delete the *Career Department* folder by completing the following steps:
   a. Right-click the *Career Development* folder in the list box.
   b. At the shortcut menu that displays, click <u>D</u>elete.
   c. At the message asking if you are sure you want to remove the folder and all of its contents, click <u>Y</u>es.
   d. At the message telling you that the presentation is a read-only file, click the Yes to <u>A</u>ll button.
3. Close the Open dialog box.

Renaming Files

At the Open dialog box, use the Rena<u>m</u>e option from the Too<u>l</u>s drop-down menu or the shortcut menu to give a file a different name. The Rena<u>m</u>e option changes the name of the file and keeps it in the same folder. To use Rena<u>m</u>e, display the Open dialog box, click once on the file to be renamed, click the Too<u>l</u>s button on the dialog box toolbar, and then click Rena<u>m</u>e. This causes a thin black border to surround the file name and the name to be selected. Key the new name and then press Enter.

You can also rename a file by right-clicking the file name at the Open dialog box and then clicking Rena<u>m</u>e at the shortcut menu. Key the new name for the file and then press the Enter key.

1. Display the Open dialog box with the *PowerPoint Chapter 07* folder active.
2. Rename a file by completing the following steps:
   a. Click once on *Comm Pres with Table*.
   b. Click the Tools button on the dialog box toolbar.
   c. At the drop-down menu that displays, click Rename.
   d. Key **Comm Pres with Embedded Object** and then press the Enter key.
3. Close the Open dialog box.

CHAPTER summary

➤ Integration is the process of completing a file by adding parts to it from other sources.

➤ An object created in one program of the Microsoft Office suite can be copied, linked, or embedded to another program in the suite.

➤ The program containing the original object is called the source and the program the object is pasted to is called the destination.

➤ An embedded object is stored in both the source and the destination programs.

➤ Edit an embedded object by double-clicking it to open the source program's menus and toolbars.

➤ An object should be linked if the content in the object is subject to change. Linking will ensure that the content in the destination always reflects the current content in the source.

➤ A linked object is stored in the source program only. The destination program contains a code indicating the name and location of the source.

➤ The content in a link is edited by opening the document containing the linked object in the source program, making the required changes, and then saving and closing the file.

➤ When you open a document containing links, a message displays asking if you want to update the links.

➤ A link can be broken between the source and the destination program if there is no longer any need to update the destination program.

➤ Another program such as Word or Excel can be launched within a PowerPoint presentation by creating a hyperlink to a Word or Excel file.

➤ When another program is launched from a slide show, the application is opened in its own window on top of the slide show.

➤ Perform file management tasks such as creating a new folder and copying, deleting, and renaming files at the Open dialog box.

➤ Presentation files should be grouped logically and stored in folders. A folder can be created within a folder (a subfolder). The main folder on a disk or drive is called the root folder. Additional folders are created as a branch of this root folder.

➤ Create a new folder by clicking the Create New Folder button located on the Open dialog box toolbar.

➤ Use the Shift key while selecting files to select multiple adjacent files and use the Ctrl key to select multiple nonadjacent files.

➤ Use the Copy and Paste options from the shortcut menu at the Open dialog box to copy a file from one folder to another folder or drive.

➤ When you copy a file into the same folder, PowerPoint names the duplicated file(s) "Copy of xxx" (where xxx is the original file name).

➤ To delete a file, select the file and then click the Delete button on the dialog box toolbar; click Tools, and then click Delete at the drop-down menu; or right-click the file to be deleted, and then click Delete at the shortcut menu.

COMMANDS review

Command	Mouse
Display Paste Special dialog box	Click Edit, Paste Special
Display Links dialog box	Click Edit, Links
Display Action Settings dialog box	Click Slide Show, Action Settings
Display New Folder dialog box	Click Create New Folder button on Open dialog box toolbar

CONCEPTS check

Completion: On a blank sheet of paper, indicate the correct term, symbol, or command.

1. The process of completing a document by adding parts from other sources is referred to as this.
2. To link or embed an object, open this dialog box in the destination program after copying the source object.
3. An object can be duplicated in a destination program by copying, embedding, or this.
4. Do this with the mouse to open an object in an editing window with the source program's menus and toolbars.
5. If an object has been linked from a Word document to a PowerPoint presentation, which program would you open to edit the content of the link?
6. Display this dialog box to disconnect the source program link from the destination object.
7. A file from another program can be opened from a PowerPoint presentation by creating a hyperlink at this dialog box.
8. File management tasks such as copying or deleting files can be performed at this dialog box.
9. Select multiple adjacent files by clicking the first file, holding down this key, and then clicking the last file.
10. Select multiple nonadjacent files by holding down this key while clicking each file name.

SKILLS check

Assessment 1

1. In PowerPoint, open Telephone Presentation (located in the *PowerPoint Chapter 07* folder on your disk).
2. Save the presentation with Save As in the *PowerPoint Chapter 07* folder on your disk and name the presentation Enhanced Telephone Pres.
3. Create a new Slide 6 with the following specifications:
   a. Use the Title Only slide layout.
   b. Insert the title *Placing Calls with Voice Mail*.
   c. Open Word and then open the document named Voice Mail Etiquette located in the *PowerPoint Chapter 07* folder on your disk.
   d. Copy and embed the bulleted list from the Word document to Slide 6. *(Hint: The bulleted list is not in a table. You will need to select all of the bulleted items.)*
   e. Double-click the embedded object, press Ctrl + A to select all of the text in the object, and then change the font size to 16 points.
   f. Click outside the text to remove the Word editing tools.
   g. With the text object selected, resize and move the text object so it fills most of the slide below the title.
   h. Click the button on the Taskbar representing Word, close the Voice Mail Etiquette document, and then exit Word.
4. Create a new Slide 3 with the following specifications:
   a. Apply the Title Only slide layout to the new Slide 3.
   b. Key **Average Time by Region** as the slide title.
   c. Open Excel and then open the workbook named Calls Workbook from the *PowerPoint Chapter 07* folder on your disk.
   d. Select the chart and then copy and embed it in Slide 3 in the Enhanced Telephone Pres.
   e. Resize the chart as large as possible.
5. Print only Slide 3 of the presentation.
6. Double-click the chart and then change the chart type to Column.
7. Run the presentation beginning with Slide 1.
8. Print the presentation as handouts with all slides on one page.
9. Save and then close Enhanced Telephone Pres.
10. Click the button on the Taskbar representing Excel, close the Calls Workbook, and then exit Excel.

Assessment 2

1. In PowerPoint, open Enhanced Telephone Pres.
2. Display Slide 2 in the Slide pane, select the title text *Answering Calls*, and then hyperlink the text to the Word document named Verbal Skills.
3. Apply an animation scheme of your choosing to all slides in the presentation.
4. Run the presentation beginning with Slide 1. At Slide 2, click the hyperlink to view the Word document Verbal Skills.
5. Review the Verbal Skills document and then exit Word.
6. Navigate through the remainder of the slide show.
7. Save and then close Enhanced Telephone Pres.

Assessment 3

1. In PowerPoint, open Funds Pres with Links. (You edited this presentation in exercise 3. If you did not complete exercise 3, open Funds Presentation.)
2. At the message telling you that the presentation contains links, click the Update Links button.
3. Open Microsoft Excel and then open Excel Workbook 03 from the *PowerPoint Chapter 07* folder on your disk.
4. Save the workbook with Save As and name it Funds Workbook 03.
5. Copy and link the chart to Slide 4 in the presentation.
6. Increase the size of the chart in the slide so it fills a good portion of the slide below the title.
7. Print only Slide 4.
8. Save and then close Funds Pres with Links.
9. Click the button on the Taskbar representing Excel.
10. Close Funds Workbook 03 and then exit Excel.

Assessment 4

1. Open Excel and then open Funds Workbook 03.
2. Make the following changes to the data in cells in Funds Workbook 03:
   a. Change B2 from *5%* to *12%*
   b. Change B4 from *10%* to *15%*
   c. Change B6 from *8%* to *17%*
3. Save the workbook again with the same name (Funds Workbook 03).
4. Close Funds Workbook 03 and then exit Excel.
5. With PowerPoint the active program, open Funds Pres with Links. At the message telling you that the presentation contains links, click the Update Links button.
6. Add an animation scheme of your choosing to all slides in the presentation.
7. Run the presentation beginning with Slide 1.
8. Print the presentation as handouts with all slides on one page.
9. Save and then close Funds Pres with Links.

Assessment 5

1. Use PowerPoint's Help feature to learn how to copy slides with the Slide Finder feature.
2. After reading the information, insert slides from one presentation into another by completing the following these basic steps:
   a. Open Communication Presentation.
   b. Display Slide 6 in the Slide pane.
   c. Using the information you learned in the Help files, insert all of the slides in the Telephone Presentation into the current presentation. *(Hint: Make sure you use the Slide Finder feature to do this.)*
   d. Check the inserted slides and make any minor adjustments necessary.
3. Save the presentation with Save As in the *PowerPoint Chapter 07* folder on your disk and name the presentation Combined Comm Pres.
4. Run the presentation beginning with Slide 1.
5. Print the presentation as handouts with six slides per page (the second page will contain five slides).
6. Close Combined Comm Pres.

SHARING PRESENTATIONS

PERFORMANCE OBJECTIVES

Upon successful completion of chapter 8, you will be able to:
- Send a presentation for review
- Edit a presentation sent for review
- Accept/reject changes from reviewers
- Insert comments in a presentation
- Print comments
- Save a presentation for use on another computer using the Pack and Go Wizard
- Embed fonts used in a presentation when saving
- Save a presentation as a Web page
- Preview a Web page
- Format a Web page
- Broadcast a presentation online

PowerPoint Chapter 08

If you want to share your presentation with others, you can send the presentation for review and then merge the changes in the original presentation. the process for merging changes into the original presentation varies depending on whether you are using Microsoft Outlook or another e-mail program. In this chapter, you will learn about the review cycle, and the steps to merge changes to a presentation using the Compare and Merge Presentations feature. you will learn how to insert a comment in a presentation that you are sending our for review, as well as how to delete, edit and print comments.

Use the Pack and Go Wizard to save a PowerPoint presentation for use on another computer that does not have PowerPoint installed. Fonts can be embedded into the presentation file if the computer that will be used to deliver the presentation does not have the same fonts installed. Slides can also be converted to HTML for viewing as Web pages in a static presentation. Along with on-screen slide shows, presentations can be delivered live by broadcasting them online. You will learn how to set up and schedule an online broadcast of your PowerPoint presentation.

Sending a Presentation for Review

Some employees in a company may be part of a *workgroup*, which is a networked collection of computers sharing files, printers, and other resources. In a workgroup, you generally make your files available to your colleagues. With the Windows operating system and Office programs, you can share and distribute your files quickly and easily to members of your workgroup from your desktop computer.

If you are part of a workgroup, you may want to send a copy of a PowerPoint presentation to other members of the workgroup for review. To do this, you would set up a review cycle for reviewing the presentation. This cycle consists of the following general steps:

1. Send a separate copy of the presentation to each person who is to review the presentation using Microsoft Outlook or using other e-mail programs.
2. Each reviewer makes changes to his or her own copy of the presentation.
3. Each reviewer sends his or her own edited presentation back to you.
4. You compare each edited presentation with the original presentation and determine if you want to accept or reject changes.

If you are using Microsoft Outlook to send the presentation, click File, point to Send To, and then click Mail Recipient (for Review). Specify to whom you want the presentation sent and then click the Send button. If you are using an e-mail program other than Outlook, you would complete these general steps to send a presentation for review:

1. Open the presentation
2. Click File and then Save As.
3. At the Save As dialog box, key a new name for the presentation in the File name text box.
4. Click the down-pointing triangle at the right side of the Save as Type option box and then click *Presentation for Review* at the drop-down list.
5. Click the Save button.
6. Close the presentation.

exercise 1

SENDING A PRESENTATION FOR REVIEW

1. Open Job Search Presentation (located in the *PowerPoint Chapter 08* folder on your disk).
2. Save the presentation with Save As in the *PowerPoint Chapter 08* folder on your disk and name it Original Job Search Pres.
3. Save the presentation for review by Suzanne Nelson by completing the following steps:
   a. Click File and then Save As.
   b. At the Save As dialog box, key **Job Srch Pres Edited by SN** in the File name text box.
   c. Make sure the *PowerPoint Chapter 08* folder on your disk is the active folder.
   d. Click the down-pointing triangle at the right of the Save as type option box and then click *Presentation for Review* in the drop-down list.

e. Click the Save button.
4. Save the presentation for review by Michael Ramsey by completing steps 3a through 3e, except save the presentation with the name *Job Srch Pres Edited by MR* in step 3b.
5. Close Original Job Search Pres.

Editing a Presentation Sent for Review

When a presentation is saved as a presentation for review, PowerPoint inserts a link in the copy of the presentation back to the original presentation. When you open the copy of the presentation, a message displays asking if you want to merge changes to the copy of the presentation back into the original presentation. Click Yes if you want changes you make to the copy of the presentation to apply to the original. Click No if you do not want the original presentation to reflect the changes you make to the copy. Make the desired changes to the presentation and then save it in the normal manner.

In exercise 3, you will be reviewing changes made by two reviewers to two different copies of the job search presentation. PowerPoint uses different colors to identify reviewers. In exercise 2, you will specify a user name at the Options dialog box with the General tab selected and then make changes to a copy of the job search presentation. You will then change the user name at the Options dialog box and then make changes to another copy of the presentation.

To change the user name, click Tools and then Options. At the Options dialog box, click the General tab. At the Options dialog box with the General tab selected, select the name in the Name text box and then key the new name. Select the initials in the Initials text box and then key the new initials. Click OK to close the dialog box.

EDITING PRESENTATIONS SENT FOR REVIEW

1. At the blank PowerPoint screen, change the user name and initials by completing the following steps:
   a. Click Tools and then Options.
   b. At the Options dialog box, click the General tab. (Make a note of the current name and initials. You will reenter this information later in this exercise.)
   c. At the Options dialog box with the General tab selected, select the name in the Name text box and then key **Suzanne Nelson**.
   d. Select the initials in the Initials text box and then key **SN**.

e. Click OK to close the dialog box.
2. Edit the job search presentation as Suzanne Nelson by completing the following steps:
   a. Open the Job Srch Pres Edited by SN presentation located in the *PowerPoint Chapter 08* folder on your disk.
   b. At the message asking if you want to merge changes in Job Srch Pres Edited by SN back into Original Job Search Pres, click <u>N</u>o.

   c. Make the following changes:
      1) Edit the title in Slide 1 so it reads *JOB SEARCH* (instead of *JOB SEARCH STRATEGIES FOR THE NEW MILLENNIUM*).
      2) Display Slide 3 and then insert the text *Include any volunteer experience* between the first and second bulleted text.
      3) Display Slide 5 and then edit the second bulleted item so it reads *Locate newspaper ads*.
      4) Display Slide 6 and then edit the fourth bulleted item so it reads *Bring at least three references*.
3. Save the presentation with the same name (Job Srch Pres Edited by SN).
4. Print the presentation as handouts with all nine slides on one page.
5. Close Job Srch Pres Edited by SN.
6. At the blank PowerPoint screen, change the user name and initials by completing the following steps:
   a. Click <u>T</u>ools and then <u>O</u>ptions.
   b. At the Options dialog box, click the General tab.
   c. At the Options dialog box with the General tab selected, select the name in the <u>N</u>ame text box and then key **Michael Ramsey**.
   d. Select the initials in the Initia<u>l</u>s text box and then key **MR**.
   e. Click OK to close the dialog box.
7. Edit the job search presentation as Michael Ramsey by completing the following steps:
   a. Open the Job Srch Pres Edited by MR presentation located in the *PowerPoint Chapter 08* folder on your disk.
   b. At the message asking if you want to merge changes in Job Srch Pres Edited by MR back into Original Job Search Pres, click <u>N</u>o.
   c. Make the following changes:
      1) Edit the subtitle in Slide 1 so it reads *Strategies for Employment Search*.
      2) Display Slide 5 and then edit the last bulleted item so it reads *Locate resources on the Internet*.
      3) Display Slide 6 and then edit the second bulleted item so it reads *Be on time for the interview*.
      4) Display Slide 9 and then edit the last bulleted item so it reads *Establish personal work goals*.
8. Save the presentation with the same name (Job Srch Pres Edited by MR).
9. Print the presentation as handouts with all nine slides on the same page.
10. Close Job Srch Pres Edited by MR.
11. Change the name and initials in the User information back to the original information by completing the following steps:
    a. Click <u>T</u>ools and then <u>O</u>ptions.

b. At the Options dialog box with the General tab selected, key the original name in the Name text box.
c. Press the Tab key and then key the original initials in the Initials text box.
d. Click OK to close the dialog box.

Accepting/Rejecting Changes from Reviewers

When you open a presentation saved as a presentation for review, a message displays asking if you want to merge changes to the copy of the presentation back into the original presentation. If you click Yes, the changes made to the copy are automatically made to the original (this is because of the link established between the presentations). If you want control over what changes are made to the original presentation, click No (this is what you did in exercise 2).

If you used Outlook to distribute presentations for review, combine the review by double-clicking the attached reviewed presentation. At the dialog box that displays, click Yes and PowerPoint will automatically combine the reviewed presentation with the original presentation.

If you used another e-mail program to distribute presentations for review, use PowerPoint's Compare and Merge Presentations feature to combine changes. To use this feature, open the original presentation, click Tools, and then click Compare and Merge Presentations. At the Choose Files to Merge with Current Presentation dialog box, click to select all reviewed presentations, and then click the Merge button. This displays the original presentation with change markers identifying changes made by each reviewer. The Revisions Pane also displays at the right side of the PowerPoint screen as shown in figure 8.1 along with the Reviewing toolbar, which displays immediately below the Formatting toolbar.

HINT PowerPoint identifies reviewer changes that conflict. You decide what changes to make when a conflict exists.

HINT Click the End Review button on the Reviewing toolbar to end a review and permanently end the ability to combine reviewed presentations with the original.

FIGURE

8.1 *Original Presentation Merged with Reviewed Presentations*

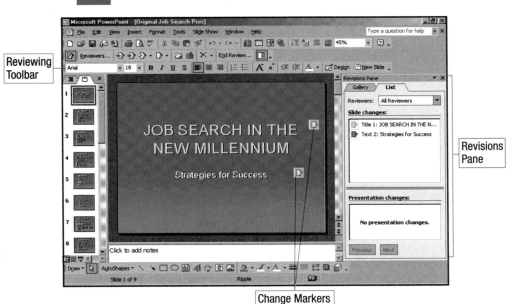

Changes made by each reviewer display in a change marker in the original presentation. Change markers for each reviewer display in a different color. This helps you identify who has suggested what change.

The Revisions Pane contains two tabs—Gallery and List. The Revisions Pane with the List tab selected displays changes in the Slide changes list box. You can also display a list of reviewers by clicking the down-pointing triangle at the right side of the Reviewers option box. By default, all reviewers are selected. If you do not want to view changes made by a specific reviewer, remove the check mark by the reviewer's name.

Click the Gallery tab and the Revisions Pane displays the current slide as slide miniatures for each reviewer showing the changes made by the reviewer. Above each pane is the reviewer's name preceded by a check box. Click this check box to accept all changes to the slide made by that specific reviewer.

To accept a change to a slide, click the change marker and a box displays containing a check box followed by a description of the change. Move the mouse pointer over the description, and the location of the change is identified in the slide by red marks. Accept the change by clicking the check box located in the change marker box to insert a check mark. You can also accept a change by clicking the Apply button on the Reviewing toolbar. Move to the next change by clicking the Next button located toward the bottom of the Revisions Pane or click the Next Item button on the Reviewing toolbar.

To accept all changes made to a slide, click the down-pointing triangle at the right side of the Apply button on the Reviewing toolbar, and then click *Apply All Changes to the Current Slide* at the drop-down list. To accept all changes made by one reviewer on one slide, click the Gallery tab at the Revisions Pane. Click the check box that displays for the specific reviewer above the slide miniature. You can also point to a slide miniature of the reviewer whose changes you want to accept, click the down-pointing triangle that displays at the right side of the miniature, and then click _A_pply Changes By This Reviewer at the drop-down list. To accept all changes made to the presentation, click the down-pointing triangle at the right side of the Apply button on the Reviewing toolbar, and then click *Apply A_l_l Changes to the Presentation*.

exercise 3

| COMPARING AND MERGING CHANGES INTO THE ORIGINAL PRESENTATION |

1. Open Original Job Search Pres.
2. Click _T_ools and then Compare and Merge Presentations.
3. At the Choose Files to Merge with Current Presentation dialog box, make sure the *PowerPoint Chapter 08* folder on your disk is the active folder and then click *Job Srch Pres Edited by MR*. Hold down the Ctrl key and then click *Job Srch Pres Edited by SN*. (This selects both presentations.)
4. Click the _M_erge button located in the lower right corner of the dialog box. (This displays Slide 1 in the Slide pane, displays the Reviewing toolbar below the Formatting toolbar, and also displays the Revisions Pane at the right side of the screen. Notice the two changes markers [in two different colors] that display in Slide 1.)
5. Make the following changes to Slide 1:
   a. Click the change marker located at the right side of the Slide 1 title. (This displays a description of the change followed by the reviewer's name *Suzanne Nelson*.)

b. You do not want to make this change, so click in the slide outside the change description box.

c. Click the change marker located at the right side of the Slide 1 subtitle.

d. Accept the changes to the subtitle by clicking the check box preceding the text *All changes to Text 2*.

6. Click the Next Item button on the Reviewing toolbar to display the next change (located on Slide 3).

7. Accept the change to Slide 3 by clicking the check box preceding the description of the change (this inserts a check mark and accepts the change).

8. Click the Next Item button on the Reviewing toolbar. (This displays Slide 5).

9. Accept the changes by completing the following steps:

a. Click the Gallery tab at the Revisions Pane. (This displays slide miniatures in the pane showing changes made by each reviewer.)

b. Accept the changes made to Slide 5 by Michael Ramsey by clicking in the check box that displays above the top slide miniature.

c. Accept the changes made to Slide 5 by Suzanne Nelson by clicking in the check box that displays above the bottom slide miniature.

10. Click the Next Item button on the Reviewing toolbar. (This displays Slide 6.)

11. Accept all changes made to Slide 6 by clicking the down-pointing triangle at the right side of the Apply button on the Reviewing toolbar and then click *Apply All Changes to the Current Slide* at the drop-down list.

12. Click the Next Item button on the Reviewing toolbar. (This displays Slide 9.)

13. Accept the change to Slide 9 by clicking the Apply button on the Reviewing toolbar.

14. Display Slide 1 and then run the presentation.

15. Save the presentation with Save As and name it Merged Job Search Pres.

16. Print the presentation as handouts with all nine slides on one page.

17. Close Merged Job Search Pres.

Inserting Comments

If you are sending out a presentation for review and want to ask reviewers specific questions or provide information about slides in a presentation, insert a comment. To insert a comment, display the desired slide and then position the insertion where you want the comment to appear. Click Insert on the Menu bar

Insert Comment

and then click Comment and a comment box displays similar to the one shown in figure 8.2. You can also insert a comment by clicking the Insert Comment button on the Reviewing toolbar. Display this toolbar by clicking View, pointing to Toolbars, and then clicking Reviewing.

8.2 *Comment Box*

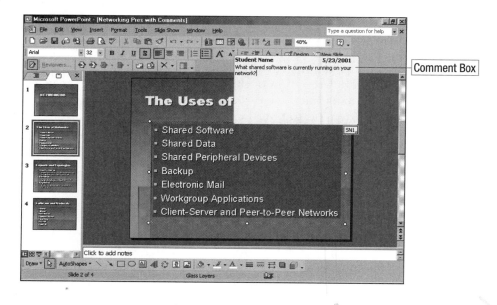

HINT

To edit a comment, double-click the comment box, make the desired changes, and then click outside the box.

HINT

Move a comment by selecting the comment box and then dragging it to the desired location.

HINT

Turn on or off the display of comment boxes with the Markup button on the Reviewing toolbar. The Markup button is a toggle button. The button is active when it displays with a blue border and light gray shading.

After keying the desired comment, click outside the comment box. A small yellow box displays at the right side of the slide aligned horizontally with the position where the comment was inserted. The user's initials display in the yellow box followed by a number. Comments by individual users are numbered sequentially beginning with 1.

To delete a comment from a slide, click the small box containing the user's initials and comment number and then click the Delete Comment button on the Reviewing toolbar. You can also right-click the box containing the initials and then click Delete at the shortcut menu.

To print comments, display the Print dialog box, choose how you want slides printed with the Print what option, and then insert a check mark in the Include comments page check box. Comments print on a separate page after the presentation is printed.

1. Open Networking Presentation.
2. Save the presentation with Save As in the *PowerPoint Chapter 08* folder on your disk and name the presentation Networking Pres with Comments.
3. Insert comments by completing the following steps:
    a. Display Slide 2 in the Slide pane.
    b. Turn on the Reviewing toolbar by clicking <u>V</u>iew, pointing to <u>T</u>oolbars, and then clicking Reviewing.
    c. Click immediately right of *Shared Software* (the first bulleted item). (This moves the insertion point immediately right of *Software*.)
    d. Click the Insert Comment button on the Reviewing toolbar.
    e. Key the following in the comment box: **What shared software is currently running on your network?**
    f. Display Slide 3 in the Slide pane.
    g. Click immediately right of *Star Network* (the second bulleted item).
    h. Click the Insert Comment button on the Reviewing toolbar.
    i. Key the following in the comment box: **Please include examples of star networks with which you have experience.**
    j. Click outside the comment box to deselect it.
4. Print the presentation and comments by completing the following steps:
    a. Click <u>F</u>ile and then <u>P</u>rint.
    b. At the Print dialog box, click the down-pointing triangle at the right side of Print <u>w</u>hat and then click *Handouts*.
    c. Make sure *6* displays in the Slides pe<u>r</u> page text box.
    d. Click in the Incl<u>u</u>de comment pages check box to insert a check mark.
    e. Click OK.
5. Run the presentation beginning with Slide 1.
6. Save and then close Networking Pres with Comments.

Saving a Presentation to Use on Another Computer

The safest way to transport a PowerPoint presentation to another computer to do a slide show is to use PowerPoint's Pack and Go Wizard. The Pack and Go Wizard will bundle a presentation onto a disk or network location including all of the linked files, fonts used, and the PowerPoint Viewer program in case the destination computer does not have PowerPoint installed on it. To start the Pack and Go Wizard, click <u>F</u>ile and then Pac<u>k</u> and Go.

If you do not have any information about the computer you will be using to do the slide show, select <u>E</u>mbed TrueType fonts and include the <u>V</u>iewer for Windows. If you reach your destination and the other computer does not have

HINT

Include the Microsoft PowerPoint Viewer when packaging a presentation if you plan to run the presentation on a computer without PowerPoint.

PowerPoint or the same fonts installed that you used in the presentation, the packed file will have copies of what you need. If you have charts or other linked documents incorporated in the presentation, select Include linked files to avoid a disaster if you forget to copy these other files yourself. If you pack a presentation using Pack and Go and then make modifications to the presentation file, you will have to run the wizard again to update the packed files. In exercise 5, you will work through the steps in the Pack and Go Wizard dialog boxes.

exercise 5

PACKING A PRESENTATION WITH PACK AND GO

1. Open E-commerce Presentation from the *PowerPoint Chapter 08* folder on your disk.
2. Run the Pack and Go Wizard to save the presentation as a packed file including the fonts used by completing the following steps:

   a. Click File and then Pack and Go.
   b. At the first dialog box telling you what the Pack and Go Wizard will do, click Next>.
   c. At the second dialog box with Active presentation selected, click Next>.
   d. At the third dialog box with drive A selected, click Next>.
   e. At the fourth dialog box, click Embed TrueType fonts to insert a check mark. Make sure a check mark appears in the Include linked files check box and then click Next>.
   f. At the fifth dialog box, click Viewer for Windows™, and then click Next>.
   g. At the sixth dialog box, click Finish.
   h. The Pack and Go Status dialog box will display the progress as the presentation is packaged onto the disk in drive A. Click OK when the message displays that Pack and Go has successfully packaged your presentation.
3. Close E-commerce Presentation.

When you reach the destination computer, the presentation has to be unpacked before it can be viewed as a slide show. To do this, complete the following steps:

1. Launch Windows Explorer, select drive A, and then double-click the icon for **Pngsetup.exe**.
2. Key the name of the destination folder to which you want the file unpacked and then click OK.
3. The Pack and Go Setup will display a message that the presentation was successfully installed and ask if you want to run the slide show now. Click Yes and the first slide in the presentation slide show will display on the screen.

POWERPOINT

Embedding Fonts in a Presentation File

The available fonts will vary from computer to computer due to printer selections, installation configurations, and third-party font software. If you create a presentation on one computer that will be used on another computer, you can embed the fonts used when you save the file. The file size will be considerably larger, but will ensure that the presentation displays the same on both computers.

To embed the fonts in the presentation file, display the Save As dialog box, click Tools on the Save As toolbar, and then click Save Options. At the Save Options dialog box shown in figure 8.3, click Embed TrueType fonts to insert a check mark in the check box, and then click OK. At the Save As dialog box, key a name for the presentation, and then press Enter or click the Save button.

FIGURE

8.3 *Save Options Dialog Box*

Insert a check mark in this check box to embed fonts in the presentation file.

EMBEDDING FONTS WHEN SAVING A PRESENTATION

1. Open E-commerce Presentation from the *PowerPoint Chapter 08* folder on your disk.
2. Embed the fonts used in the presentation by completing the following steps:
   a. Click File and then Save As.
   b. Click Tools on the Save As toolbar and then click Save Options at the drop-down menu.

Step 2b

c. At the Save Options dialog box, click Embed TrueType fonts to insert a check mark in the check box.

d. Click OK to close the dialog box.

e. At the Save As dialog box, key **Embedded E-commerce Pres** in the File name text box and then press Enter.

3. Close Embedded E-commerce Pres.

4. Complete the following steps to determine the difference in file sizes between the original E-commerce Presentation and the file with the embedded fonts by completing the following steps:

a. Display the Open dialog box with *PowerPoint Chapter 08* the active folder.

b. Click the down-pointing triangle at the right of the Views button on the Open dialog box toolbar and then click Details at the drop-down menu.

c. Notice the difference in file size between E-commerce Presentation and Embedded E-commerce Pres.

d. Click the down-pointing triangle at the right of the View button and then click List at the drop-down menu.

e. Close the Open dialog box.

5. Display the Open dialog box, delete the Embedded E-commerce Pres, and then close the Open dialog box.

Step 2c

Step 4b

Saving a Presentation as a Web Page

The Internet is fast becoming a preferred choice as a presentation medium. Once a presentation has been published to the Internet, anyone around the world with Internet access can view your presentation. If you are traveling to several remote locations to deliver a presentation you can access the slides from any computer with Internet access instead of transporting disks or portable computers.

Presentations are published to the Internet directly through PowerPoint if you are connected to a Web server or company intranet, or through a two-step process if you are not directly connected. In the first step you convert the PowerPoint file to HTML file format. The second step requires that the HTML files be copied to a Web server. *HTML* is an acronym for Hypertext Markup Language, which is the programming language used to code pages to display graphically on the World Wide Web. HTML is a collection of instructions that include *tags* applied to text and graphics to instruct the Web browser software how to properly display the page.

Fortunately, PowerPoint will translate the slides into Web pages for you so you can publish presentations to the Internet without having to learn HTML programming statements. To do this, open the presentation you want to convert to HTML, click File, and then click Save as Web Page. At the Save As dialog box shown in figure 8.4, the name in the File name text box will default to the presentation file name (with the extension *.htm*). Also, the Save as type option defaults to *Web Page*.

POWERPOINT

8.4 Save As Dialog Box

Click the Publish button to display the Publish as Web Page dialog box where you specify what you want published and the desired browser.

Save as type option changes to Web Page.

Click the Publish button and the Publish as Web Page dialog box displays as shown in figure 8.5. If you do not want to convert all of the slides in the presentation, specify the starting slide number in the Slide number text box and the ending slide number in the through text box in the Publish what? section. You can convert to specific versions of Web browser software with the options in the Browser support section as shown in figure 8.5. Click the Web Options button to display the Web Options dialog box displayed in figure 8.6.

8.5 Publish as Web Page Dialog Box

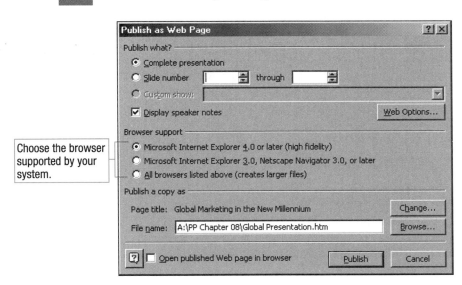

Choose the browser supported by your system.

FIGURE
8.6   **Web Options Dialog Box**

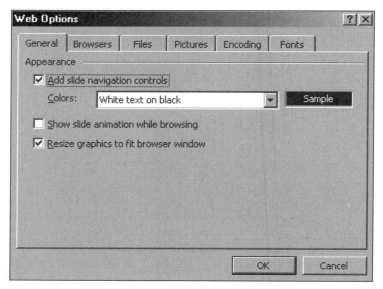

When PowerPoint converts the presentation to HTML format, navigation buttons are created for users to navigate through the slides in the Web browser. The default colors for the navigation buttons are *White text on black*. You can select different color schemes with the Colors option at the Web Options dialog box with the General tab selected. If the target browser is Microsoft Internet Explorer version 4.0 or later, you can select Show slide animation while browsing.

Click the Files tab at the Web Options dialog box and options display for determining how the Web page files will be organized. By default, PowerPoint creates a folder in the conversion process and stores all of the files in the folder. The screen size can be set at the dialog box with the Pictures tab selected. Click the down-pointing arrow to the right of the Screen size text box and then click a screen resolution from the drop-down list. Use options at the Web Options dialog box with the Encoding tab selected to specify a different language code for saving the Web page.

When a presentation is converted to HTML with All browsers listed above as the Browser support option, additional files are created from the original presentation as follows: Separate graphic files are created for each slide; separate graphic files are created for the navigation buttons and other navigation assistance tools; separate HTML files are created for each slide; a text-only version is created for each page for browser software that does not support graphics; and finally, an outline page is created that becomes the index frame where the user can select the page titles for each slide. The outline page is the opening page in the left frame that is displayed in the Web browser. A single presentation file can result in several files being created after conversion to Web pages.

If you are directly connected to a company intranet or Web server, contact the system administrator to find out the destination folder you need to specify in the Publish a copy as File name text box. Use the Browse button next to the File name text box to navigate to the correct folder. If you are not directly connected to an intranet or Web server, specify a folder on your system to copy the files to which you can later send to a Web server by modem or disk.

Click the Publish button in the Publish as Web Page dialog box to begin the conversion once all of the options have been set. If you would like to view the completed Web pages in your Web browser software when the conversion is complete, click the Open published Web page in browser check box before clicking Publish. The presentation opens in the browser window in a manner similar to what you see in figure 8.7 (your browser window may vary). Navigate through the presentation using the slide titles in the left frame of the browser window or the navigation buttons located along the bottom of the window.

FIGURE

8.7 *Presentation in Web Browser Window*

Click a slide title to display that slide.

Use these navigation buttons to display the previous or next slides.

Full Screen Slide Show

SAVING A PRESENTATION AS A WEB PAGE

1. Open Global Presentation from the *PowerPoint Chapter 08* folder on your disk.
2. Save the presentation as a Web page by completing the following steps:
   a. Click File and then Save as Web Page.
   b. At the Save As dialog box, click the Publish button.
   c. At the Publish as Web Page dialog box, click the Web Options button in the Publish what? section.
   d. At the Web Options dialog box with the General tab selected, click the down-pointing triangle next to the Colors text box in the General tab, and then click *Black text on white* at the drop-down list.

Step 2d

e. Click OK to close the Web Options dialog box.

f. Choose the target browser in the Browser support section that applies to your school. Check with your instructor if you are not sure which target browser you should be using. The default selection is Microsoft Internet Explorer 4.0 or later.

g. Click the Browse button next to the File name text box, make sure the correct folder is displayed for storing the HTML files, and then click OK.

h. Click the Open published Web page in browser check box to insert a check mark.

i. Click the Publish button.

j. In a few moments, the conversion will be complete and the Microsoft Internet Explorer or other default browser window will open with the opening page of the presentation displayed.

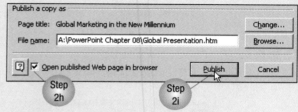

3. Navigate through the presentation by clicking the slide titles along the left frame, or using the Next Slide and Previous Slide navigation buttons along the bottom of the window. (Refer to figure 8.7.) When you have finished viewing all of the slides, close the Internet Explorer or other browser window.

4. Save and then close Global Presentation.

5. Display the Open dialog box with the *PowerPoint Chapter 08* folder active.

6. Double-click the *Global Presentation_files* folder in the list box and then look at the HTML files saved in the folder.

7. Click the down-pointing triangle at the right side of the Views button on the Open dialog box toolbar and then click Details. Scroll through and look at the file types and names for the files that were created in the conversion process.

8. Click the down-pointing triangle at the right side of the Views button and then click List.

9. Click the Up One Level button to display the *PowerPoint Chapter 08* folder contents.

10. Close the Open dialog box.

To make a presentation available to others on the Internet, the HTML files need to be copied to a *Web server*. A Web server is a computer connected to the Internet that is set up to store Web pages that can be accessed by other Internet users by referencing an address such as www.microsoft.com. The system administrator for the Web server would provide you with instructions on where and how to copy the HTML files. You may be assigned an account name and password for the Web server by the administrator and will probably use File Transfer Protocol (FTP) to send the files to the server.

Previewing a Web Page

If you want to see how the presentation displays in your Web browser, view the presentation in Web Page Preview. To do this, open the presentation you have saved as a Web page, click File, and then click Web Page Preview. This displays the first slide in the Web browser as shown in figure 8.7.

When you first display the presentation in Web Page Preview, you may need to click the Maximize button located in the upper right corner of the Web browser window. Scroll through the slides in the presentation by clicking the Next Slide button located toward the bottom of the browser window (see figure 8.7).

Click the Previous Slide button to view the previous slide. The Outline pane displays at the left side of the browser. Move to various slides in the presentation by clicking the title of the desired slide in the Outline pane. If you want the slide to fill the entire screen, click the Full Screen Slide Show button located in the lower right corner of the browser window. Run the presentation as you would any other presentation.

exercise 8

VIEWING A PRESENTATION IN WEB PAGE PREVIEW

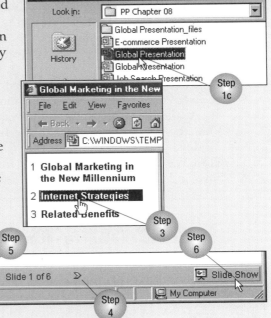

1. Open Global Presentation that was saved as a Web page by completing the following steps:
   a. Display the Open dialog box.
   b. Make sure *PowerPoint Chapter 08* is the active folder.
   c. Double-click the HTML presentation named Global Presentation (see figure at right). (Notice that the HTML Global Presentation displays in the Open dialog box preceded by an icon of a yellow page containing a blue globe behind the normal PowerPoint presentation icon.)
2. Click <u>F</u>ile and then We<u>b</u> Page Preview.
3. At the browser window, click the slide title *2 Internet Strategies* to display the next slide in the presentation.
4. Click the Next Slide button located toward the bottom of the window to display Slide 3.
5. Click twice on the Previous Slide button to display Slide 1.
6. With Slide 1 displayed, run the presentation by completing the following steps:
   a. Click the Full Screen Slide Show button located in the lower right corner of the window.
   b. When Slide 1 fills the screen, navigate through the presentation by clicking the left mouse button.
   c. Continue clicking the mouse button until the Web browser window displays.
7. Close the Web browser window.
8. Close Global Presentation.

Formatting Web Pages

A presentation that has been converted to HTML can be edited in PowerPoint by opening the original presentation file, editing and/or formatting the presentation, and then saving it as a Web page to republish the Web pages. You can also directly open the HTML presentation, edit as required, and then use the regular Save command to update the Web pages. However, you should use the first method described to ensure the original source file and the HTML files have the same content.

1. Open the original Global Presentation from the *PowerPoint Chapter 08* folder on your disk.
2. Edit the content and format the original presentation by completing the following steps:
   a. Apply the Network design template to the presentation.
   b. Change to the Slide Master view and then make the following changes:
      1) Make sure the Network Title Master miniature is selected.
      2) Click the text *Click to edit Master title style*.
      3) Change the font to 40-point Tahoma.
      4) Click the Network Slide Master miniature.
      5) Click the text *Click to edit Master title style* and then change the font to 32-point Tahoma.
   c. Change back to the Normal view.
   d. Delete Slide 5. (To do this, click Slide 5 in the Outline/Slides pane with the Slides tab selected, and then press the Delete key.)
3. Update the revised HTML files by completing the following steps:
   a. Click File and then Save as Web Page.
   b. At the Save As dialog box, click the Publish button.
   c. At the Publish as Web Page dialog box, click the Publish button. (The options that were used when the presentation was originally published will be saved.)
   d. At the message asking if you want to replace the existing Web page, click Yes.
4. View the revised Web pages in the Internet Explorer window or other browser software window.
5. Close the Internet Explorer or other browser window.
6. Save and then close Global Presentation.

Broadcasting a Presentation Online

A slide show can be delivered to audience members in remote locations or dispersed to more than one conference room by broadcasting it using the Web. The presentation can be recorded and saved for viewing later, scheduled for a live viewing at a preset day and time, or a live viewing can be started instantaneously. Video and/or audio can be included if the host computer has a video camera and/or microphone connected. PowerPoint initiates invitations to the broadcast via a meeting request message through Microsoft Outlook.

The presentation is saved in HTML format, so that the audience members can view the presentation in their Web browser software. The online broadcast feature requires that members have Internet Explorer version 5.1 or later and access to the server where the broadcast files are stored. You would complete the following basic steps to set up and schedule a live broadcast:

1. Open the presentation that you want to broadcast.
2. Click Slide Show, point to Online Broadcast, and then click Schedule a Live Broadcast.
3. The Schedule Presentation Broadcast dialog box opens as displayed in figure 8.8.

POWERPOINT

8.8 *Schedule Presentation Broadcast Dialog Box*

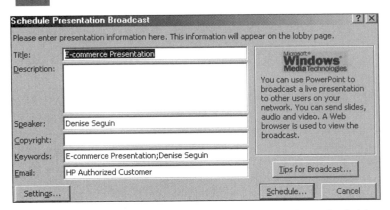

4. Key the welcome message that you want displayed on the lobby page for the broadcast in the <u>D</u>escription text box, the name of the presenter in the Speaker text box, and the contact person's e-mail address in the <u>E</u>mail text box.
5. Click the Settings button to display the Broadcast Settings dialog box with the Presenter tab selected as shown in figure 8.9.

8.9 *Broadcast Settings Dialog Box*

6. Key the server name and folder name for the broadcast files in the <u>S</u>ave broadcast files in text box in the File location section, or, click <u>B</u>rowse and navigate to the server and folder name in the Choose Directory dialog box. The file location must be a shared folder that can be accessed by the audience participants.
7. If necessary, change the Audio/Video settings, change Slide sho<u>w</u> mode from Full Screen to Resizable Screen, or, click the Display s<u>p</u>eaker notes with the presentation check box in the Presentation options section.
8. Click OK.
9. Click <u>S</u>chedule in the Schedule Presentation Broadcast dialog box to start Microsoft Outlook and set up a meeting request to identify the broadcast participants, message, and the start and end times.

When you are ready to begin the broadcast, open the presentation, click Slide Show, point to Online Broadcast, and then click Start Live Broadcast Now. If you are a participant in the broadcast, a reminder message will appear in Outlook when the presentation is to begin. If Outlook is not your e-mail program, open the invitation e-mail message and then click the URL for the broadcast.

STEPS TO SET UP AND SCHEDULE AN ONLINE BROADCAST (OPTIONAL EXERCISE)

(Note: Before completing this exercise, check with your instructor for further details on the online broadcast. You will either be given a server name and folder name location for the broadcast HTML files and a list of whom to invite to the broadcast, or you will be instructed to complete the steps up to step 2e only and then click Cancel to return to the PowerPoint screen.)

1. Open E-commerce Presentation.
2. Set up and schedule an online broadcast by completing the following steps:
   a. Click Slide Show, point to Online Broadcast, and then click Schedule a Live Broadcast.
   b. Click in the Description text box and then key the following text:

      Welcome to Global Marketing in the New Millennium.

   c. Press Tab and then key your first and last names in the Speaker text box.
   d. Press Tab three times and then key your e-mail address in the Email text box.
   e. Click the Settings button.
   f. At the Broadcast Settings dialog box, key the server and folder location that you were given by your instructor in the Save broadcast files in text box. (The file location name should be in the format *servername\foldername*.)

   g. Click OK to close the Broadcast Settings dialog box.
   h. At the Schedule Presentation Broadcast dialog box, click the Schedule button.
   i. Microsoft Outlook will open with a meeting request message window open. Enter the e-mail addresses of the audience participants in the To. . . text box.
   j. Key a description for the meeting in the Subject text box.
   k. Click the This is an online meeting using check box and then click *Windows Media Services* in the drop-down list.
   l. Enter the start time, end time, and reminder information as per instructions from your instructor.
   m. Click Send.
3. If you will be viewing a broadcast, your instructor will provide instructions on how to participate.
4. Close E-commerce Presentation.

This feature works for an online broadcast to 10 or fewer audience members at a time. To broadcast to a larger audience, a Windows Media Server that supports streaming media (such as video and audio) is required.

CHAPTER summary

➤ If you want to share a presentation with others, send the presentation for review and then merge the changes in the original presentation. The process for merging changes varies depending on whether you are using Outlook or another e-mail program.

➤ One method for sending a presentation for review is to display the Save As dialog box, key a name for the presentation, change the Save as type option to *Presentation for Review*, and then click the Save button.

➤ In a presentation saved as a presentation for review, PowerPoint inserts a link back to the original presentation. When you open a presentation sent for review, you can choose whether or not you want changes reflected in the original presentation.

➤ One method for merging reviewers' changes is to use the Compare and Merge Presentations feature. To use this feature, open the original presentation, click Tools, and then click Compare and Merge Presentations. At the Choose Files to Merge with Current Presentation dialog box, select all reviewed presentations, and then click the Merge button.

➤ Changes made by each reviewer display in a change marker in the original presentation.

➤ Use the change markers, buttons on the Reviewing toolbar, or options at the Revisions Pane to accept and/or reject reviewer changes.

➤ Insert a comment in a slide by clicking the Insert Comment button on the Reviewing toolbar or by clicking Insert and then Comment. Key the comment text in the comment box that displays.

➤ To print comments, display the Print dialog box, choose how you want slides printed, and then insert a check mark in the Include comments page check box. Comments print on a separate page after the presentation is printed.

➤ Use the Pack and Go Wizard to save a presentation for use on another computer.

➤ Fonts used in a presentation can be embedded within the presentation file.

➤ If you are saving a presentation file to display on another computer and are not sure if the other computer has the same fonts, you can embed the fonts as you save the file.

➤ Save a presentation as a Web page by clicking File and then Save as Web Page. At the Save As dialog box, click the Publish button to display the Publish as Web Page dialog box where you specify what you want published and identify the supported browser.

➤ Preview a presentation in the default Web browser by clicking File and then Web Page Preview.

➤ Format Web pages directly in PowerPoint using the regular features you would use to format slides.

➤ You can broadcast a presentation using the Web to an audience in remote locations or dispersed to more than one conference room. The online broadcast feature requires that audience members are using Internet Explorer 5.1 or later and have access to the server where the broadcast files are stored.

➤ Schedule an online broadcast with options at the Schedule Presentation Broadcast dialog box. Specify broadcast settings with options at the Broadcast Settings dialog box.

➤ To begin the broadcast, open the presentation, click Slide Show, point to Online Broadcast, and then click Start Live Broadcast Now.

COMMANDS review

Command	Mouse/Keyboard
Display Choose Files to Merge with Current Presentation dialog box	Click Tools, Compare and Merge Presentations
Insert comment	Click Insert Comment button on Reviewing toolbar; or click Insert, Comment
Display Reviewing toolbar	Click View, Toolbars, Reviewing
Begin Pack and Go wizard	Click File, Pack and Go
Display Save Options dialog box	Click Tools button on Save As toolbar, then click Save Options
Save as Web page	Click File, Save as Web Page
Preview Web page	Click File, Web Page Preview
Display Schedule Presentation Broadcast dialog box	Click Slide Show, Online Broadcast, Schedule a Live Broadcast
Display Broadcast Settings dialog box	Click Settings button at Schedule Presentation Broadcast dialog box

CONCEPTS check

Completion: On a blank sheet of paper, indicate the correct term, symbol, or command.

1. To send a presentation out for review, display the Save As dialog box, key a name for the presentation, change the Save as type option to this, and then click the Save button.
2. Change user's information at this dialog box with the General tab selected.
3. To display the Choose Files to Merge with Current Presentation dialog box, click Tools and then click this option.
4. Accept or reject reviewers' changes with buttons on the Reviewing toolbar or with options at this pane.
5. Accept a reviewer's change, click the change marker, and then click this button on the Reviewing toolbar.
6. Move to the next change in a presentation by clicking this button on the Reviewing toolbar.
7. Insert a comment in a presentation by clicking Insert and then Comment or by clicking the Insert Comment button on this toolbar.
8. To print comments, display the Print dialog box, specify how you want the presentation printed, and insert a check mark in this option check box.
9. Use this wizard to transport a PowerPoint presentation to another computer.
10. To embed fonts in a presentation, display this dialog box, insert a check mark in the Embed TrueType fonts check box, and then click OK.
11. *HTML* is an acronym for this, which is the programming language used to code pages to display graphically on the World Wide Web.

12. To begin the process of saving a presentation as a Web page, click File on the Menu bar and then click this option at the drop-down menu.

13. Click File on the Menu bar and then click this option to see how a presentation displays in your Web browser.

14. Display the Schedule Presentation Broadcast dialog box by clicking Slide Show, pointing to this option, and then clicking Schedule a Live Broadcast.

SKILLS check

Assessment 1

1. Open Communication Presentation (located in the *PowerPoint Chapter 08* folder on your disk).

2. Save the presentation with Save As in the *PowerPoint Chapter 08* folder on your disk and name it Original Comm Pres.

3. Save the presentation for review by Jennifer Riley with the name Comm Pres Edited by JR. *(Hint: Change the Save as type option at the Save As dialog box to Presentation for Review.)*

4. Save the presentation for review by Greg Lui with the name Comm Pres Edited by GL.

5. Close Original Comm Pres.

6. At the blank PowerPoint screen, display the Options dialog box with the General tab selected, key **Jennifer Riley** in the Name text box, key **JR** in the Initials text box, and then close the dialog box.

7. Edit the communication presentation as Jennifer Riley by completing the following steps:
   a. Open the Comm Pres Edited by JR presentation located in the *PowerPoint Chapter 08* folder on your disk.
   b. At the message asking if you want to merge changes in Comm Pres Edited by JR back into Original Comm Pres, click No.
   c. Make the following changes:
      1) Display Slide 2 and then edit the first bulleted item so it reads *Clearly identify to the audience what you need to communicate*.
      2) Display Slide 3 and then edit the third bulleted item so it reads *Decide whether to communicate verbally or in writing*.
      3) Display Slide 4 and then edit the first bulleted item so it reads *Gather and organize relevant facts*.

8. Save the presentation and then print it as handouts with all six slides on one page.

9. Close Comm Pres Edited by JR.

10. At the blank PowerPoint screen, display the Options dialog box with the General tab selected, key **Greg Lui** in the Name text box, key **GL** in the Initials text box, and then close the dialog box.

11. Edit the communication presentation as Greg Lui by completing the following steps:
    a. Open the Comm Pres Edited by GL presentation located in the *PowerPoint Chapter 08* folder on your disk.

    b. At the message asking if you want to merge changes in Comm Pres Edited by GL back into Original Comm Pres, click <u>N</u>o.

    c. Make the following changes:

      1) Display Slide 2 and then insert a new bulleted item at the beginning of the bulleted list that reads *Identify the intended audience*.

      2) Display Slide 3 and then edit the second bulleted item so it reads *Determine what the audience already knows*.

      3) Display Slide 5 and delete *Voice mail* in the Verbal section.

12. Save the presentation and then print it as handouts with all six slides on one page.

13. Close Comm Pres Edited by GL.

14. Display the Options dialog box with the General tab selected, change the name and initials in the User information back to the original information, and then close the dialog box.

Assessment 2

1. Open Original Comm Pres.

2. Display the Choose Files to Merge with Current Presentation dialog box, select *Comm Pres Edited by GL*, select *Comm Pres Edited by JR*, and then click the <u>M</u>erge button.

3. Apply the following changes to slides:

    Slide 2 = Apply change made by Jennifer Riley

             Do not apply change by Greg Lui

    Slide 3 = Apply all changes

    Slide 4 = Apply all changes

    Slide 5 = Do not apply changes

4. Apply an animation scheme of your choosing to all slides in the presentation.

5. Run the presentation beginning with Slide 1.

6. Save the presentation with Save As and name it Merged Comm Pres.

7. Print the presentation as handouts with all six slides on one page.

8. Close Merged Comm Pres.

Assessment 3

1. Open Global Presentation.

2. Save the presentation with Save As in the *PowerPoint Chapter 08* folder on your disk and name the presentation Global Pres with Comments.

3. Insert the following comments:

    Slide 1 = Click immediately right of the subtitle *How does the Internet impact our business?* and then insert the comment **Change this from a question to a statement.**

    Slide 2 = Click immediately right of the bulleted item *Think "global"* and then insert the comment **Define global markets.**

    Slide 4 = Click immediately right of the bulleted item *Netscape and Microsoft* and then insert the comment **Include browser versions.**

4. Print the presentation as handouts with all five slides on one page and also print the comments page.

5. Save and then close Global Pres with Comments.

Assessment 4

1. Open Skills Presentation (located in the *PowerPoint Chapter 08* folder on your disk).
2. Save the presentation file as a Web page. Accept the default name for the presentation and select the option to display the Web page in the Web browser window when the conversion is complete.
3. View the entire presentation in the Web browser window.
4. Close the Web browser window.
5. Save and then close Skills Presentation.

Assessment 5

1. Open Skills Presentation. (Open the normal Skills Presentation and not the HTML Skills Presentation.)
2. Apply a different color scheme of your choosing to the presentation.
3. Delete slide 8.
4. Replace the existing Web pages for the presentation and view the results in the Web browser window.
5. Close the Web browser window.
6. Print the presentation as handouts with all seven slides on one page.
7. Save and then close Skills Presentation.

Assessment 6

1. In this and previous chapters, you have learned how to save presentations in different file formats. Use PowerPoint's Help feature to learn about the various file formats for saving presentations. Learn specifically about the Windows Metafile format.
2. Open Global Presentation and then save only Slide 5 in the Windows Metafile format in the *PowerPoint Chapter 08* folder on your disk and name the slide file Home Computers.
3. Open Word and then open the document named Global Marketing located in the *PowerPoint Chapter 08* folder on your disk.
4. Position the insertion point at the beginning of the third paragraph (begins with *Call Global Marketing today…*).
5. Click the Insert Picture button on the Drawing toolbar.
6. At the Insert Picture dialog box, navigate to the *PowerPoint Chapter 08* folder on your disk and then double-click *Home Computers*.
7. Print the document by clicking the Print button on the Standard toolbar.
8. Save the document with the same name (Global Marketing).
9. Close Global Marketing and then exit Word.

WORKPLACE Ready

ASSESSING proficiency

In this unit, you have learned to add visual elements to presentations such as WordArt, organizational charts, diagrams, charts, tables, and sound and video clips. You also learned methods for sharing objects and files such as copying and pasting, copying and embedding, copying and linking, using action buttons, and creating hyperlinks. Techniques for sending presentations for review and then merging reviewers' comments were introduced as well as information on how to insert and print comments in a presentation and save a presentation as a Web page.

Assessment 1

1. Open Telecom Presentation (located in the *PowerPoint Unit 02* folder on your disk).
2. Save the presentation with Save As in the *PowerPoint Unit 02* folder on your disk and name the presentation Telecom Pres with Terms.
3. Create a new Slide 7 (with the Title and Text slide layout) with the following specifications:
   a. Click the text *Click to add title* and then key **APPLICATIONS**.
   b. Click the text *Click to add text* and then copy text from Word and paste it into Slide 7 by completing the following steps:
      1) Open Word and then open Word Concepts 01.
      2) Display the Clipboard Task Pane by clicking <u>E</u>dit and then Office Clip<u>b</u>oard. (Make sure the Clipboard Task Pane is empty. If not, click the Clear All button.)
      3) Select *RECEIVING* and the paragraph below it and then click the Copy button.
      4) Select *STORING* and the paragraph below it and then click the Copy button.
      5) Select *TRANSMITTING* and the paragraph below it and then click the Copy button.
      6) Click the button on the Taskbar representing Telecom Pres with Terms.
      7) Display the Clipboard Task Pane by clicking <u>E</u>dit and then Office Clip<u>b</u>oard.
      8) Make sure the insertion point is positioned in the bulleted list placeholder in Slide 7 and then click the *TRANSMITTING* item in the Clipboard Task Pane.

9) Press the Enter key and then click the *RECEIVING* item in the Clipboard Task Pane.

10) Clear the Clipboard Task Pane by clicking the Clear All button located in the upper right corner of the task pane.

11) Close the Clipboard Task Pane.

12) If necessary, make adjustments to the inserted text in the placeholder.

4. Apply an animation scheme of your choosing to all slides in the presentation.

5. Print the presentation as handouts with all seven slides on one page.

6. Run the presentation beginning with Slide 1.

7. Save and then close Telecom Pres with Terms.

8. Make Word the active program, close the Clipboard Task Pane, close Word Concepts 01, and then exit Word.

Assessment 2

1. Make sure PowerPoint is open and then open Word.

2. With Word the active program, open Word Outline 03.

3. Import the text into PowerPoint.

4. Make PowerPoint the active program.

5. Make the following changes to the presentation:

   a. Change the slide layout for Slide 2 to Title Slide.

   b. Change the slide layout for Slide 3 to Title Slide.

   c. Change the slide layout for Slide 6 to Title Slide.

   d. Apply a design template of your choosing.

   e. Insert a clip art image related to "software" in Slide 5. If necessary, recolor the image to follow the color scheme of the design template.

   f. Check each slide and make any formatting changes to enhance the slide.

   g. Create the following hyperlinks for the text in Slide 6:

   Apple Computer = http://www.apple.com
   Microsoft Corporation = http://www.microsoft.com

   h. Insert the action button named *Action Button: Home* (links to first slide) at the bottom of Slide 3, Slide 4, and Slide 5.

   i. Insert the action button named *Action Button: Return* (links back to last slide viewed) at the bottom of Slide 1.

6. Apply a transition and sound of your choosing to all slides in the presentation.

7. Save the presentation and name it Apex Presentation.

8. Run the presentation beginning with Slide 1. (When Slide 3 displays, click the Home action button. After viewing Slide 1, click the Return action button. Continue in this manner with Slide 4 and Slide 5. If you are connected to the Internet, click the *Apple Computer* hyperlink in Slide 6. At the Apple Computer Web site, click a few hyperlinks that interest you and then close the Web browser. Click the *Microsoft Corporation* hyperlink in Slide 6. At the Microsoft Corporation Web site, click a few hyperlinks that interest you and then close the Web browser.)

9. Print all six slides on one page.
10. Close Apex Presentation.
11. Make Word active, close Word Outline 03, and then exit Word.

Assessment 3

1. Create a presentation with the following specifications:
   a. Use a design template of your choosing.
   b. Create the first slide with the following specifications:
      1) Choose the Blank slide layout.
      2) Use WordArt to create the text *International Securities*. (You determine the shape and formatting of the WordArt text.)
   c. Create the second slide with the following specifications:
      1) Choose the Title Slide layout.
      2) Key **2003 SALES MEETING** as the title.
      3) Key **European Division** as the subtitle.
   d. Create the third slide with the following specifications:
      1) Choose the Title Only slide layout.
      2) Key **REGIONAL SALES** as the title.
      3) Open Excel and then open Excel Workbook 04.
      4) Save the workbook with Save As and name it Sales Workbook.
      5) Select cells A1 through D5 (the cells containing data) and then copy and embed the cells in Slide 3.
      6) Increase the size of the cells to fill the slide.
   e. Create the fourth slide with the following specifications:
      1) Make sure the slide contains the Title and Text slide layout.
      2) Key **2003 GOALS** as the title.
      3) Key the following as the bulleted items:
         • **Increase product sales by 15 percent.**
         • **Open a branch office in Spain.**
         • **Hire one manager and two additional account managers.**
         • **Decrease production costs by 6 percent.**
   f. Create the fifth slide with the following specifications:
      1) Choose the Title and Content slide layout.
      2) Key **HIRING TIMELINE** as the title.
      3) Click the Insert Table button in the content placeholder and then create a table with two columns and five rows.
      4) Key the following text in the cells in the table. (You determine the formatting of the cells.)

Task	*Date*
Advertise positions	**03/01/03 – 04/30/03**
Review resumes	**05/15/03 – 06/01/03**
Perform interviews	**06/15/03 – 07/15/03**
Hire personnel	**08/01/03**

   g. Create the sixth slide with the following specifications:
      1) Choose the Title Only slide layout.
      2) Key **PRODUCTION EXPENSES** as the title.

      3) Make Excel the active program and then close Sales Workbook.
      4) Open Excel Workbook 05.
      5) Save the workbook with Save As and name it Expenses Workbook.
      6) Copy and then link the pie chart in Expenses Workbook to Slide 6.
      7) Increase the size of the pie chart to better fill the slide. (Be sure to maintain the integrity of the chart.)
      8) Make Excel active, close Expenses Workbook, and then exit Excel.
  h. Create the seventh slide with the following specifications:
      1) Choose the Title and Content slide layout.
      2) Key **OFFICE STRUCTURE** as the title.
      3) Click the Insert Diagram or Organization Chart button in the content placeholder and then create an organizational chart with the following text:

Ricardo Miraflores
Manager

Audrina Chorrillos	**Hector Palencia**	**Jules Verde**
Account Manager	**Account Manager**	**Account Manager**

      4) Apply an autoformat of your choosing to the organizational chart.
2. Save the presentation and name it Securities Presentation.
3. Add an animation scheme of your choosing to all slides in the presentation.
4. Run the presentation beginning with Slide 1.
5. Print the slides as a handout with all slides on one page.
6. Save and then close Securities Presentation.

Assessment 4

1. Open Excel and then open Expenses Workbook.
2. Make the following changes:
  a. B2: Change *38% to 41%*
  b. B3: Change *35% to 32%*
  c. B4: Change *18% to 21%*
  d. B5: Change *9% to 6%*
3. Save the workbook again with the same name (Expenses Workbook).
4. Print and then close Expenses Workbook.
5. Exit Excel.
6. With PowerPoint the active program, open Securities Presentation. (At the message that displays, click the Update Links button.)
7. Display Slide 3, double-click the cells to display Excel editing tools, and then make the following changes to the data in the embedded cells:

a. C2: Change *2,678,450* to *2,857,300*
b. C3: Change *1,753,405* to *1,598,970*
c. C5: Change *2,315,600* to *2,095,170*
8. Print the slides as a handout with all slides on one page.
9. Save and then close Securities Presentation.

Assessment 5

1. Open Telecom Presentation.
2. Save the presentation with Save As in the *PowerPoint Unit 02* folder on your disk and name it Original Telecom Pres.
3. Save the presentation for review by Marcus Cook with the name Telecom Pres Edited by MC. *(Hint: Change the Save as type option at the Save As dialog box to Presentation for Review.)*
4. Save the presentation for review by Naomi Holden with the name Telecom Pres Edited by NH.
5. Close Original Telecom Pres.
6. At the blank PowerPoint screen, display the Options dialog box with the General tab selected, key **Marcus Cook** in the Name text box, key **MC** in the Initials text box, and then close the dialog box.
7. Edit the presentation as Marcus Cook by completing the following steps:
   a. Open the Telecom Pres Edited by MC presentation located in the *PowerPoint Unit 02* folder on your disk.
   b. At the message asking if you want to merge changes in Telecom Pres Edited by MC back into Original Telecom Pres, click No.
   c. Make the following changes:
      1) Edit Slide 1 so the subtitle reads *Technology Concepts*.
      2) Display Slide 2 and then edit the second bulleted item so it reads *Digital Camera* (instead of *35mm Camera*).
      3) Display Slide 5 and then add a new bulleted item at the end of the list that reads *Amplifier*.
8. Save the presentation and then print it as handouts with all six slides on one page.
9. Close Telecom Pres Edited by MC.
10. At the blank PowerPoint screen, display the Options dialog box with the General tab selected, key **Naomi Holden** in the Name text box, key **NH** in the Initials text box, and then close the dialog box.
11. Edited the communication presentation as Naomi Holden by completing the following steps:
   a. Open the Telecom Pres Edited by NH presentation located in the *PowerPoint Unit 02* folder on your disk.
   b. At the message asking if you want to merge changes in Telecom Pres Edited by NH back into Original Telecom Pres, click No.
   c. Make the following changes:
      1) Display Slide 2 and then edit the fourth bulleted item so it displays as *Pointing Devices* (rather than *Mouse*) and add a new bulleted item at the end of the list that reads *Keyboard*.
      2) Display Slide 3 and then delete the second bulleted item

Telephone and then insert a new bulleted item at the end of the list that reads *Monitoring Systems*.

     3) Display Slide 4 and then insert a new bulleted item between the third and fourth items that reads *Twisted-Pair and Coaxial Cable*.

12. Save the presentation and then print it as handouts with all six slides on one page.
13. Close Telecom Pres Edited by NH.
14. Display the Options dialog box with the General tab selected, change the name and initials in the User information back to the original information, and then close the dialog box.

Assessment 6

1. Open Original Telecom Pres.
2. Display the Choose Files to Merge with Current Presentation dialog box, select *Telecomm Pres Edited by MC*, select *Telecom Pres Edited by NH*, and then click the Merge button.
3. Apply the following changes to slides:

        Slide 1 = Do not apply changes
        Slide 2 = Apply change made by Marcus Cook
                        Do not apply change by Naomi Holden
        Slide 3 = Apply all changes
        Slide 4 = Do not apply changes
        Slide 5 = Apply all changes

4. Save the presentation with Save As and name it Merged Telecom Pres.
5. Apply a transition and sound of your choosing to all slides in the presentation.
6. Print the presentation as handouts with all six slides on one page.
7. Use the Rehearse Timings feature to set the following times for the slides to display during a slide show:

        Slide 1 = 3 seconds
        Slide 2 = 4 seconds
        Slide 3 = 5 seconds
        Slide 4 = 5 seconds
        Slide 5 = 6 seconds
        Slide 6 = 5 seconds

8. Set up the slide show to run continuously.
9. Run the presentation beginning with Slide 1. Watch the slide show until the presentation has started for the second time and then end the show.
10. Save and then close Merged Telecom Pres.

Assessment 7

1. Open Apex Presentation.
2. Save the presentation with Save As in the *PowerPoint Unit 02* folder on your disk and name the presentation Apex Pres with Comments.
3. Insert the following comments:

        Slide 4 = Click immediately right of the third bulleted item and then insert the comment **Include specific timeline on hiring new personnel.**

Slide 5   =   Click immediately right of the last bulleted item and then insert the comment **Specify the percentage of business for each category.**

4. Print the presentation as handouts with all six slides on one page and also print the comments page.
5. Save and then close Apex Pres with Comments.

Assessment 8

1. Open Telecom Presentation.
2. Save the presentation file as a Web page. Accept the default name for the presentation and select the option to display the Web page in the Web browser window when the conversion is complete.
3. View the entire presentation in the Web browser window.
4. Close the Web browser window.
5. Save and then close Telecom Presentation.

WRITING activities

The following activities give you the opportunity to practice your writing skills along with demonstrating an understanding of some of the important PowerPoint features you have mastered in this unit. Use correct grammar, appropriate word choices, and clear sentence structure.

Activity 1

Using PowerPoint's Help feature, learn more about file formats for saving and importing in presentations and then prepare a PowerPoint presentation with the information by completing the following steps:

1. Use the PowerPoint Help feature to look up and then print information on the following topics:
   - File formats for saving presentations
   - File formats PowerPoint can import
   - Graphic file types and filters
2. Read the information you printed on file formats and then prepare a PowerPoint presentation that includes *at least* the following information:
   - Slide containing the title of presentation and your name
   - Two slides containing available file formats for saving presentations including the file format type, extension, and what it is used to save
   - Slide containing information on what file formats PowerPoint can import
   - Slide containing information on graphic file types and filters
3. Apply an animation scheme of your choosing to all slides in the presentation.
4. Save the completed presentation and name it File Formats Presentation.
5. Run the presentation.
6. Print the presentation as handouts with all slides on one page (if possible).
7. Close File Formats Presentation.

Activity 2

1. Open Word and then open and print Travel Vacations. Close Travel Vacations and then exit Word. Looking at the printing of this document, create a presentation in PowerPoint that presents the main points of the document. Apply an animation scheme of your choosing to all slides in the presentation.
2. Save the presentation and name it Travel Presentation.
3. Run Travel Presentation.
4. Print the slides as handouts with six slides per page.
5. Close Travel Presentation.

INTERNET project

Presenting Office XP

Make sure you are connected to the Internet and then explore the Microsoft Web site at www.microsoft.com. Browse the various categories and links on the Web site to familiarize yourself with how information has been organized.

Create a PowerPoint presentation that could be delivered to someone who has just purchased Office XP and wants to know how to find more information about the software from the Microsoft Web site. Include points or tips on where to find product release information and technical support. Include hyperlinks to important pages on the Microsoft Web site. Add formatting and enhancements to make the presentation as dynamic as possible. Save the presentation and name it Microsoft Presentation. View the slide show. Print the presentation as handouts with all slides on one page (if possible). Close Microsoft Presentation.

JOB study

Creating a Skills Presentation

Your manager has asked you to prepare a PowerPoint presentation explaining to a group of new employees the skills they will be trained in as they begin a position with your company. Your presentation should include at least one table (use Job Skills Table in the *PowerPoint Unit 02* folder on the CD that accompanies this text), one hyperlink to a Web site, one hyperlink to a file, and one linked or embedded object that can be updated automatically from within the presentation.

Create at least 10 slides, as well as a summary slide, for a total of at least 11 slides. You will need to insert action buttons to move to the next page for the first slide through the second to last slide. On your final slide, create an action button to return to the first slide.

Save and run the presentation. Print the slides as handouts with six slides per page. Send your presentation to Microsoft Word, then save and print an outline of your presentation.

INDEX